CCEA BUSINESS STUDIES for GCSE

SECOND EDITION

HOPE KERR

Farm

HODDER EDUCATION
AN HACHETTE UK COMPANY

Orders: please contact Bookpoint Ltd, 130 Milton Park, Abingdon, Oxon OX14 4SB.
Telephone: (44) 01235 827720. Fax: (44) 01235 400454. Lines are open from
9.00 to 5.00, Monday to Saturday, with a 24-hour message answering service.
You can also order through our website www.hoddereducation.co.uk

If you have any comments to make about this, or any of our other titles, please send them to educationenquiries@hodder.co.uk

British Library Cataloguing in Publication Data
A catalogue record for this title is available from the British Library

ISBN: 978 0 340 98581 6

First Edition Published 2003
This Edition Published 2009
Impression number 10 9 8 7 6 5 4 3 2
Year 2012, 2011, 2010, 2009

Typeset by Pantek Arts Ltd, Maidstone, Kent.

Printed in Italy for Hodder Education, an Hachette UK Company, 338 Euston Road, London NW1 3BH

Contents

Acknowledgements

Every effort has been made to trace the copyright holders of quoted material. The publishers apologise if any sources remain unacknowledged and will be glad to make the necessary arrangements at the earliest opportunity. The authors and publishers would like to thank the following for permission to reproduce copyright photos:

Title page © Kronick / iStockphoto.com; p.2 Clara Molden/PA Archive/PA Photos; p.5 © Stockbyte / Photolibrary Group Ltd; pp.9–12 Robert & Hope Kerr; p.15 Peter Cavanagh / Alamy; p.20 Robert & Hope Kerr; p.21 Justin Kase zelevenz / Alamy; p.22 David Cook / blueshiftstudios / Alamy; p.24 Robert Mayne / Alamy; p.26 © Photodisc / Getty Images; p.28 Robert & Hope Kerr; p.29 (top) City Living / Alamy, (bottom) Kim Nayler/Divine; p.38 (top) Phoenix Natural Gas, (bottom) Culloden Hotel; p.48 Greg Balfour Evans / Alamy; p.52 Robert & Hope Kerr; p.53 (pushchair) © Julián Rovagnati – Fotolia.com, (chair) © Maksym Bondarchuk / iStockphoto.com, (speakers) © Aliaksandr / iStockphoto.com, (crisps) Robert & Hope Kerr; p.56 Ros Drinkwater / Alamy; p.57 Ted Horowitz/CORBIS; p.59 Robert & Hope Kerr; p.60 WoodyStock / Alamy; p.68 Steffan Hill / Alamy; pp.69–70 Robert & Hope Kerr; p.72 AA World Travel Library / Alamy; p.74 Jacky Parker / Alamy; p.94 © green308 – Fotolia.com; p.102 Robert & Hope Kerr; p.103 Peter Panczyk; p.104 (top) Advertising Archives, (bottom) Robert & Hope Kerr; p.106 Advertising Archives; p.108 Pukka Pies; p.110 sciencephotos / Alamy; p.112 GUSTOIMAGES / SCIENCE PHOTO LIBRARY; p.118 Rex Features; p.120 vario images GmbH & Co.KG / Alamy; p.121 Chris Laurens / Alamy; p.122 Phoenix Natural Gas; p.123 Nigel Cattlin / Alamy; p.130 (left) Bob Battersby, (right) Robert & Hope Kerr; p.133 © The British Standards Institution 2009; p.156 Paul Rapson / Alamy; p.169 Dungannon and South Tyrone Borough Council; p.170 Robert & Hope Kerr; p.173 Mika/zefa/Corbis; p.187 Robert & Hope Kerr; p.194 Photofusion Picture Library / Alamy; p.208 Robert & Hope Kerr; p.214 WoodyStock / Alamy; p.215 Robert & Hope Kerr; p.217 © Photodisc / Getty Images; p.220 Simon Marcus/Corbis; p.221 imagebroker / Alamy; p.222 david pearson / Alamy; p.227 © Ingram Publishing Limited.

Introduction

This book is dedicated to the memory of my beloved husband Robert, who I miss so much.

This second edition of *GCSE Business Studies for CCEA revises*, amends and updates the original textbook in line with the new CCEA GCSE Business Studies specification which is due to be taught for the first time in September 2009.

Owing to the uncertain nature of the national economy at the time of writing, it has been thought less appropriate to use as many case studies as in the previous edition, since such studies might appear out of date in the future.

In the interests of simplicity, this revised textbook accurately follows the order of the new specification. Like the specification, the book is divided into two main units which, in turn, are divided into themes to provide the coverage of the necessary material. This in no way aims to dictate the order in which the specification should be approached. However, it is understood that the two units will be examined separately.

At a few points in the book, some detail in addition to that which is required for GCSE (CCEA) has been included. There are two reasons for this – first, it may encourage some students to undertake further reading on the subject and second, experience has shown that the book will be used by some business students taking other examinations.

It is not possible to include previous examination questions since the pattern of the examination will alter to conform to the new specification. However, as Chief Examiner, the author understands that many candidates do not answer questions appropriately because they fail to recognise the requirements of the command words used in questions. For this reason, a section on command words is included at the end of the book. It should be noted that only three assessment objectives now have to be met instead of the original four and this is reflected in the list of command words.

In addition, each theme includes activities which have been designed to reinforce learning and to make the student think further about the knowledge-based material provided as well as to give opportunities to develop the skills of application, analysis and evaluation. The author is aware of the wide range of ability in the candidature for this particular examination, so activities have been designed to cater for these varying abilities.

Each theme ends with an indication of the key facts which should be understood at that stage and the glossary provides an easy reference for revision.

Hope Kerr

1

BUSINESS START-UP

Theme 1.1

Entrepreneurs

Starting up any business begins with an entrepreneur – a person who has an idea for a new business and is prepared to take risks to make that business work.

Two well-known entrepreneurs are Richard Branson, who founded the very successful Virgin Group, and Bill Gates, who started up Microsoft. However, entrepreneurs do not have to have such huge businesses to be successful.

Patricia O'Hagan was recently named as Northern Ireland's 'Entrepreneur of the Year' on the BBC television programme 'Chasing the Dollar' and has been described as a role model for others thinking of starting up their own businesses. Patricia is managing director of Core Systems, a small business based in Duncairn Gardens, Belfast. Core Systems has developed a unique product, known as an 'Inmate Information Centre', for use in prisons in the United States. The product is a multi-purpose interactive kiosk which incorporates fingerprinting technology and where prisoners can access personal information and make service requests. Patricia is confident of the future since there are over 2 million prisoners in the United States and the company's turnover is showing substantial increases.

What it means to be enterprising

To be enterprising means to be able to spot a good business opportunity and to have the vision and drive to make that business succeed. In order to do this, the entrepreneur has to be prepared to take calculated risks.

So what are the characteristics of an entrepreneur?

- An entrepreneur contributes original ideas which give the business an edge on its competitors
- An entrepreneur has self-confidence and a passion about his/her venture
- An entrepreneur has the ability to work independently and develop his/her ideas
- An entrepreneur is committed and willing to make personal sacrifices for the benefit of his/her business
- An entrepreneur is a creative thinker and shows initiative
- An entrepreneur has vision of what the business could become and works single-mindedly towards that goal
- An entrepreneur has the energy to work hard and make sure that the business achieves its full potential
- An entrepreneur is willing to take calculated business risks and to encourage other financiers such as banks to lend money to the enterprise
- An entrepreneur has good leadership qualities

- An entrepreneur can motivate others in the work team and inspire them with enthusiasm
- An entrepreneur is not discouraged by failures and setbacks and understands that many good business ideas do not succeed, perhaps because it is the wrong place or time.

Why the government encourages enterprise

The government is keen to encourage enterprise and to develop an 'enterprise culture' in this country. For these reasons it has set up various schemes to help entrepreneurs to succeed. People are encouraged to try their ideas in business and to establish their own businesses rather than be unemployed.

There are several reasons why the government encourages enterprise:

- It reduces unemployment
- New ideas may succeed and provide fresh opportunities
- People feel motivated
- Competition ensures a healthier business environment.

Activity

Have you got what it takes to be an entrepreneur? Answer the following questions truthfully to find out! The good entrepreneur's answers are given at the end.

1 What do you do if you find a task difficult?
  a Keep trying until you get it right
  b Give up
  c Ask for help

2 Can you make decisions?
  a Always
  b Never
  c Depends on the circumstances

3 If you won the lottery, which of the following would you do?
  a Tour the world
  b Treat all your friends to the greatest party ever
  c Invest it

4 How single-minded are you? When you are working, are you
  a easily distracted?

b oblivious to everything around you?
c able to concentrate – but only if you like the work?

5 How energetic do you think you are?
a Very energetic at everything
b Energetic at the things I enjoy
c There are lots of things I can't be bothered with

6 How well do you work with people?
a I'd rather work on my own
b I love being in a team
c I must be the team leader

Answers: 1a, 2a, 3c, 4b, 5a, 6c

Checklist

At this stage you should understand:

- key characteristics of entrepreneurs
- what it means to be enterprising
- why the government encourages enterprise.

Theme 1.2

Resources of business

Theme 1.1 explained how important enterprise is as one resource in business. Altogether there are four resources which are necessary in any business.

The factors of production

There are four resources which are essential in every business. They are known as the 'factors of production'. Those factors of production are land, labour, capital and enterprise.

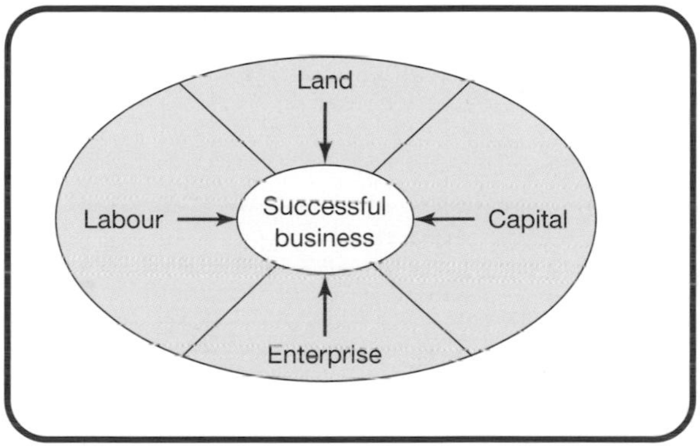

Land

A basic need in business is the land on which to place the business premises, houses, roads and farms. However, 'land' is used more widely in this economic sense and includes not only the surface of the land but also the oceans and all natural resources and raw materials which are contained either on, above or in the earth. Such resources and raw materials would include oil, gas, trees, water, fish, coal and minerals.

Supplies of land are limited, which makes it a very valuable resource.

Labour

The term 'labour' refers to the human resource in the business – the workers who are employed to manufacture the product or provide the service for which the business has been set up. The labour used in the business may be physical labour or mental labour, depending on the nature of the firm's final product. Supplies of labour with the appropriate skills are also limited.

Capital

Capital is defined as 'wealth which is employed in the creation of further wealth'. It is the element contributed by capitalists – the owners – to set up and maintain the business. Capital includes the money which the owners invested in the business at the beginning, but also includes the items which were bought with that original investment – items such as premises and machinery.

Capital is always in short supply and capitalists will risk investing it only in safe business projects.

Enterprise

You learned in the previous section that enterprise is contributed to a business by people known as entrepreneurs. They are the managers and they play a most essential role in business, estimating future demand and ensuring that production is at the correct level to meet that demand.

It is the role of the entrepreneur to organise the capital, the land and the labour in the correct proportions to run the business successfully. For example, some businesses such as large factories require vast amounts of capital and land but, because they are heavily mechanised, they may require proportionately less labour. Other businesses such as large department stores may be very labour intensive. For this reason, they would use a large amount of labour but proportionately less land.

Each of the people who contribute the factors of production has to be rewarded. The following table shows how.

A business would not be successful unless it had all four factors of production.

A person might have adequate amounts of capital but unless that person has enterprise, he/she would not be able to start a business.

Equally, an entrepreneur may have great ideas for a successful business but unless he/she has land on which to start the business and labour to operate it, there will be no business.

On the other hand, a landowner may own large areas of land but without the ideas contributed by enterprise or sufficient amounts of capital, he/she would not have a business.

Factor of production	Contributed by	Rewarded by
Land	Landlords	Rent
Labour	Employees	Wages and salaries
Capital	Capitalists	Interest
Enterprise	Entrepreneurs	Profit

Activity

Cecil has come up with a good idea for a new business. He knows that the business would be successful but his difficulty is that he would need finance and premises. Some friends agree to join the business. Fred will provide the necessary finance, Eric has premises which he will allow the business to use and Roy will work in the business.

Using the spaces provided, show the role of each person and the rewards which he can expect.

Name	Role	Reward
Cecil		
Fred		
Eric		
Roy		

Checklist

At this stage you should be able to:

- understand the factors of production: land, labour, capital and enterprise
- analyse how businesses use resources differently.

Business ownership – private sector

Any business which is owned by private people is known as a private sector business.

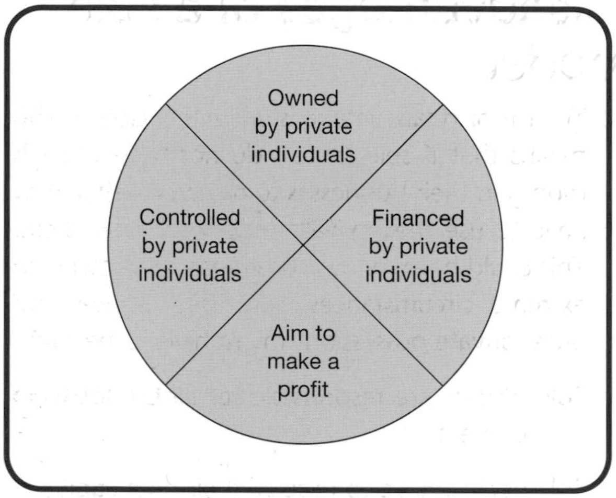

Introduction to private sector businesses

Some of these businesses may be small and owned by just one person – that person is called a sole trader. In some cases the business may be slightly larger and two or more people may have put money into it and perhaps joined together to work in the business. That is an example of a partnership.

Other businesses may be even larger and money would be needed from many people to keep them going. A large business would be organised as a private limited company, and the largest business of all would be organised as a public limited company.

There is one other type of business in the private sector – a franchise.

Theme 1.3 studies each of these types of business organisation in turn. At this stage, it is important for you to remember that private sector businesses are owned and controlled by private people who aim to make a profit from the money they have invested in the businesses.

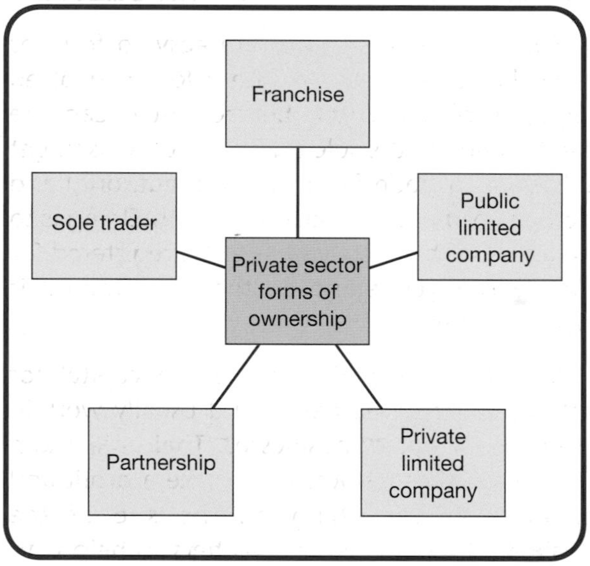

Sole trader

This is the most common form of business ownership. Sole traders are found in every town and district throughout Northern Ireland running small and medium-sized shops as well as providing services such as hairdressing, plumbing, dressmaking, painting or electrical work.

It is a popular form of business organisation because sole traders are their own bosses and own the businesses themselves. For this reason, they are also sometimes called sole proprietors.

Sole traders' businesses are easy to form as they do not have to provide a lot of involved legal documentation before they can be established. All the sole trader has to do is to get a licence to trade from the local authority and perhaps planning permission if the building is to be altered. The business has to be registered for VAT with Revenue and Customs and then it is ready to open.

Sole traders provide the entire capital for setting up their businesses and usually work in their own shops or businesses. Their major aim in running the business is to make a profit and to expand. Depending on the size of the business, they may employ others to help with the work.

Sole traders are entitled to keep any profits made but also are responsible for losses incurred. They have unlimited liability, which means that if they do not have enough money in their businesses to pay their debts, they have to use their private funds to meet them.

Advantages of a sole trader

- The business is cheaply and easily formed without involved legal procedures
- The owner can keep all the profits made in the business
- The owner can make all the decisions and can make them quickly without having to call committee meetings
- Because the business is usually small, the sole trader has very close links with the customers and employees
- The financial affairs of the business do not have to be published, although tax authorities must have access to them.

Disadvantages of a sole trader

- The major disadvantage is unlimited liability. This means that if sole traders do not have enough money in their businesses to pay their debts, they have to use their private money to meet them. This could have serious consequences because, in extreme circumstances, their cars, houses and other private possessions might have to be sold
- Sole traders are responsible for all the losses in the business
- Sole traders have to raise all their own capital
- The amount of capital which sole traders have is limited, so their businesses are likely to be small
- Because their businesses are small, banks are less willing to lend money to sole traders than they would be to large businesses
- Being limited, it is more difficult for sole traders to compete with the large business organisations as they cannot take advantage of economies of scale
- The business is very dependent on one person. The sole trader in a shop, for example, is expected to have expertise in sales, purchasing, advertising, accounting, window dressing, deliveries and stocktaking. This means they work very long hours
- If the sole trader becomes ill or is on holiday, there is often no one to call on
- The sole trader frequently does not have anyone with whom to discuss problems.

Activity

Read the short case study and answer the questions which follow.

Gillian Morton is an excellent hairdresser who has been working at 'Best Cuts', a very good hair salon in Newcastle. She loves her job but has always dreamed of setting up her own salon. For several weeks she had noticed an empty shop which had a notice in the window saying it was available for renting.

Her mother helped her to clean and paint it. Her father put up some mirrors, installed basins and built shelves and cupboards. Gillian had saved enough to be able to buy dryers and other necessary items of small equipment. Her brother offered to lend her money, if necessary.

On 1 October Gillian opened her new business, which she named 'Hair Line'.

1 Outline the difficulties she might have in her new business.

2 State the advantages which Gillian will have as a sole trader.

3 How might Gillian use extra money in the business?

Usually the size of a business is determined by the capital available, but in some cases the owner has made a conscious choice to remain small.

Read about Susanna in the following case study.

Susanna runs a small catering business from home. She caters for business lunches in companies' own premises, dinner parties in private houses and small family parties to celebrate events such as birthdays, christenings and anniversaries. She likes to do all the buying and cooking herself but employs Rebecca and Emma sometimes to help as waitresses at the functions.

Susanna has learned from experience that she can cater each week for a maximum of four lunches for twelve people each, as well as a maximum of two evening parties of approximately the same size. This calculation is based on the amount of freezer space she has, the size of her cookers and other kitchen equipment, and the room in her car for transporting her food.

She has built up a very good reputation and has as many customers as she can cope with. In fact, the quality of her catering is so high that she is having to refuse work and some customers are anxious to employ her for larger functions such as wedding receptions. Sometimes Susanna wonders if she should expand.

Activity

Read the case study above and then answer these questions:

1 Give details of two major items of expenditure Susanna would have if she decided to take on extra work.

2 What risk would Susanna take if she did decide to expand her business?

3 Name two advantages Susanna would gain by expanding.

4 What advice would you give Susanna about the future of her business? Give your reasons.

Partnership

Partnerships are most frequently found in professional businesses such as doctors, dentists, veterinary surgeons, accountants and solicitors. Just think of the doctor, dentist or vet you go to – do they work on their own or in partnerships? If you are unsure, have a look at the nameplates outside their doors or their headed paper. If they show a number of names, then the business is a partnership.

Partnerships are also commonly found in trades such as plumbers, hairdressers and electricians. They are popular in all of these businesses because expertise can be shared and each doctor, solicitor or hairdresser, for example, can take responsibility for one area of work.

A partnership consists of a minimum of two people (partners) and a maximum of twenty who jointly own a business. On some occasions an additional partner may be brought in to contribute capital but not to work in the business or to take any part in its organisation. This person is known as a 'sleeping partner'.

The partners:

- agree between themselves how they will run and organise their business
- are jointly responsible for any debts incurred in the business
- provide the entire capital for setting up their business

These are name plates of partnerships

- aim to make a profit and to expand
- are entitled to keep any profits made but also are responsible for losses incurred.

Like the sole trader's business, a partnership is easy to set up and requires only the agreement of the partners about how their business will be organised.

Partnership Act, 1890

The partnership is governed by the Partnership Act, 1890, which states that:

- any profits or losses made in the business would be equally shared between them
- no partner would be paid a salary.

The Partnership Act, however, does not take into consideration the individual situation in each business. For example, one partner may have contributed much more capital to the business than the others, so it would be only fair to give that partner more of the profits. The other way of rewarding that partner would be to pay him/her interest on capital. One partner may work full time in the business while the other partners may carry on their careers elsewhere. In this case it is unfair that the partner working full time cannot be paid a salary.

For all of the above reasons, the partners are advised to draw up a Deed of Partnership, which is a legal document setting out the terms and conditions under which that particular business would operate.

Deed of Partnership

If a Deed of Partnership is drawn up it takes the place of the Partnership Act for that business and states:

- how the profits and losses are to be shared
- the amount of capital which each partner will contribute
- if salaries are to be paid and the amount to be paid
- whether interest on capital is payable
- how the duties and responsibilities are to be shared
- how new partners might be introduced to the firm
- how the partnership could be dissolved and, in the event of this happening, how the assets would be shared.

Darren Anderson and Jamie Moore were good friends who both loved working with cars. Even before they left school they had earned pocket money for themselves by washing cars in the large yard at the side of Jamie's home. They quickly built up a good reputation as very capable workers and their business was increasing all the time.

The boys realised that their hobby could be turned into a profitable business so, soon after leaving school, they decided to open a car wash and valeting business in Garvagh.

Market research had shown that there was no local competition and they had proved that there was a demand for this service.

Darren had a substantial sum of money which he had inherited from an uncle and he was willing to invest some of it in the new business. Jamie was able to borrow £2,000 from his father and the boys were allowed to continue to use the yard at Jamie's house for a small rental.

They consulted a business adviser who helped them to plan the details of their business and also drafted their Deed of Partnership. Darren and Jamie thought the Deed was unnecessary since they were such good friends but the business adviser insisted.

Deed of Partnership
between
Darren Anderson
and
Jamie Moore

Trading name of the business:
Garvagh Car Valet Service

The function of the business will be to provide the services of:
- Power washing and waxing all road vehicles
- Cleaning vehicles in preparation for Motor Vehicle Testing
- Valeting vehicle interiors

Business Capital:
- The total capital of the business will be £4,000
- Each partner will contribute £2,000

Share of Profits or Losses:
- All profits or losses will be shared equally by Darren Anderson and Jamie Moore

Wages and Interest Payable:
- Each partner will be entitled to draw equal wages from the partnership as agreed annually between them
- No interest will be payable on capital

Banking
- The bank account will be in the name of Garvagh Car Valet Service
- Each cheque must be signed by both Darren Anderson and Jamie Moore

The Duties of the Partners will be as follows:
- Darren Anderson will undertake all accounting and banking
- Jamie Moore will undertake all purchasing of materials and machinery
- Both partners will share equally the work of washing, waxing and valeting

Dissolution of the Partnership
- The partnership may be dissolved by mutual consent between the two partners
- In this event, the assets will be shared equally between the two partners

Advantages of a partnership

- There is more capital in the business, which allows it to expand
- Specialisation is possible as the partners may bring different skills to the business
- The owners can share responsibility for decision making and discuss the problems which occur in the business
- If one partner is ill or on holiday the business can carry on
- The financial affairs of a partnership do not have to be published, although tax authorities must have access to them.

Disadvantages of a partnership

- As in the case of the sole trader, the major disadvantage in a partnership is unlimited liability. This means that if the partners do not have enough money in their business to pay their bills, they have to use their own private money. This puts their private possessions at risk. Each partner is liable in this way even if the debt was created by one of the other partners
- If one partner is dishonest or inefficient, all partners are held liable for that partner's actions or decisions. It is important therefore that partnerships are formed only between people who know each other well and trust each other totally
- The partners have to raise their own capital
- When compared with a large company, the amount of capital in a partnership business is small. They have the same difficulty as a sole trader in borrowing money from banks and cannot take advantage of economies of scale
- There is the possibility of conflict between the partners
- The death or bankruptcy of one partner may cause the break-up of the business. Otherwise the remaining partner has to 'buy him out'. This is known as 'lack of continuity'.

Activity

Gillian Morton's hairdressing business in Newcastle, 'Hair Line', has been very successful. She now employs two juniors to do shampoos and act as receptionists, and her own skills are in great demand as a hairdresser.

However, Gillian is annoyed at having to turn away customers because she is too busy. She knows there is enough work for two qualified hairdressers and has thought of employing another one to work with her. The difficulty is lack of space and she does not want to borrow money in case she could not repay it.

Gillian's friend, Charles Doherty, also a qualified hairdresser, has discussed the possibility of forming a business partnership with her. Eventually they decide to go for it. They also decide to retain the name 'Hair Line', to make it a unisex salon, to keep the two juniors and to move to larger premises which are available in the town. They have agreed to contribute £10,000 each as capital and wish to draw up a Deed of Partnership.

1. **Design a Deed of Partnership suitable for Gillian Morton and Charles Doherty.**
2. **Name any advantages which Gillian will gain by moving into a partnership.**
3. **What new problems may arise for Gillian in the new business arrangement?**

Limited companies

A company is a group of people who have joined together to form a business. You may be thinking that that sounds like a partnership. Right so far – but read on to see the differences between companies and partnerships.

It is legally possible to form a company with as few as two shareholders and one director and there is no limitation on how large it may become. While there are many small companies in Northern Ireland, there are also many which are extremely large. Businesses on this scale could not possibly raise the amount of capital required if they remained as sole traders or partnerships.

Lidl – one of the large limited companies operating in Northern Ireland

Shares and shareholders

In order to raise the vast amount of capital required, members of the public are invited to become members of the company and invest money in it. They do this by buying shares on the Stock Exchange. This makes them shareholders – or part-owners – in the company. From the company's point of view this has the advantage of providing large amounts of capital, while the shareholder benefits by becoming a part-owner of the company and being entitled to a share of its profits at the end of the year.

There are two types of shares:

- **Ordinary shares**. These shares are not guaranteed a dividend (share of the profit) at the end of the year. Whether they get a dividend depends on how successful the company has been during the year. Owners of ordinary shares are given voting rights in the company which gives them a say in the election of the Board of Directors.
- **Preference shares**. These shares are less common and are safer because they are guaranteed a fixed dividend out of the profits before any payment is made to the ordinary shareholders. Preference shareholders usually are not given voting rights in the company because their investment is not at as much risk.

Ownership and control of a company

Although the shareholders are the owners of the company, obviously it is impossible for them to run the company. The shareholders are entitled to attend the company's annual general meeting to elect a Board of Directors who run the business on their behalf. In practice, few shareholders actually attend the annual general meeting.

Although the Board of Directors has overall responsibility for the running of the company, they employ managers to undertake its day-to-day running. This situation is often referred to as a 'divorce of ownership and control', because the people who own the company do not control its running and the people who run it may not be its owners.

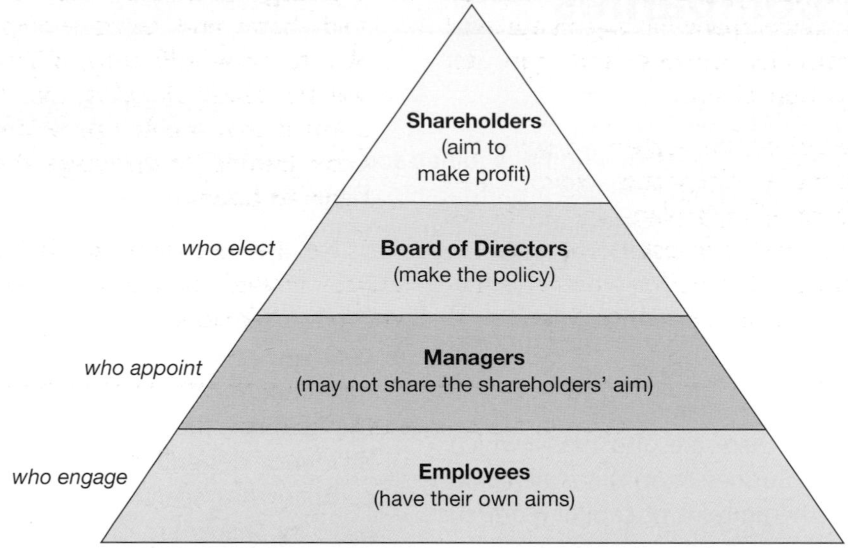

Activity

1 Explain the phrase 'divorce of ownership and control'.

2 Explain the effect this might have on the company.

Main features of limited companies

Apart from the increased capital you have already learned about, companies have two other important advantages over sole traders and partnerships.

1 Limited liability. The most significant feature of the limited company is that it has limited liability. This means that people who invest in a company cannot lose any money other than the amount they put into it. If the business should fail, the shareholders' liability is limited to the amount of their original investment – their private possessions cannot be taken. (You will remember that sole traders and partners risked losing everything if their businesses failed.)

2 Separate legal existence (incorporation). A limited company is considered to be quite separate from its owners in law – it is said to be incorporated. Being incorporated gives creditors the right to sue the company without affecting the owners of the company. Equally the company could sue its debtors if the need arose. This is very different from the situation of the sole trader or partners, who could be taken to court as owners of the business.

Forming a limited company

Setting up a limited company is a lengthy legal procedure and the company must be registered with the Registrar of Companies. The following documents have to be completed before trading may commence:

- **Memorandum of Association**. This has six clauses which state the official name of the company, the country in which the company will be situated, the work the company will be doing and the amount of capital with which the company is to start. The Memorandum also has a liability clause which states that members' liability is limited and an association clause which is a declaration by at least two people that they wish to form a company.
- **Articles of Association**. These show the voting rights of the shareholders, the method of election of directors, how profits will be divided, how meetings are to be conducted and the duties of the directors.

- **Certificate of Incorporation**. This is issued to show that the company has a separate legal existence from its owners and can act independently from them.
- **Prospectus**. Before shares can be sold, the company issues a Prospectus which gives details of the company's plans and its hopes for the future. Possible investors will read the Prospectus and use it to decide whether or not the company is a worthwhile investment.
- **Trading Certificate**. After the company has sold shares and raised enough capital to be able to trade efficiently, a Trading Certificate will be issued showing that the Registrar is satisfied that the company is in a position to begin trading. At that stage, the company may begin to trade.

There are two types of limited company: a private limited company and a public limited company. See figure.

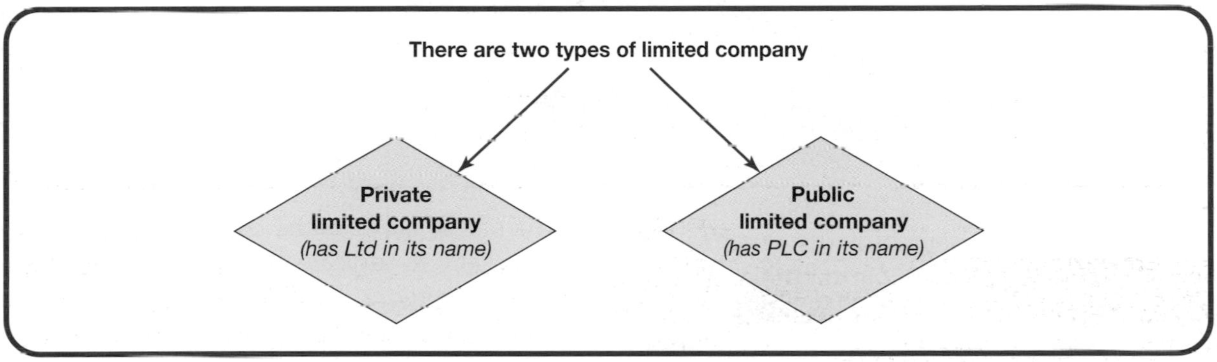

Private limited company

A private limited company is called 'private' because its shares cannot be bought by members of the public. Instead shares in a private limited company are held by a small group of people (very often members of one family) who are able to keep control of the business. Shareholders in a private limited company may only sell their shares privately and with the consent of the other shareholders. Each year the shareholders are entitled to a share of the profits which is paid in direct proportion to the number of shares each one holds.

A private limited company is attractive to shareholders because they retain control of the business while at the same time enjoying the benefits of limited liability. This gives them all the advantages they would have had in a partnership but with the added security of limited liability. You can now see why the partnership is less popular to trading businesses. The official name of the company includes either 'Limited' or 'Ltd' to indicate that the liability of the owners is limited.

Advantages of a private limited company

- The amount of capital available is much greater than in sole traders and partnerships
- Because the business is on a larger scale, it is usually easier for it to borrow money
- As a larger business, it can benefit from economies of scale
- It has limited liability
- The business has a separate legal identity from its owners and may take legal action on its own behalf without involving the owners
- The business has continuity. This means that if one shareholder dies the business is not affected
- There are a number of directors and managers in the business so responsibility and workloads are shared
- There are opportunities for specialisation and division of labour

- Control of the business is retained by a small group of shareholders.

Disadvantages of a private limited company

- Some of the financial information of a private limited company must be available for inspection by members of the general public. This may give competitors valuable insights into the affairs of the business
- Shares are not available for wider sale, so expansion may be difficult
- Shareholders are entitled to receive a share of the profit in the form of dividends
- The process of forming the company is more involved than it is in business organisations such as sole traders and partnerships.

Public limited company

A public limited company (PLC) is the largest type of private sector organisation and must have a minimum capital of £50,000. Shares in a public limited company may be sold to members of the public – that is how it gets its name. Shares are bought and sold on the Stock Exchange all the time, but although ownership of the shares may change, the actual amount of capital in the business does not alter. The value of the shares rises and falls according to how successful the company is at that particular time and according to the general economic conditions in the country.

A public limited company may have thousands of owners although the number of shares owned by each person may be quite small. However, the total capital in the company is very large. The liability of the shareholders is limited to the amount which they invested in the firm and they have the confidence of knowing that they cannot lose more than that. Each year a dividend is declared and shareholders are paid a share of the dividend in proportion to the number of shares they own.

The official name of the company includes the initials 'PLC' to indicate that the liability of the owners is limited.

Advantages of a public limited company

- Public limited companies are very powerful organisations with great influence in the market

- Shareholders have limited liability
- The capital available is very large, which gives the business all the benefits of easier borrowing and economies of scale
- A public limited company has the resources necessary for growth and expansion
- Because the business has a separate legal identity from its owners, it can take legal action without involving the shareholders
- The business has continuity and shareholders may buy and sell their shares without affecting the business
- Each director and manager has his/her own area of responsibility in the business, giving the benefits of specialisation and division of labour.

Disadvantages of a public limited company

- The shareholders are the owners of the business but the directors and managers make all the decisions. Therefore the owners of the company have no real say in its running
- The formation of a public limited company involves a lengthy legal procedure
- The financial information of a public limited company must be published for the information of the general public
- In some public companies top management and employees feel out of touch with one another
- Decision making in large companies is frequently slow because a series of meetings has to be held and numerous people have to be consulted.

Activity

The following extracts from letterheads indicate the type of business ownership in each of the businesses. Study the letterheads and complete the question for each business.

1

JONATHAN LOWRY
Plumber and Electrician
88 Middle Street
CRUMLIN
Co Antrim

2

MARIE LONG & KIM SHORTT
Qualified Hairdressers
101 Top Road
DROMORE
Co Down

3

PREMIER PRINTERS LTD
PREMIER PRINTERS LTD
66 Low Avenue
MARKETHILL
Co Armagh

4

ALPHA MUSIC MAKERS PLC
15 Beta Drive
CASTLEDERG
Co Tyrone

The type of business ownership is ....

How many people might it be owned by? ....

What, in your view, is the greatest advantage of this type of organisation?

....

What, in your view, is the greatest disadvantage of this type of organisation?

....

Franchise

A franchise is an excellent way for someone to set up in business. This method gives the person the opportunity to sell a well-known set of products, but without the risks attached to opening as a sole trader and having to start from scratch.

Franchising originated in America and has become popular all over the world. It is a system through which successful business ideas can be hired out to other businesses. A franchise gives permission to the franchisee (person who is buying the franchise) to set up a business using an established business name and idea. The business can also use the established trademark and image. A franchisee's liability depends on whether the business is organised as a sole trader, partnership or limited company.

You are familiar with and use many of these franchised businesses:

McDonald's is a favourite franchise. Some of the other franchises operating in Northern Ireland are shown here.

Another of the well-known franchises in Northern Ireland is Benetton – you probably shop there yourself!

Just imagine that, at some time in the future, you are setting up a new Benetton shop in your local area. Very simply, you would reply to an advertisement and apply to Benetton for a licence to sell their goods and operate a business using their name.

Benetton would consider your application – for example, they have to be sure that you have the experience and qualifications to run one of their retail outlets and that the new outlet would not be too close to one of their existing shops.

If your application is successful, you (the franchisee) would pay an agreed sum of money as capital for the use of the Benetton trademark and image, and Benetton (the franchiser) would provide shop fittings, stock, premises and design. They would also train you in the techniques which they apply to selling their products.

You would be expected to buy an agreed percentage of goods solely from Benetton, to reach a certain sales target and to organise the business according to the Benetton guidelines. In addition, you would have to pay a royalty to the franchiser – this is really a share of the profit made and would be a set percentage.

Advantages of a franchise

The franchisee gains:

- from having reduced risks and capital investment
- the sole right to sell a well-known set of products and brand in that particular area
- increased sales as consumers know the quality of that particular established brand
- use of a brand name
- training provided by the franchiser
- the right to be his/her own boss in the shop
- the benefits of national advertising and promotions
- continuous support from the franchiser
- increased borrowing power from the bank because franchised businesses are usually profitable.

The franchiser gains:

- increased opportunities for expansion
- further benefits from economies of scale
- a percentage profit from all sales in that particular shop
- another retail outlet which is run without any increased capital investment
- by having the retail outlet run and managed for them.

Disadvantages of a franchise

The franchisee loses:

- any individuality. All shops are decorated and organised in the same way in order to be instantly recognisable by the public

- independence as he must organise the business according to the rules given by the franchiser. In many ways he could be seen more as a manager than an owner
- the right to sell the business without approval from the franchiser
- the right to buy stock from other sources which may be cheaper
- royalties which must be paid annually to the franchiser.

The franchiser loses:

- management of the day-to-day running of the shop. If the local service is poor, the reputation of the franchise is damaged.

The Frying Squad

The Frying Squad is a fish and chip shop franchise which was founded by Michael Neill, a businessman from Bangor. He already has two outlets in Bangor, one in Carrickfergus and one in Larne. He has plans to open an additional six sites in 2009 in Belfast, Lisburn, Armagh, Ballycastle, Ballymena and Enniskillen.

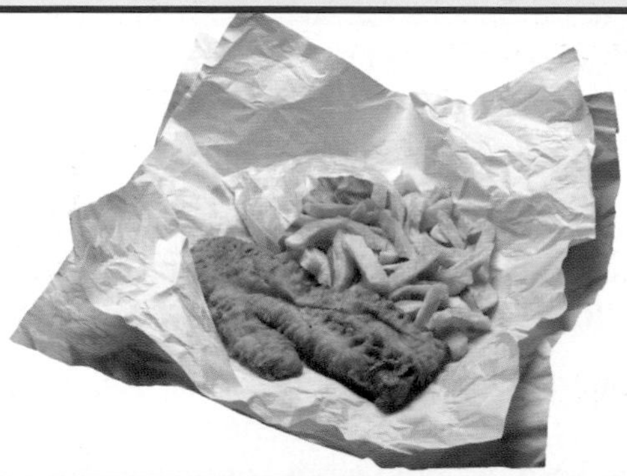

Activity

The following people all want to set up in business and ask you to advise them which type of business ownership is best suited to their needs. Complete the table with the appropriate names.

Person	Individual needs	Suitable type of business organisation
Phillip	I want to be my own boss	
Peter	I want to run a McDonald's fast food restaurant	
Brian	I want to operate a fleet of ten jets	
Lawrence	I want to go into business with my cousin	
Barbara	I need to have limited liability	
Olive	I want to be part of a really big business with lots of capital	
Dorothy	I would love to open up a little home bakery and do the work myself	
Florence	My sister and I could set up a dressmaking business. We work well together	
Christopher	I dream of owning a leisure centre with my four friends but I do want limited liability	

Activity

Complete the following table to show details of businesses in the private sector.

	Type of liability	Number of owners	Source of capital	Use of profits	Who controls the business?
Sole trader					
Partnership					
Private limited company (Ltd)					
Public limited company (PLC)					
Franchise					

Checklist

At this stage you should be able to:

- understand why and how a business starts
- identify and describe different types of business organisation
- understand the advantages and disadvantages of each type of ownership
- compare different types of ownership in terms of ownership, control, decision making, finance and liability.

Theme 1.4

Other forms of business ownership

General overview of public sector ownership

Any business which is owned by the country as a whole and run on behalf of the people is known as a public sector business. The government takes over the running and control of vital activities such as law and order or defence. Other activities such as education and the health service are also administered by government because it is important that every citizen has use of these services. If they were left in private ownership, it could be that those services would be too expensive and not everyone would have access to them.

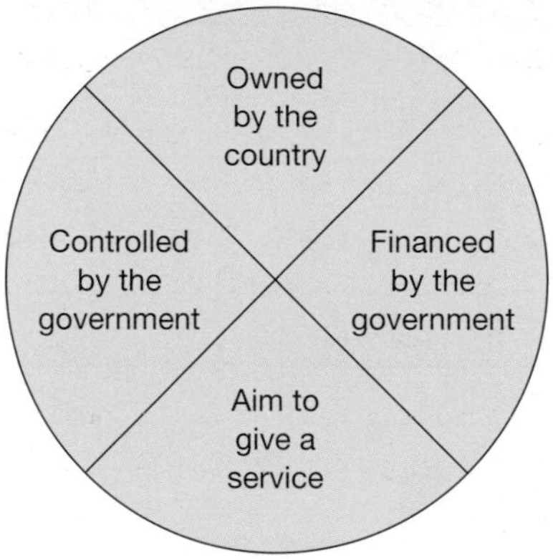

Some public sector enterprises are run by the central government of the country, either in Westminster or by the Northern Ireland Assembly in Stormont. Others, known as municipal undertakings, are run by local authorities (councils).

Although the government or local authorities run and control public sector businesses, they are owned by the country.

The finance for public sector businesses is found by either central or local government, and their aim is to give a service for the people of either the country as a whole or for those who live in the local authority area.

Parliament Buildings, Stormont

Differences between public and private sector businesses

Public sector businesses differ from private sector businesses in several important ways:

- Private sector businesses are owned by private people but public sector businesses are owned by the country as a whole. There are no individual owners in the public sector
- Private sector businesses are controlled by the people who own them or by directors and managers appointed to do so, but public sector businesses are controlled by the government or local authority
- Capital is raised differently. In private sector businesses, the capital is invested by private people but in public sector businesses the capital is either borrowed from the government's central funds – the Treasury – or taken out of the local rates
- The profits of the business are used differently and losses are met differently. In private sector businesses, at least some of the profits are distributed to the owners and they also bear the losses, but in public sector businesses, any profits are handed back to the government and their losses are offset by the Treasury
- Their aims are very different. Private sector businesses aim to maximise profits for their owners. In public sector businesses the aim is to give a service to the people and less emphasis is placed on profit making, although they are expected to break even.

This information is summarised in the following table.

	Private sector	**Public sector**
Ownership	Private individuals	Country or state
Control	Private owners or directors and managers working on their behalf	National government or local authority
Capital	Raised by private owners	Comes from Treasury or from rates
Use of profits	Distributed to owners	Handed back to government or local authority
Aim	To make profit	To give a service

The most usual form of public sector ownership are public corporations which are run by the government, and municipal undertakings which are run by local authorities.

Public corporations

Public corporations are defined as government-controlled market bodies. (A market body is one which produces goods and services for sale, and at least 50% of its income comes from sales.)

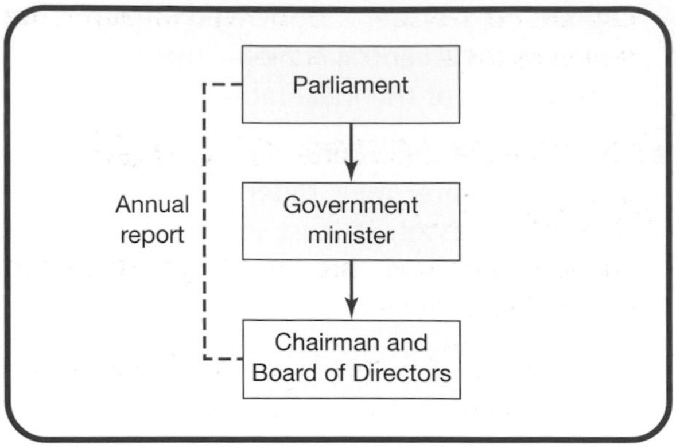

Control of a public corporation

Examples of public corporations in the United Kingdom include British Nuclear Fuels, Royal Mint, Bank of England, British Broadcasting Corporation, British Waterways Board and the Civil Aviation Authority.

You can see immediately that these activities are too important to be left to private individuals.

There are several reasons why these industries have been taken over:

- Some services are essential and must be provided, but their costs are so high that a privately-owned firm would not be interested in them because they would not make profit
- In many cases the capital investment needed would be too great for any privately owned business to afford
- It would be unsafe for private people to run dangerous industries such as the provision of atomic energy
- Nationalisation prevented large, powerful, privately-owned monopolies from existing and being able to set very high prices for their services
- In some instances, the business was failing, so the government took it over in order to save jobs
- There are examples where it would be wasteful to have several organisations duplicating services.

Aims of public corporations

The overriding aim of a public corporation is to give a service. At one time little or no emphasis was placed on profit making, however that situation has changed and nowadays public corporations are expected, at least, to break even.

Financial targets are set by the government and the corporations are now expected to meet those targets and to be able to pay for any new investment they may require.

Control

The government has overall control of the public corporation and appoints a government minister to take responsibility for it. The minister appointed would be the one whose department is most closely linked to the work of the corporation. For example, Railtrack is accountable to the Minister of Transport. The minister would oversee the appointment of a chairman and board of directors and they would become responsible for the day-to-day running of the industry.

The chairman of the board of directors must report annually to the minister who, in turn, presents the report in parliament where it is publicly debated and later published for the information of the general public.

Finance

Public corporations are financed in the following way:

- Most of the money for public corporations comes through grants from the Treasury which is the government department responsible for the country's finance

- In addition, the corporation may borrow from the Treasury
- If the corporation makes profit from its activities, some may be ploughed back into the business
- Public corporations get revenue from charging for the services they provide.

Advantages of public corporations

- The government ensures that the country's essential services are provided
- The government is in a good position to plan the overall provision for the country
- Services are not duplicated and resources are not wasted
- Any profits made could benefit taxpayers by reducing the level of taxation.

Disadvantages of public corporations

- Public corporations are very large which can lead to inefficiencies
- It is difficult to motivate employees in an impersonal organisation such as this
- The taxpayer has to meet higher tax payments if the corporation makes a loss
- The running of the corporation could be politically influenced.

Activity

In the following table link the first part of the sentence with its correct ending. The first one is done for you as a guide.

A public corporation is	to give a service
Public corporations are financed	that it may be inefficient
One advantage of a public corporation is	controlled by the government
A disadvantage of a public corporation is	by the Treasury
Public corporations aim	that services are not duplicated

Municipal undertakings

The word 'municipal' refers to local government so municipal undertakings are activities organised by the local councils.

Each district council has elected representatives who have been voted onto the council to represent the people and to work with the council staff to provide and maintain key services throughout the area.

The services for which local authorities are responsible may vary slightly from area to area, but all are expected to provide:

- refuse collection and disposal
- street cleaning

- health and environmental services
- parks and recreational facilities
- local housing
- parking areas
- maintenance of local roads.

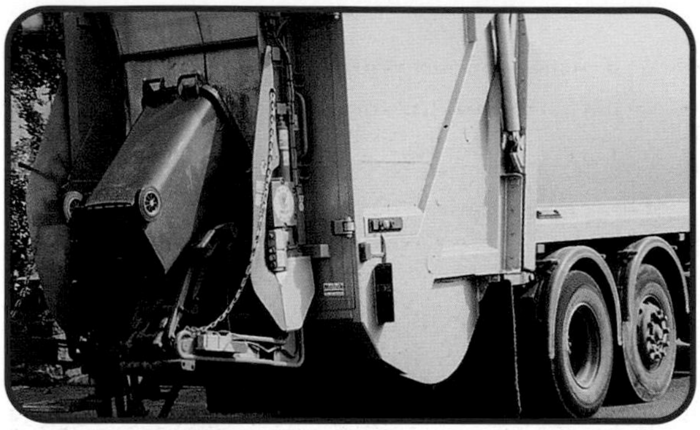

In addition, they support:

- the arts
- tourism
- economic development.

Main sources of finance for municipal undertakings

1 Government grant

The government gives a capital grant to the local authority to assist it with essential building work. It is unusual for the government to finance the project any further

2 Rates

Some of the money required to run local government enterprises comes from the rates. Rates are paid by each householder and each business in the area according to the size of their properties.

3 Charge for the activity

An entrance fee is charged to each person using the facilities provided by the council in the area – for example a swimming pool or leisure centre.

Activity

This activity is based on your own local authority. You should arrange for one member of your class to contact the local authority in order to find the necessary information. Alternatively, if you have access to the internet, you could find some information there.

Write the answers to the following questions in your notebook.

1 Give the name of your local authority
2 Write down the address of its main offices
3 Find out the name of the Chief Executive of the Council
4 Find out the name of the councillor who is responsible for the area where you live
5 Make a list of the business activities your local council undertakes.

The role of social enterprise

A social enterprise is a business which has social aims and reinvests a large proportion of its profits into the community or back into the enterprise. It does not have as its primary aim the need to make maximum profits for its shareholders or owners. A social enterprise makes its money in a socially responsible way and can be in any sector or any type of business. It competes alongside other businesses but uses business principles to achieve social aims and promote ethical trading.

A social enterprise is not to be confused with a charity. A charity depends on donations to survive whereas a social enterprise is self-sustaining.

Many social enterprises were originally set up to meet social needs such as unemployment in the area or to solve an environmental problem. A social enterprise often offers a more flexible approach to working and can be of particular benefit to groups of people such as the long-term unemployed, people with learning disabilities, minority ethnic groups or disabled people.

Fifteen

Fifteen is one of the most famous social enterprises and is a restaurant in London set up by the celebrity chef, Jamie Oliver. The restaurant trains disadvantaged young people who are interested in becoming chefs. Many of the young people accepted for training had criminal records, were drug addicts or were homeless. If they were committed to improving themselves and were hard-working they were given a year-long placement at the restaurant. The restaurant is very successful and every year new trainees start the course. Those finishing the course go on further work placements or sometimes open their own restaurants.

Divine Chocolate

Divine Chocolate was launched in 1998 to produce chocolate which was Fairtrade, farmer-owned and an affordable price. The enterprise has been very successful and the profits are passed on to the producers in Ghana of the cocoa from which the chocolate is made. Customers are keen to buy the chocolate products in our shops not only because the goods are affordable but also because they know they are ensuring a fair deal for the producers in Ghana who otherwise would receive much less for their cocoa.

Checklist

At this stage you should:

- be aware of the role of the public sector
- understand the role of social enterprise.

Theme 1.5

Sources of finance

The entrepreneur may need finance for the business not only when starting up but also at times during the life of the business. For example, new expensive machinery may be needed. Sometimes large sums may be required for a long period while, at other times, small amounts for a short time may do.

The time for which the finance is needed may be:

Short term	Medium term	Long term
May be used to:	May be used to:	May be used to:
• Buy extra Christmas stock • Avail of special offers • Help when trade is poor	• Buy short-life assets such as vehicles	• Buy long-life assets such as premises

At this stage, before you learn about sources of finance, it is helpful for you to do a little more work on 'capital'.

Capital can be thought of as the money invested in a business when it is first opened. That money is then used to buy whatever machinery, equipment or other items which are needed in the business.

These items become part of the assets (items owned) of the business. For example if the new business is a shop, the owner will need to buy equipment such as display cabinets and cash tills before the shop can be opened.

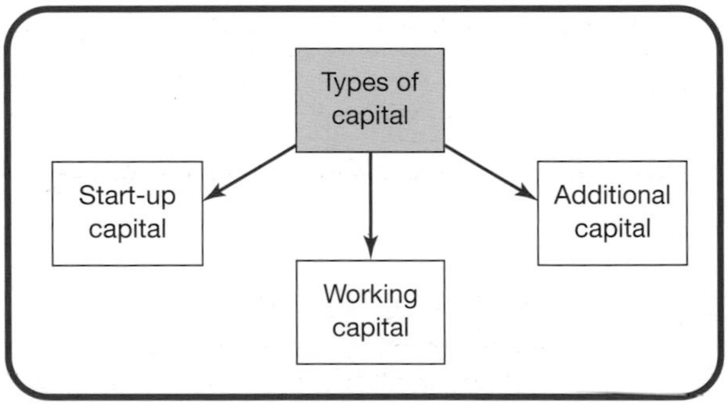

Types of capital

There are three types of capital.

Start-up capital

Start-up capital is the finance needed to get a business started. At the very beginning of its life, the business needs capital to get 'off-the-ground'.

For example, the owner of any new business must be able either to buy or to rent premises, to buy the basic equipment necessary for that particular type of business and to buy stock in order to trade.

Additional capital

Most businesses need additional (or more) capital at some stage. For example, if the business is successful, the owner may decide to expand it. In order to expand, the owner would have to purchase more assets such as vehicles or machinery, and recruit more employees.

Additional capital might also be required to extend a business into different areas or to start trading in new lines of goods. Other reasons for needing additional capital are the rebuilding or refurbishment of premises, or perhaps the decision to purchase premises which have previously been rented.

Working capital

Working capital is necessary to pay for the day-to-day running expenses of the business and to pay bills such as electricity and telephone.

If a business does not have sufficient working capital it will have cash-flow problems which could cause its total failure.

Lack of working capital would mean that the business could not pay its bills and eventually its creditors (people to whom it owes money) would have to take legal action to get their money. In extreme cases, the court would have the business wound up and its assets sold in order to raise money to pay the creditors.

Activity

Which type of capital would be appropriate in each of the following cases? The first one has been done for you.

Money to develop a new market	**Additional capital**
Money to buy stock to start trading	
Money to pay creditors	
Money to pay the rates bill	
Money to replace the computers	
Money to redecorate the offices	
Money to pay the suppliers	

Sources of finance

There are several methods by which businesses may raise necessary finance. The method which they choose depends on how much they wish to borrow and how long they wish to borrow it for.

Money can be raised both internally – inside the business – or externally – from sources outside the business.

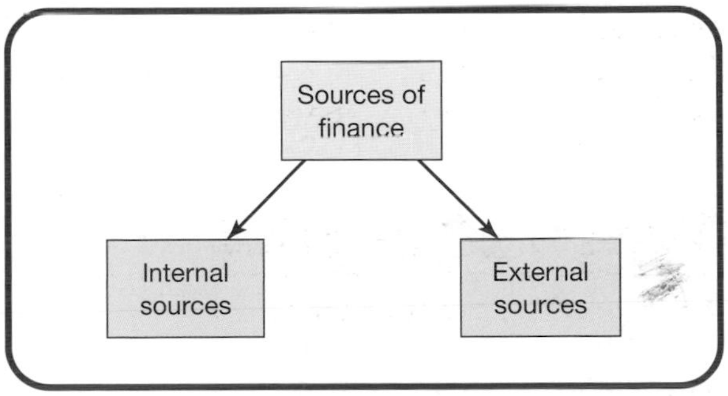

Internal sources of finance

There are five major internal sources – that means the money is raised *inside* the business. This is the cheapest method of raising finance because there are no interest charges.

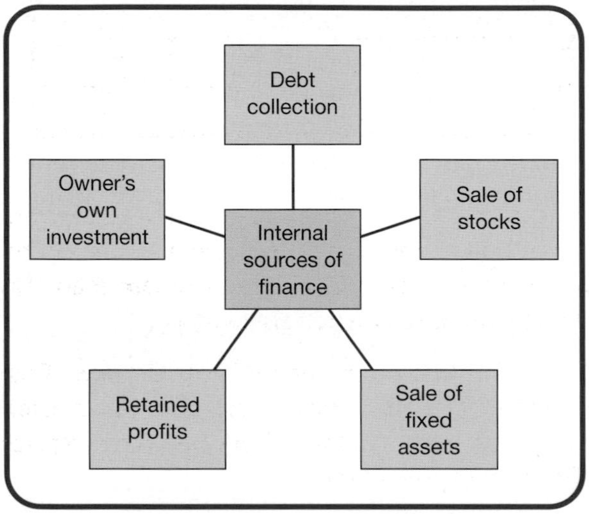

Owner's own investment

In this case, the owners draw on their own private financial resources and invest their private money into the business.

Using the owner's own capital has the advantages of remaining private and does not have to be repaid. On the other hand, not all owners have additional capital to call on.

This method would be used if the money were required long term.

Retained profits

Sometimes the owners may decide to 'plough back' profits from previous years instead of taking them out of the business for their own use.

This method also has the advantages of remaining private and does not have to be repaid. However, not all businesses make enough profit to be able to do this.

Retained profits would be used if the money were required in the medium or long term.

Sale of fixed assets

Businesses have large sums of money invested in their fixed assets and sometimes choose to sell some surplus assets – perhaps a machine or a building – in order to raise finance. However, new or small businesses are unlikely to have any surplus assets to sell and even a business which has surplus assets would find the method slow. There is also a limit to the number of assets which a business can sell before it starts to affect its production.

Selling fixed assets would be done if the money were required in the medium term.

Sale of stocks

Every manufacturing firm and every shop has stocks of goods which have not been sold. The firm can raise finance quickly by holding a sale and offering the goods to the public at a discount. In this way the business gets its money quickly and can use this money to manufacture or buy new stock. We are all familiar with the January sales in shops which clear the winter stock, and also raise money and create space for the new spring stock.

Selling stock would be done if the money were required in the short term.

Debt collection

Most businesses have debtors – people who have bought goods and have not paid for them. It is common practice for businesses to allow thirty days' credit although all the large supermarkets sell only for cash. The money which is owing by debtors is not working for the business, so the business has to have a system of credit control to chase debtors and get the money it is owed.

Debt collection is useful if the money were required in the short term.

Activity

Name one advantage and one disadvantage of each of the sources of finance named.

Source of finance	Advantage	Disadvantage
Owner's own capital		
Retained profits		
Sale of fixed assets		
Sale of stocks		
Debt collection		

External sources of finance

For GCSE you are required to study eight external sources – that means the finance is raised *outside* the business. External sources are usually more expensive because they often incur interest charges.

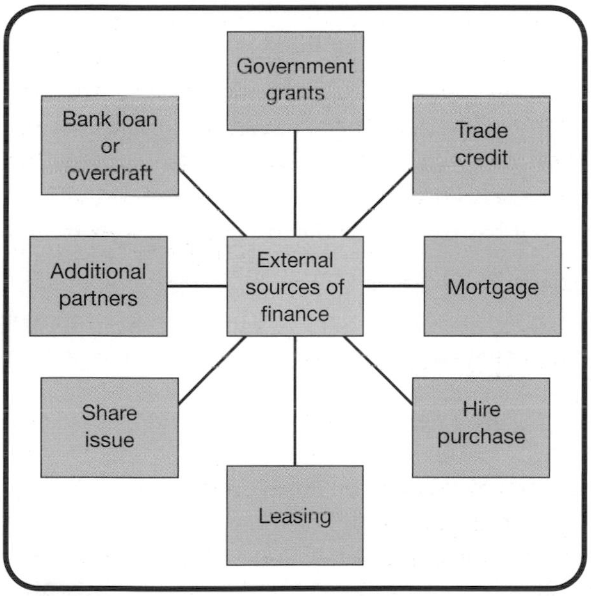

A bank loan is suitable as a medium- or long-term source of finance. The bank agrees to lend a set sum of money to the business for an agreed period of time. In return, the bank charges interest at a rate which is fixed for the entire period of the loan. For this reason a bank loan can be an expensive way to raise finance.

The bank requires security for its loans. This means that the bank has the right to sell an asset belonging to the business if the loan is not repaid within the agreed time.

A bank overdraft is a short-term means of finance. This is an arrangement with the bank whereby the business is allowed to pay cheques from its bank account beyond the amount which has been lodged in the account.

Interest is paid on the amount actually overdrawn each day and therefore getting a bank overdraft is usually cheaper than a bank loan which has a fixed rate of interest.

Additional partners

If a partnership needs extra finance the partners can agree to invite an additional partner to join the business.

The new partner will contribute capital which can be used to finance the purchase of assets or whatever the extra finance is required for in the business. However, the new partner is entitled to a share of the profits of the business.

Activity

Apart from the additional finance which the new partner would contribute to the firm, there are other advantages and disadvantages which taking on a new partner would have for the business.

1. **Write down one other advantage which introducing an additional partner would have for the business.**
2. **State one possible disadvantage for the business of introducing an additional partner.**

Share issue

In the case of a limited company, extra finance may be raised by issuing new shares in the company and inviting members of the public to become shareholders.

This is a long-term source of finance for the company and no interest is payable although all shareholders are entitled to dividends (share of the profits).

Leasing assets

Leasing is a method of acquiring assets and is a medium-term method of finance. Leasing is similar to renting and the business does not have to pay a lump sum as it would have to do if it were buying the asset.

The lease is arranged by a finance company and the business makes regular payments to it for the use of the asset. These payments can be very high because they include profits for the finance company. The asset remains the property of the finance company which is another disadvantage of leasing.

Despite these disadvantages, leasing is commonly used in business because it enables firms to have the use of up-to-date equipment (the asset will be updated regularly) and the business is able to get the asset immediately. In addition, maintenance and repair costs are usually paid by the finance company. A common example is a fleet of company cars, which are frequently leased.

Hire purchase

Hire purchase is another method of medium-term finance which is used for the purchase of assets. In the case of hire purchase, the business pays a deposit on the asset and agrees to pay off the balance in equal instalments over an agreed period of time. The business has the use of the asset while it is paying it off – or hiring it.

The major difference between hire purchase and leasing is that in the hire purchase system, the business eventually becomes the owner of the asset once it has paid off all the instalments.

Hire purchase is a popular method of buying assets because the business can have very modern equipment without having to part with a large sum of money at the outset, and it will eventually own the asset.

The major disadvantage is that the total cost of the asset is much higher than if it were bought for cash.

Activity

Andrew owns an earth-moving business and is hoping to obtain a new digger soon. He is unsure whether to use hire purchase or leasing and has come to you for advice.

Complete the following table to show Andrew the advantages and disadvantages of both hire purchase and leasing to help him to decide which of these two sources of finance would be better for him to use.

Advantages of hire purchase	Disadvantages of hire purchase	Advantages of leasing	Disadvantages of leasing

On the basis of your work, which method would you advise him to use?

Mortgage

A mortgage is a very long-term method of raising finance and is most often used to help in the purchase of premises.

The mortgage is arranged with a building society or a bank over a long period of years (usually twenty to twenty-five) and the sum borrowed, plus interest charges, has to be repaid in instalments over that period. This makes the purchase more expensive than if it were bought for cash. The premises act as collateral which means that the premises can be taken and sold by the building society or bank should the business fail to make repayments.

The big advantage of a mortgage is that the business has the use of the premises from the beginning and can carry on its work there while making repayments. Another advantage is that the premises eventually become the property of the business when all the payments have been made.

Trade credit

Trade credit is a short-term means of finance, and is where suppliers allow their customers to have a period of time (usually thirty days) in which to pay for the goods they have received.

Trade credit gives an advantage to buyers because they have the immediate use of the goods. This would help the working capital of a small shop, for example, because the shop could buy the goods on credit, and then sell them and raise money from them before having to pay the supplier.

Trade credit has the added advantage of being free. However, suppliers usually give discount for cash payment which would be lost by using the trade credit facility.

Government grants

Several systems of government grants apply in Northern Ireland to assist businesses financially. These are paid either through the Assembly, the national government or the European Union. Details change regularly so you are advised to keep up-to-date.

Such grants usually do not have to be repaid although they usually do have conditions. It is common, for example, that the government would specify the location of the business so that some of the unemployment problems in a certain area might be solved.

Government grants are given for a number of reasons but the most usual is to create employment in a depressed area in order to regenerate that area. Such government assistance may take the form of tax allowances, rates reduction or help with re-location costs.

Activity

In each of the circumstances described here you are asked to identify the most appropriate source of finance to use. Write down your answer in your notebook and give reasons for your choice of source.

1 A company wishes to obtain five new cars for its sales representatives.

2 A small shopkeeper needs to increase his working capital temporarily.

3 A business needs short-term help to buy extra stock for the Christmas market.

4 Elaine and Martin cannot raise enough money for their business to be able to compete with other businesses in their area.

5 A limited company wishes to expand its market and needs more long-term capital.

6 A large company needs to up-date its machinery but does not have enough money available immediately.

7 A business has plans to buy modern premises which would allow it to expand production.

8 A French company is planning to set up a new business in Northern Ireland in an area where there is high unemployment.

Checklist

At this stage you should be able to:

- understand internal sources of finance – owner's own capital, retained profits, sale of stock, sale of fixed assets and debt collection
- understand external sources of finance – bank loan or overdraft, additional partners, share issue, leasing, hire purchase, mortgage, trade credit and government grants
- identify the most appropriate source of finance to be used in particular circumstances.

Theme 1.6

Mission statement and business aims

When entrepreneurs start up new businesses, they will have aims which they set out in order to give a focus to their activities. These aims then become their targets and they can judge their progress against their stated aims.

Having aims is helpful to a business because they:

- define what a business is and what it aspires to be
- serve as a guide for the firm's activity in the future
- provide targets for the business to achieve
- act as a standard against which the business may compare its progress.

In order to be successful, the firm's aims have to be **SMART**:

Specific

Measurable

Attainable

Realistic

Timed

Mission statement

The firm's aims are summarised in a short statement known as a mission statement. This statement sets out the purpose of the business. The mission statement shows members of the public what the business stands for and what its guiding principles are.

Now study the following selection of mission statements and answer the questions at the end.

McDonald's*

McDonald's vision is to be the UK's best quick service restaurant experience. This will be achieved through five strategies:

Development:	Lead the Quick Service Restaurant market by a programme of site development and profitable restaurant openings
Our people:	Achieve a competitive advantage through people who are high calibre, effective, well motivated and feel part of the McDonald's team in delivering the company's goals
Restaurant excellence:	Focus on consistent delivery of quality, service and cleanliness through excellence in our restaurants
Operating structure:	Optimise restaurant performance through the selection of the most appropriate operating, management and ownership structures
The brand:	Continue to build the relationship between McDonald's and our customers in order to be a genuine part of the fabric of British society

*As widely quoted in 2002

Phoenix Natural Gas

Our aim is to make natural gas the fuel of choice for all energy consumers in Northern Ireland

PHOENIX NATURAL GAS

CULLODEN hotel

MISSION STATEMENT

Through our commitment to excellence, we will guarantee that every visit to The Culloden Hotel will be a special occasion.

Built for a Bishop . . . . . Fit for a King.

Culloden Hotel

VISION AND VALUES

Culloden Hotel, the flagship of Hastings Hotels will be internationally renowned as the premier hotel in Ireland.

We will enhance the magnificence and splendour of the Culloden Hotel by:

- *the warmth, friendliness and professionalism of our dedicated team;*
- *continually investing in the quality of our guests' comfort and staff development;*
- *anticipating and exceeding our guests' expectations*

Activity

The Culloden Hotel is situated in Cultra, Co Down in the former residence of a bishop. It is one of the very few five-star hotels in Ireland. In what way does the hotel's mission statement convey the quality of the hotel?

Activity

Answer the following questions in your notebook:

1. What do McDonald's expect of their members of staff?
2. What would you, as a customer, be entitled to expect in a McDonald's restaurant?
3. Suggest one way in which McDonald's could become 'a genuine part of society'.
4. From reading the Phoenix Gas mission statement, what do you think is a very important aim in that company?

Activity

Find out whether your school has a mission statement.

If it does, you should study it and comment on how it is being implemented.

If your school does not have a mission statement, you should design an appropriate one.

The aims of each business will be different according to the size and type of the organisation, although there are usually some general aims and common ideas in most of them. The usual aims are detailed here.

Business aims

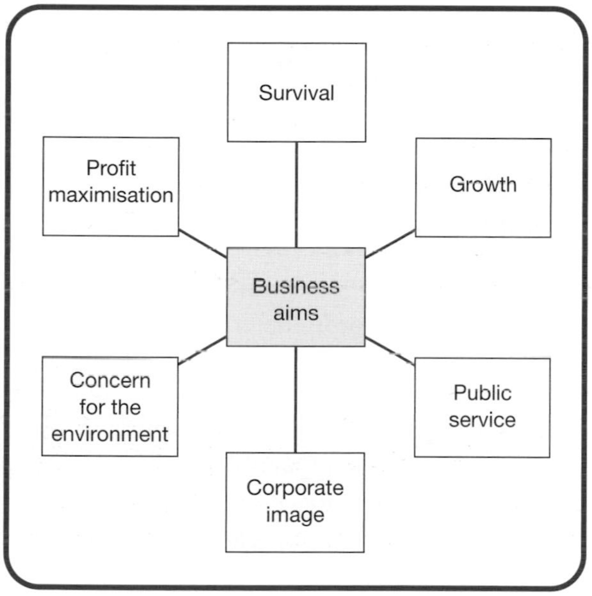

Survival

When a business first opens it takes some time for it to become established in the market. During the period when it is becoming established it is unlikely to be in a profit-making position, and its basic aim, at the early stage, would simply be to survive.

There are other times when established firms may have difficulty in making sales and even staying in business. This would occur at times when the country's interest rates are high making it difficult for people to borrow money. The result is that consumers are able to buy fewer and less expensive goods.

At such times the firm simply aims to survive and stay afloat until economic conditions improve. In order to do so, the business may reduce prices as low as possible to hold on to their customers or it may reduce other expenditure as far as possible.

Profit maximisation

One of the most basic aims for a business is to make profit and to improve on the profit levels of previous years. Everyone involved in the business benefits – the owners and shareholders get larger returns on their investments, customers will have an improved variety of goods on offer in the firm, while employees have job security and their morale is improved. In addition, making profit is the best way of guaranteeing the firm's survival and it also has other benefits for the business since it allows it to expand in the future and to take advantage of economies of scale.

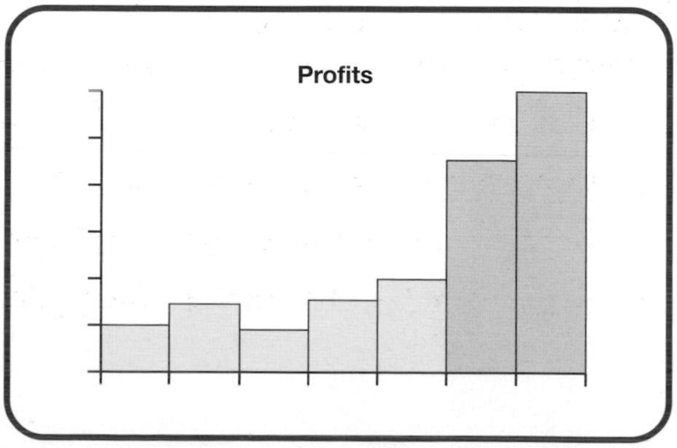

However, businesses have to be careful that, in trying to maximise profit, they do not price their goods so highly that consumers leave and take their custom away. This would cause the profit levels to fall and the custom would go to competitors instead.

The most successful business is one which is able to price and sell good quality items at prices which are fair. This will retain customers who will return to the business, thereby ensuring that it makes further profit.

Growth

If a business is successful it will aim to grow and expand its market into new areas by opening more branches, by taking over other businesses, or by extending its range of products. A business would have several reasons for wishing to expand in these ways.

By opening new branches the firm would have access to a larger market which would normally lead to increased sales and profits. Extension of the range of products, if successful, also would lead to increased profits. Higher profits lead to greater job security for employees and to greater consumer confidence in the firm.

Corporate image

For many businesses the need to have a good corporate image is very important. This means that the business wants to be thought well of by its customers, by other companies and by members of the general public.

In order to enhance and maintain its image, a business may provide a number of customer services such as a restaurant or a crèche. It may also contribute generously to the local community and have a high profile there.

Public service

Businesses in the public sector are set up with the aim of providing a public service rather than making a profit – although they are expected to break even (cover their expenses). The services which the public sector provides – such as electricity, water and sewerage – would not be economic for the private sector to provide throughout the whole country. Other public organisations such as hospitals, libraries and schools also exist to provide services to members of the public.

Charitable organisations, such as Save the Children Fund or Cancer Research Campaign, are established expressly to render a service. Their aim is to raise funds to help those in need.

Increasingly, businesses in the private sector are also becoming more aware of their public responsibility. As a result, many private sector businesses sponsor public and sporting events and play a part in the public life of their communities.

Concern for the environment

Concern for the environment and global warming have become major issues for all of us. All responsible businesses are aware of their responsibility to reuse and recycle. For example, all large supermarkets have either stopped using plastic bags or at least have limited their use by charging customers for them. Some businesses place great emphasis on caring for their local environment and enhancing the area surrounding their premises. In order to do this they landscape their grounds attractively and plant trees around their buildings which provide food for birds. Sometimes they sponsor competitions and work in the local schools in order to draw attention to the environment.

Most firms also use recycled paper and packaging materials and are careful that effluent and chemicals from their places of work do not contaminate local rivers and lakes. They also control their levels of noise and toxic waste.

Activity

Match the most appropriate aim to the businesses listed giving a reason for your choice. The first one is done for you as an example.

Description of business	Appropriate aim	Reason
Small boutique just starting up for the first time	Survival	As the business is new it will take some time to become established
Large popular supermarket		
Factory situated in an area of natural beauty		
Hospital		
Hotel which is proud of its reputation for high quality		
Farmer who has been badly affected by poor weather and foot and mouth disease		
Hairdresser who is well established and has regular customers		

Activity

The following list gives details of a number of businesses and names one aim which is important to each business. You are asked to complete the third column to show how that aim would affect the activities of that business. The first one has been done for you.

Description of business	Aim of business	How the business activities would be affected
Large grocery shop	Concern for the environment	Would plant trees in its grounds Would provide litter bins
Social enterprise	Public service	
Travel agency – during a recession	Survival	
International car manufacturer	Growth	
Small business which undertakes painting and decorating work	Profit improvement	
Up-market fashion store	Corporate image	

How the aims of a business may be in conflict

On occasions a business may find that its aims may be in conflict with one another. Keeping one aim can sometimes cause tension between the stakeholders or even with another aim. For example, shareholders are most interested in profit improvement and may be unhappy about some of the profits being given to a worthy cause such as the Third World. On the other hand, the donation to the Third World would improve the firm's corporate image, which is another of its aims.

To illustrate this point let us consider the following business.

A large meat processing factory is situated near a residential area of a major town. The factory is prosperous, profits are good and it provides employment for over one hundred local people. However, the local residents are unhappy because heavy traffic to the factory is causing dangers for the children and is damaging the road past their houses. They also complain about a bad smell coming into their houses from the factory.

The factory was due to be extended because it is so successful. The directors also had plans to install new processing machinery which would eliminate the smell. The residents formed a pressure group and have asked their MLA and the local council to help them to ensure that the factory does not get planning permission for the extension.

It seems impossible to satisfy all the stakeholders.

Activity

Consider each of the following courses of action and complete the spaces to show one group who would be satisfied with the action and a second group who would be unhappy with that action.

Action	Satisfied stakeholders	Dissatisfied stakeholders
The factory closes and moves to a different town	....	....
The factory expands on its present site and installs the new processing machinery	....	....
The factory stays as it is	....	....

Action	Satisfied stakeholders	Dissatisfied stakeholders
The factory spends a large sum of money widening and improving the road	....	....

If you were the managing director of this factory which cause of action would you recommend to your board?

Distinction between public sector and private sector aims

There is a distinction between the aims of businesses in the private sector and businesses in the public sector. In general, the differences are as follows:

Type of sector	Aims
Private sector – ● Sole trader ● Partnership ● Limited companies	● To create and improve profit ● To grow and expand ● To give customer satisfaction ● To have a good corporate image
Public sector	● To provide a service ● To break even
Social enterprise	● To contribute to the community ● To relieve social problems

Ethical and moral issues associated with business aims

Obviously the majority of businesses wish to make profit – that is the basic reason for being in business. However, they also want to deal fairly and honestly with their customers, employees and suppliers. That is their moral duty.

Quite apart from morals, would you ever go back to a business which had treated you dishonestly by giving you shoddy goods and refusing to change them, or by giving you less change than you were entitled to? Of course not, and businesses know that customers will return to them if they are treated fairly and honestly. Businesses do not pursue the aim of 'profit creation' at the expense of these issues and will be willing to reduce their profit a little for that reason.

Most businesses have 'care of the environment' among their aims. We are all responsible for the environment and businesses share that responsibility. For this reason, they landscape their grounds, plant trees, provide litter bins and encourage people to use them.

There are other moral and ethical issues which the majority of businesses see as important even though they may reduce the overall profit slightly:

- Most businesses pay their employees fair wages
- Many businesses refuse to buy goods which have been made in countries where workers are exploited
- Many businesses sell 'Fair Trade' products

- Many businesses use recycled paper and packaging and sell biodegradable products in their shops
- The Body Shop has always refused to sell any product which was tested on animals.

Checklist

At this stage you should be able to:

- know and understand business aims
- understand how the aims of a business affect its activities
- understand how, on occasions, these aims may be in conflict
- distinguish between public sector aims and private sector aims
- analyse how social enterprise aims differ from those of other organisations
- understand the ethical and moral issues associated with business aims.

Stakeholders

Stakeholders in a business are people who affect, or may be affected by, the actions of that business.

The following are the main stakeholders in business:

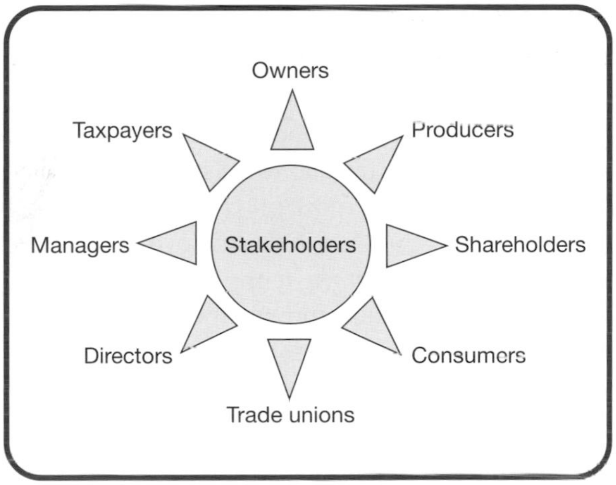

Owners

The owners of a business are those who have invested money in it. They may have contributed the total capital for the business as in the case of a sole trader or a partnership. In a small business, the owners may also manage and run the business.

Owners have the greatest interest in the progress of the business since a large part of their money is invested in it and, in the majority of cases, the owners depend on the business for their livelihood.

The reward which owners get from the business is in the form of profit but they also risk having to bear any loss incurred in the business.

Shareholders

Shareholders are those people who invest money in a business which is a limited company. Their investment is in the form of shares and this makes them part owners of the company. Shareholders do not take any part in the management of the company although they are entitled to attend the annual general meeting and vote for the Board of Directors.

The reward which shareholders receive from the business is in the form of a dividend which is a share of the annual profit. If the company is not in a profit-making position, the shareholders risk losing their shares. However, they have limited liability which means that their loss is limited to the amount they invested in the shares.

Directors

Directors are appointed to the Board of a limited company and their function is to be responsible for the overall running of the company. Directors make the policy decisions and have the ultimate power in the company. It is usual for a company to have a managing director and a number of other directors each of whom looks after a certain area of the firm's operation, for example sales, finance or production.

The reward which a director receives from the business is in the form of a salary, although it is possible for directors also to be shareholders in which case they would also receive a dividend.

Managers

Managers are the second layer of authority below the directors, and they have responsibility for the day-to-day running of the business. Managers oversee the work being done in the company, and the workers and supervisors report to them.

Managers are rewarded with a salary and they have a great interest in the success of the business since their employment depends on it.

Producers

Producers of materials to a business also have a stakeholding in it and want to see it succeed. This is because producers do not want to lose any of their customers but want to ensure that they are prosperous and able to pay their accounts.

Producers are rewarded by high levels of sales which adds to the profits of their own businesses.

Consumers

Consumers are the firm's customers and therefore are vital to its success. The business depends on consumers for its income and needs them to purchase its goods or services. If consumers do not buy the firm's products, the business will experience a loss and may eventually have to close.

Consumers have a stake in a business since it probably is situated in a convenient place for them and they will support it if it supplies goods at suitable prices. They also have an interest in seeing that the business succeeds because they have a greater number of firms to deal with which improves the competition and the variety of goods on offer.

Taxpayers

Taxpayers indirectly are stakeholders in business and therefore wish to see general business prosperity. Everyone pays tax in some way. Those who are earning pay income tax and we all have to pay Value Added Tax (VAT) on most purchases. If businesses are successful, there is full employment in the country so workers have more money to spend. This, in turn keeps government spending down on items such as unemployment benefits and therefore the government has less need to increase taxation.

Trade unions

A trade union is an organisation which represents the interests of the workers in the firm and negotiates with management on their behalf. The trade union has an interest in seeing a business succeed because it ensures the safety of its members' jobs. If the business loses profit or fails altogether it will have to make workers redundant. Those workers would then depend on the trade union to try to save their jobs or to find work for them elsewhere.

Activity

Name the stakeholder who is most likely to have said the following:

1 I want the business to succeed so that they will continue to buy my products.

2 We want our members to have secure jobs in that business.

3 I want to make profit from my investment in the business

4 I want the business to succeed because my job depends on it.

5 If the business fails there would be less wealth in the area.

6 I want the business to remain open because it is convenient for me to use.

How the aims of stakeholders may be in conflict

Here are some possible situations in which conflict may arise:

Owners, shareholders and directors want to make maximum profit from the business. In order to do this, they may try to pay lower wages to their employees which would bring them into conflict with the trade unions who represent the employees.

They may also hope to buy their stock from producers at minimum prices. Such action would bring them into conflict with the producers.

In another attempt to maximise profits, managers may raise their selling prices which would bring them into conflict with consumers who do not wish to pay more for their goods.

Owners may wish to re-invest profits into the business while shareholders may wish to have the profits shared out to them.

The local authority or taxpayers who live near the business may be in conflict with the business because of noise, waste pollution or additional traffic.

Activity

Complete the following table to show why each stakeholder would have an interest in a business.

Stakeholder	Interest
Owners	
Shareholders	
Directors	
Managers	
Producers	
Consumers	
Taxpayers	
Trade unions	

Customers

All businesses consider customers to be of the greatest importance. Quite simply, without customers the business ceases to exist. Therefore, businesses spend a lot of time and money on customer service to ensure that customers are satisfied with both their product and their service.

Businesses find that it is cheaper to retain their existing customers than to attract new ones. This is because attracting new customers requires expensive promotional activity. It involves advertising widely, and engaging in promotions such as special discounts to encourage new customers to buy the product. Keeping existing customers does not require expense but, instead, it makes the customer feel valued, is aware of their needs and tries to meet those needs, listens seriously to their views and rectifies situations where complaints have been made. This is known as customer service (see a later section in this theme).

Sir Tim Leahy is the Chief Executive of Tesco plc and he understands how important customers are. His motto is: 'Follow the customer, if they change, we change.' Perhaps that is why Tesco plc is one of the most successful retailers in the United Kingdom. Another business executive is quoted as saying 'If you don't take care of your customers, someone else will.'

Added value

Consider the following two situations.

'Good Store'	'Super Store'
'Good Store' is a typical large chain-store which sells the full range of groceries, cleaning materials, newspapers, books and magazines, DVDs, flowers, make-up and pet foods. It also has a bakery section, a butchery counter and a coffee shop. It is difficult to find any assistants in the aisles and if you do find them, they are either chatting or are too busy stacking shelves to help you to find items. Very often they block the aisles with boxes they have brought from the storeroom. The coffee shop closes two hours before the shop and cleaners begin to clean at that time. The shop has ten check-out points but usually only five are open.	'Super Store' is another typical large chain-store which sells the full range of groceries, cleaning materials, newspapers, books and magazines, DVDs, flowers, make-up and pet foods. It also has a bakery section, a butchery counter and a coffee shop. Assistants are positioned in all aisles and are trained to look after customers and to help them to find items. Shelf stacking is done early in the morning or at other less busy times. The coffee shop is bright and clean and remains open throughout the day. Cleaning is carried out at night. The shop has ten check-out points and they are all open all the time. Customers have two points added to their 'Super Store' cards for every £1 of goods they buy in the store. In addition, the store has a packing service for disabled customers and assistants will take their trolleys to their cars if requested. Prices are the same in both stores.

So which one would you go to? Of course, you would rather go to 'Super Store'. But what is the difference between the two stores? We know that the prices are the same in both stores, the range of goods is the same in both stores and the facilities are the same in both stores. The difference is the **value added**.

Value added refers to what an organisation does in addition to offering its basic product or service. It enhances the value of everyday objects or services.

Customer service

Customer service is a value added and it is customer service which is the real difference between 'Good Store' and 'Super Store'.

Customer service is the responsibility of every employee in the organisation. Everyone from part-time students working on the shop floor to the managing director must provide customer service and create a good impression.

An important part of customer service is how the business deals with complaints. It is expected that every complaint would be investigated seriously and responsibility admitted. Customers are now much more likely to bring poor products or service to the attention of the store than once was the case. If the complaint is dealt with promptly and effectively, the customer will recommend the business to others. On the other hand, they will also tell others if the complaint has been handled badly.

Effective customer service is important because:

- it gives a business a competitive advantage over other businesses
- it will be rewarded with customer loyalty – the customers will remain with that organisation
- if it deals with complaints effectively, customer loyalty is further strengthened
- this will improve sales and profit levels
- it will attract new customers
- it will make the employees more efficient
- it will improve communication in the business
- it will make customers more aware of the needs of all types of customers – different age groups, different cultural backgrounds, customers with young children and groups with other specific needs.

Customer service can be judged in three ways:

1. Timeliness – telephone calls should be answered within 20 seconds.
2. Accuracy – customers should always receive the correct order.
3. Appropriateness – if the customer has two difficulties with the firm, both of them should be solved.

Activity

In order to analyse the different ways in which organisations provide customer service, you should observe a business organisation in your local area.

1. **Make a list of the examples of good customer service you see in that business.**
2. **Suggest ways in which their customer service might be improved.**

Checklist

At the end of this theme you should be able to:

- understand the interests which the following stakeholders have in a business: owners, shareholders, directors, managers, producers, consumers, tax payers and trade unions
- consider the business from the perspective of each of these stakeholders
- analyse how the aims of these stakeholders may be in conflict
- understand how it is more expensive to attract a new customer than to
- keep an existing one
- understand how customer service adds value
- analyse different ways in which businesses provide customer service.

2

PRODUCTION

Theme 2.1

Types of production

Before you started this Business Studies course, you may have thought that 'Production' referred only to making goods. Not so. The term 'Production' more accurately refers to the creation of either goods or services. For example, the teachers in your school are involved in production – producing the service of education.

Production may be divided into three types – primary, secondary and tertiary. You are already familiar with these three words in connection with school. You started your education in a primary school – that was the first stage. You are now at the secondary level of education and if you continue into college or university, you will enter the tertiary level – the third stage.

Similarly, each industrial and business activity falls into a primary, secondary or tertiary stage.

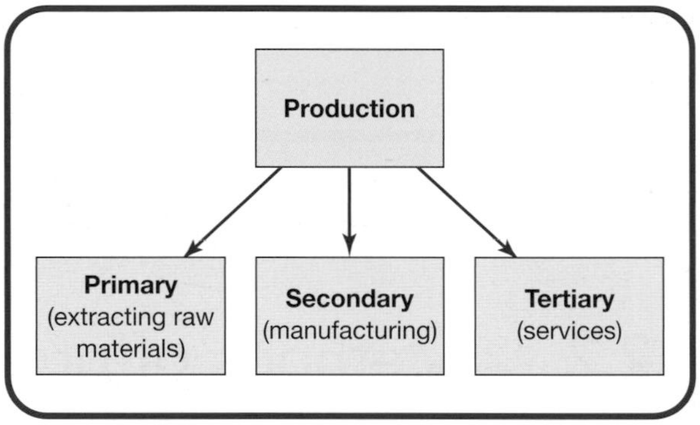

Primary industry

Primary industry is the getting of raw materials from the ground or from the sea. It is also using the earth's resources to grow items such as crops, fruit, flowers and trees.

Primary industries include farming, fishing, mining, quarrying, forestry and oil drilling.

Examples of primary production in Northern Ireland

Forestry in Fermanagh

Fishing in Kilkeel

Farming is particularly important in Northern Ireland and there are 3.5 times more people working in agriculture in Northern Ireland than in the rest of the United Kingdom.

Secondary industry

Secondary industry takes the raw material produced by the primary industries and works on it to manufacture finished goods. For example wood produced by a primary industry would be manufactured into tables and chairs by a secondary industry.

Tertiary industry

Tertiary industry provides services to all the other industries and to members of the public. These services include commercial services such as banking, marketing, insurance, transport and retail trading. It also includes all professional services such as entertainment, hospitality, education, legal, religious and medical services.

Chain of production

Farmers grow potatoes
↓
Potatoes are transported to Tayto Factory
↓
Potatoes are sorted, cooked and processed into potato crisps
↓
Crisps are filled into bags
↓
Bags of crisps are packed into boxes
↓
Boxes of crisps are distributed to shops
↓
Crisps are sold in shops to the general public

Each stage of production is dependent on the other two in order to get the finished product to the consumer – this is known as the chain of production.

The production of Tayto Potato Crisps in Tandragee illustrates the chain of production very well and shows how all three stages of production work together and are required in order to get the crisps to the consumer.

Activity

The stages involved in manufacturing potato crisps are listed here. Beside each stage, in the spaces provided on the right-hand side, write down whether it is primary, secondary or tertiary.

Farmers grow potatoes ....

Potatoes are transported to the Tayto Factory ....

Potatoes are sorted and processed into crisps ....

Crisps are filled into bags ....

Bags of crisps are packed into boxes ....

Boxes of crisps are distributed to shops ....

Crisps are sold to the general public ....

Activity

Show which type of production each of the following workers is involved in.

Occupation	Primary, secondary or tertiary
Insurance agent	
Fisherman	
Furniture manufacturer	
Teacher	
Farmer	
Shopkeeper	
Market gardener	
House builder	
Solicitor	
Coal miner	

Changing trends across the types of production

The modern trend in employment is for a shift away from the primary and secondary sectors towards employment in the tertiary sector. The service sector is the fastest growing sector of production at present. This trend, known as de-industrialisation, is affecting most developed countries.

The following two tables illustrate the changes in Northern Ireland in the number of people employed in each of the primary, secondary and tertiary sectors between March 2002 and September 2008.

Number employed in different industrial sectors in Northern Ireland in March 2002

Sector of industry	Number of employees	Percentage of total workforce
Primary	19,620	3%
Secondary	132,250	20%
Tertiary	498,700	77%
Total	**650,570**	**100%**

Source: DETI – Quarterly Employment Survey (adapted)

Number employed in different industrial sectors in Northern Ireland in September 2008

Sector of industry	Number of employees	Percentage of total workforce
Primary	14,260	2%
Secondary	131,780	18%
Tertiary	568,640	80%
Total	**714,680**	**100%**

Source: DETI – Quarterly Employment Survey (adapted)

The figures for the six years show that:

- The overall number of people in employment in Northern Ireland has risen by 64,110 during this particular period. However, this book is being written in January 2009 in a time of recession which means that future figures are likely to be much lower
- There was a decrease of 5,360 in the number employed in the primary sector in Northern Ireland even though overall employment was increased. This meant that only 2% of all people employed in Northern Ireland in September 2008 were working in the primary sector which represented a decrease of 1% over the six years
- The decrease in the number employed in the secondary sector was less than the decrease in the primary sector during these six years. However, this is the sector which is losing many jobs during this period of recession. Many factories are closing or are working three-day weeks and the construction industry is particularly badly affected
- The tertiary sector continued to grow between 2002 and 2008 and employed an additional 69,940 people. This meant that 80% of all people employed in Northern Ireland in September 2008 were working in the tertiary sector which represented an increase of 3% over the six years.

De-industrialisation is caused by several factors:

- Manufactured goods are imported cheaply from countries such as Japan, China, Malaysia and Taiwan
- The agriculture industry has had difficult times
- People are spending more on leisure activities so entrepreneurs have moved into that market
- There is now more demand for services such as education, personal banking, insurance for property and cars, investment and legal advice, therefore increasing numbers of employees are needed in these areas.

De-industrialisation: industrial areas become residential

Activity

1 On a computer create a table with four columns and twenty-two rows.

2 In the first row, label the four columns – occupation, primary, secondary, tertiary.

3 In column 1, rows 2 to 21, write the occupations of twenty people you know well – members of your family or other close friends.

4 In columns 2, 3 and 4 classify each occupation as primary, secondary and tertiary by ticking the appropriate list.

5 On row 22 total the number of occupations in each of the three sectors.

6 Study your results and say whether they reflect the percentages shown for Northern Ireland in the table above.

7 What do your results show about the area you live in?

Checklist

At this stage you should be able to:

- distinguish between the main types of production
- classify businesses according to their type of production
- understand the changing trends across the types of production.

Theme 2.2

Methods of production

There are three methods of production, and the method chosen by any business depends very much on the type of product being made and the quantity which is required. Although we shall study each of these methods separately, it should be understood that, in practice, very often a business may use a combination of the methods for some of its work.

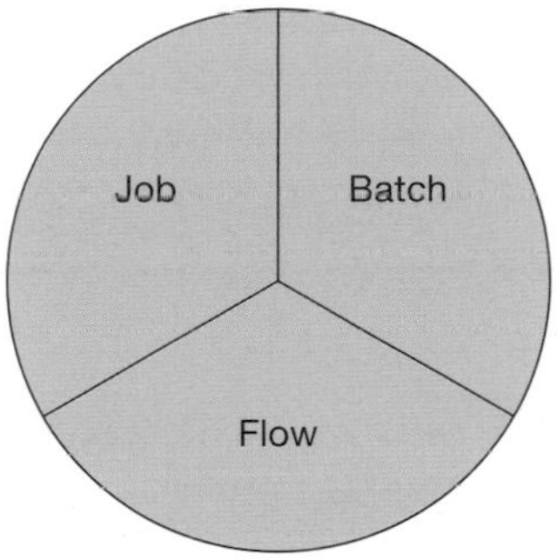

Job production

One of Joan's designs

Joan Johnston is a talented dress designer in Ballynahinch who especially enjoys designing and making wedding dresses. She works alone in a large room at the back of her house. Although her dresses are expensive, they are in great demand because they are expertly handmade and unique. Each girl comes to her with a vague idea of the design of the wedding dress she would like, and Joan draws the final design and makes the dress to suit the customer's individual requirements.

Joan gets tremendous job satisfaction from her work, and produces only one dress at a time so that it gets her full attention. Very often she changes little details of the dress during its production because the customer sometimes changes her mind. Joan is happy to do this because she wants the customer to be really pleased with the dress which is a 'one-off' and individually produced for her.

Joan's work is a good example of job production.

Job production is where one single item is made at a time and is often produced to the customer's individual specification. Each product is unique and a long time would usually have been spent on it. For this reason goods produced by this method are expensive to buy.

Job production would not be suitable for most factories but would be found in craft shops where emphasis is placed on the handmade, interesting and individual character of the product.

Examples of goods made by the job production method are:

- craft goods
- luxury cars
- designer clothes
- double glazing
- stained glass windows
- landscape gardening
- house plans
- antique furniture.

Advantages of job production

- Each piece is made to the customer's exact requirements
- Job satisfaction is high for the worker
- Quality of the goods is very high
- The design is flexible and can be changed.

Disadvantages of job production

- The products are very expensive
- The work is very time consuming.

Batch production

Cupid's is a shop in Ballynahinch which sells wedding dresses. The sales manager, Margaret Wilson, has been looking at the wedding photographs in the local newspapers. She has been very impressed with the dresses which the newspaper reports of the weddings say were made by Joan Johnston.

Margaret approached Joan and asked her to make ten dresses – all the same design, but in different sizes – for sale in Cupid's. She promised that another order would follow for ten dresses of a different style.

Joan agreed with this arrangement and had to employ two temporary dressmakers, Hazel and Joyce, to help with the additional work.

Joan has now moved into batch production.

Batch production is used where several of the same product are made in a batch. When the first batch is completed, production continues with a number of a second product and so on. All the items made in a batch are the same so production is speeded up. This reduces the cost of labour and results in the final product being less expensive for the customer.

Batch production would be suitable for businesses such as bakeries which bake a number of the same loaves and cakes every day, and where the products do not have to be individual. Newspapers are also produced by this method. The papers are printed every day and each batch must meet a deadline.

Examples of goods made by the batch production method are:

- newspapers
- bread
- clothing
- furniture

- motor car components
- books
- building of housing estates where all the houses are the same.

These houses are all identical – an example of batch production

Advantages of batch production

- Workers may specialise to some degree
- Labour costs are reduced so the final price is lower
- Machinery may be used
- Production is faster.

Disadvantages of batch production

- The work is less interesting than in job production and is repetitive
- More space is required for working and storage
- Larger stocks of raw materials must be kept
- Machines may have to be re-set between batches which loses time.

Flow production

Other shop managers in Cookstown, Ballyclare, Newcastle and Maghera have been contacting Joan Johnston to ask if she would supply wedding dresses for their shops.

Joan is certainly interested in this extra work but realises that her production method would have to change. She rents larger premises, buys additional sewing machines, makes Hazel and Joyce permanent, and employs three additional people – Evelyn, Robert and Mervyn. Joan names the business 'Wedding Belles'.

Joan organises the operation on an assembly line basis and each of the six people working in the business is responsible for his/her own separate part of the production of the wedding dresses.

Although her profits are higher, Joan regrets the fact that the larger number of dresses she now produces are all the same. She also misses the personal contact with her customers which she once enjoyed.

Joan has now moved into flow production.

Flow production is also sometimes known as mass production or assembly line production. It is the method used in factories and most modern production would employ this method.

In flow production, one product is made continuously and in large numbers. A conveyor belt or assembly line is organised and, as the product moves along the line, parts are added to it. In this way, the item starts at the beginning of the line as raw materials and is packaged and ready for sale when it reaches the end of the line.

Operation of an assembly line requires numbers of employees to sit at their particular places and perform their allocated tasks as the product moves along the line. Each employee's task is very repetitive and simple so those engaged in flow production tend to be unskilled or semi-skilled. Motivation of workers is often a problem, and strategies such as job rotation are often used in order to relieve the monotony.

Flow production is suitable for use where large numbers of identical products are being made.

This method is very dependent on machinery, therefore a large amount of capital is needed to establish the factory.

However, since large quantities are being produced in the shortest possible time, wages and other costs are kept to a minimum and the finished product is usually not expensive for the customer.

Examples of goods made by the flow production method are:

- motor vehicles
- machinery
- televisions
- inexpensive clothing
- toys.

Mass produced goods – made by the flow production method

Advantages of flow production

- Final product is inexpensive
- Large quantities can be manufactured
- The quality of the product is standardised
- Machinery can be used so labour costs are reduced
- Unskilled wages further reduce costs
- Assembly lines can run continuously
- Production is fast
- Takes full advantage of economies of scale.

Disadvantages of flow production

- The work is repetitive and boring
- There is an increased risk of accidents
- Employee motivation is low
- The products are all identical
- Large capital investment is required
- Large buildings are usually needed
- Large stocks of raw materials must be kept
- Machinery breakdown can halt production
- There is a loss of traditional skills.

Specialisation

Joan Johnston has had to allocate separate responsibilities to each of her employees in Wedding Belles.

Joan has retained responsibility for all design work. Mervyn is the cutter, and passes on the prepared parts of the dresses to Hazel and Joyce who make them up into dresses on the sewing machines. The dresses are then passed to Evelyn who is responsible for the finishing work of sewing on buttons and decorations and pressing the finished garments. Robert is responsible for packing, labelling and transporting the finished products to the shops. Robert also does all the clerical work.

Joan has now started to use specialisation.

Specialisation occurs when an employee concentrates on one particular operation, and does it all the time. It is where each worker, or group of workers, undertakes only a small section of the total work and specialises in that particular part of making the product.

It also occurs when a country concentrates on producing one particular type of goods. For example, areas of France specialise in making wine because the climate there is suitable for vineyards and wine making.

There are four types of specialisation.

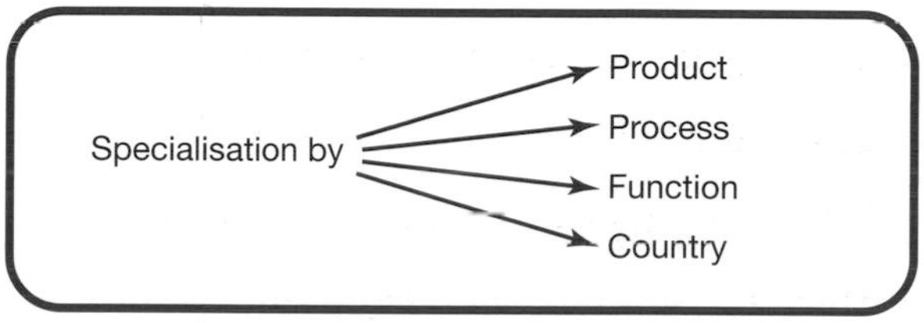

Product: for example, the Wedding Belles business specialises in the product of wedding dresses.

Process: for example, in Wedding Belles, Hazel and Joyce have specialised in the process of machining the dresses.

Function: for example, in the Wedding Belles firm, Robert has specialised in distribution and clerical work.

Country: for example, France specialises in the production of wine.

Advantages of specialisation

- People can work constantly at jobs which suit their special skills or training. In this way, each person becomes an expert
- The finished product should be of higher quality because of this expertise
- Resources can be effectively used and concentrated in one place.

Disadvantages of specialisation

- Specialised workers are trained in only one skill so it may be difficult for them to find other work if they become redundant
- Any firm concentrating on a small range of work becomes very dependent on other firms
- An area concentrating on a single industry is very badly affected if that industry should fail. For example, parts of France would suffer greatly if poor weather caused the vines not to grow.

Activity

If you are a student at a large school you will already be used to specialisation. Your teachers have all specialised in certain subjects which they concentrate on and teach all the time.

1 What is the main advantage for you as a student of having specialised teachers?

2 Which disadvantages, from the teachers' point of view, can you see in specialisation?

Division of labour

Flow production usually leads to division of labour which is a particular type of specialisation. In division of labour, the manufacture of the product is divided into a number of small stages and each employee is given a single task which may be very narrow.

I once visited a toy factory which used the practice of division of labour. I stood behind a girl whose job was to attach the heads to the bodies of dolls as they moved along the conveyor belt. That was the task which she was given, and she spent the entire day lifting a doll's head from a box with her right hand, lifting the doll's body from the conveyor belt with her left hand and attaching the two in the time the belt had halted in front of her.

Advantages of division of labour

- Each worker becomes very practised at one particular task
- Workers have to be trained for only one small task so lengthy training is avoided
- The work is faster so the costs per unit of production are reduced
- Reduced costs can be reflected in lower prices to the consumer
- Lower prices will raise sales and profits
- Time is saved because workers do not have to move between jobs
- Tools and machinery are used economically because each worker will need only the tools which are required for one particular function.

Disadvantages of division of labour

- The work can be very monotonous and boring
- Bored workers can cause accidents
- It is difficult for workers to have pride in their work since they do not see the finished product
- Delays or strikes in one section can cause stoppages throughout the production process
- There is a loss of traditional skills
- Goods produced by this method lack variety
- Workers can feel isolated from each other
- Redundant employees would have difficulty in finding other work because they are very narrowly trained.

Activity

You are the manager of a factory which makes television sets. The workers complain of boredom and you have observed that they seem to be very disinterested in their work and half asleep most of the time.

Suggest ways in which you could lessen the boredom and motivate the workers.

Stock control

Stock control is very important in any business – whether it is a manufacturing or a retail organisation. A factory will have to control the levels of two types of stock – raw materials for use in making its products and finished products ready for sale. A retail shop just has to control the level of stock of goods it has for sale.

In most modern businesses, stock control is done by computer. Details of items in stock are held in the system. As goods are sold their barcodes are recorded at the cash desk and those items are electronically deducted from the number in stock. When the computer records that the stock levels of particular items are low, those goods are automatically re-ordered. A fully computerised system means that the business can get a stock valuation at any time or see how particular items are selling.

Efficient stock control ensures that the business is not holding large stocks of goods for long periods because this would tie up finance which ought to be available for use in the business. At the same time, efficient stock control also ensures that the business is holding enough stock to keep production flowing and to meet the needs of customers. Balancing these two is the art of good stock control.

Good stock control will:

- improve efficiency because production will be constant
- enable the business always to meet demand
- give the business a competitive edge over other businesses
- ensure that capital is not lying idle.

Poor stock control may:

- mean that consumer demands cannot be met
- lose business and goodwill
- increase warehouse space required
- risk some perishable goods going out-of-date
- use finance inefficiently.

Methods of stock control

The method of stock control used varies from business to business and will depend on the type and size of business. The most usual methods are described below.

Just-in-time method of stock control

The just-in-time system originated in Japan and is widely used in that country and in Japanese factories in other parts of the world.

Using the just-in-time method:

- products are manufactured just in time for them to be sold. This prevents large stocks of finished goods having to wait to go to market
- the raw materials or parts which are needed for making the final product, are ordered and arrive just in time for use in its manufacture. Large stocks are not held in warehouses waiting to be used.

In this way the just-in-time production method saves money being tied up for long periods in unused stocks of raw materials and unsold finished products. It is therefore effective in reducing costs for the manufacturer.

On the other hand, mistakes in deliveries could hold up production because there are no reserve stocks to go on using.

Advantages of just-in-time production

- Capital is used very effectively
- Warehousing is not needed for storage
- If faults occur in supplies, the firm does not have a large number of the faulty items
- There is no waste by having excess stocks
- The finished product should be cheaper for the consumer to buy.

Disadvantages of just-in-time production

- The business is very dependent on having a very efficient ordering system
- Production could be halted if the wrong goods were delivered at the last minute
- It puts severe pressure on suppliers
- The company and its suppliers must work together closely.

Activity

Imagine that you are a Japanese manager of a new car factory being set up in Northern Ireland. You have experience of the just-in-time method of production and you wish to introduce the system into the new factory.

You plan to give a talk to the employees tomorrow to explain the system to them. Using the computer, produce the talk which you have prepared for the meeting.

Minimum stock level method

This is a simple method where the business works out the minimum amount of stock with which it can function. Stock is re-ordered when that level of stock is reached. A major difficulty with this method is that there may be a delay between ordering the goods and having them delivered.

Stock review method

In this method the business counts all the items in stock and then orders new stock to replace the stock which has been sold or used. This is usually done manually once each year. Obviously this method is slow and takes staff away from other duties. It is used only in small businesses and they sometimes close for a 'stocktaking day'.

No matter which method of stock control is used, it is difficult to always work it out accurately. For this reason, most businesses carry a 'buffer stock'.

Buffer stock

Most businesses hold buffer stock because it is difficult to make sure that exactly the correct amount of stock is being held. Buffer stock is a small amount of stock held over and above what would probably be required so that there would be no danger that supplies on supermarket shelves would run out or that production in a factory would cease just because a delivery of goods was late.

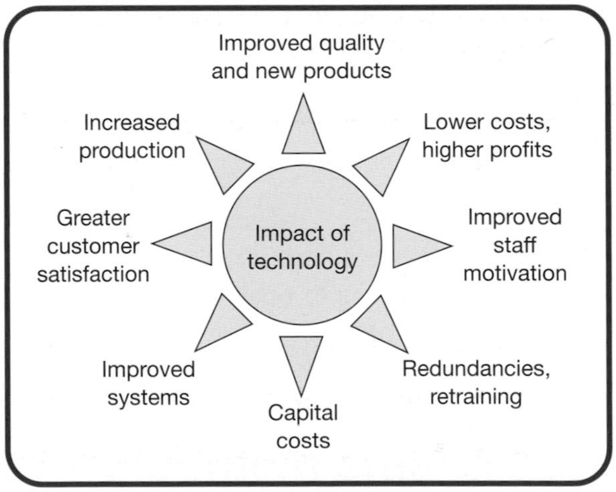

The impact of technology on production

Modern technology has been the cause of the greatest changes in modern production and businesses invest large amounts of capital in technology in order to become more successful.

The major impacts of technology on production are:

1. An improvement in the quality of the finished product. As a result of the use of technology, the quality of the products is standardised and the possibility of human error is minimised.

2 The development of new products. Improved methods of research and development would lead to new products being added to the firm's range.

3 An increase in the firm's production level. A fully mechanised business can work around the clock with no interruptions. This would have the effect of increasing the level of output.

4 A decrease in the production costs per unit. Increases in production lead to the benefits of economies of scale which reduces overall costs per unit of production.

5 Higher profit levels. Increased production and sales, as well as reduced costs lead to improved profits for the business and improved efficiency overall.

6 Greater customer satisfaction. An improvement in the quality of the firm's product and the speed of its service would lead to a larger number of satisfied customers. Computers can also monitor stock levels which would result in better customer satisfaction.

7 Improved motivation of workers. Workers enjoy being part of an organisation which is progressive and are also motivated by the opportunities provided in the business. They also benefit from constant training.

8 Improved information and communication systems. Internal and external communications are improved by the installation of the internet and e-mail systems. Access to information is improved by the provision of computer-based systems using databases and spreadsheets as well as word-processing.

9 Possible redundancies of employees. The increase of automated jobs can cause staff redundancies. Previous skills are no longer required and new ones are needed.

10 Retraining programmes. A programme of continuous training is required to keep employees abreast with the latest developments in technology. This is expensive for the business to sustain.

11 Capital costs. The installation, up-dating and maintenance of technology requires a substantial capital investment. This costly investment is often impossible for small businesses to fund.

Checklist

At the end of this theme you should be able to:

- **describe the main methods of production**
- **discuss the advantages and disadvantages of specialisation**
- **discuss the advantages and disadvantages of the division of labour**
- **identify the most appropriate methods of production in particular situations**
- **describe the main methods of stock control**
- **evaluate the impact of technology on production.**

Theme 2.3

Location of production

Several different factors influence the location of production.

Factors influencing location of production

Although much of the decision of where to situate a business depends on the type of business being opened, other factors need to be considered as well. Before we go any further, think about the following situation for a moment.

Colin Smith has always wanted to run a service station, and now has the required capital. Three sites are available for him to buy and he could afford any of them. He simply wants to go to the site where he would sell the most fuel and has no other considerations in mind. The sites are:

1 At the Belfast end of the M1 where drivers have to travel approximately forty miles to the next service station unless they leave the motorway.
2 In the small seaside town of Castlerock which has a small population but has sizeable numbers of visitors during the summer months.
3 In the very busy town of Newry which is situated on the main Belfast to Dublin route, has a large population and is a good commercial centre. However Newry is situated on the border with the Republic of Ireland, where fuel is sometimes cheaper than in Northern Ireland.

Activity

You are asked to give Colin your opinion on the best choice of site for his proposed business.

Complete the following table to list the advantages and disadvantages of each site.

SITE	ADVANTAGES	DISADVANTAGES
Belfast end of M1		
Castlerock		
Newry		

I would advise Colin to locate in:	
because:	

In your consideration of Colin's problem, you have looked at the type of business he hoped to run and then decided on the location where he would achieve the highest sales. However, decisions about location are never as straightforward as this, and other factors have to be considered.

The other influences on location are shown in the following figure.

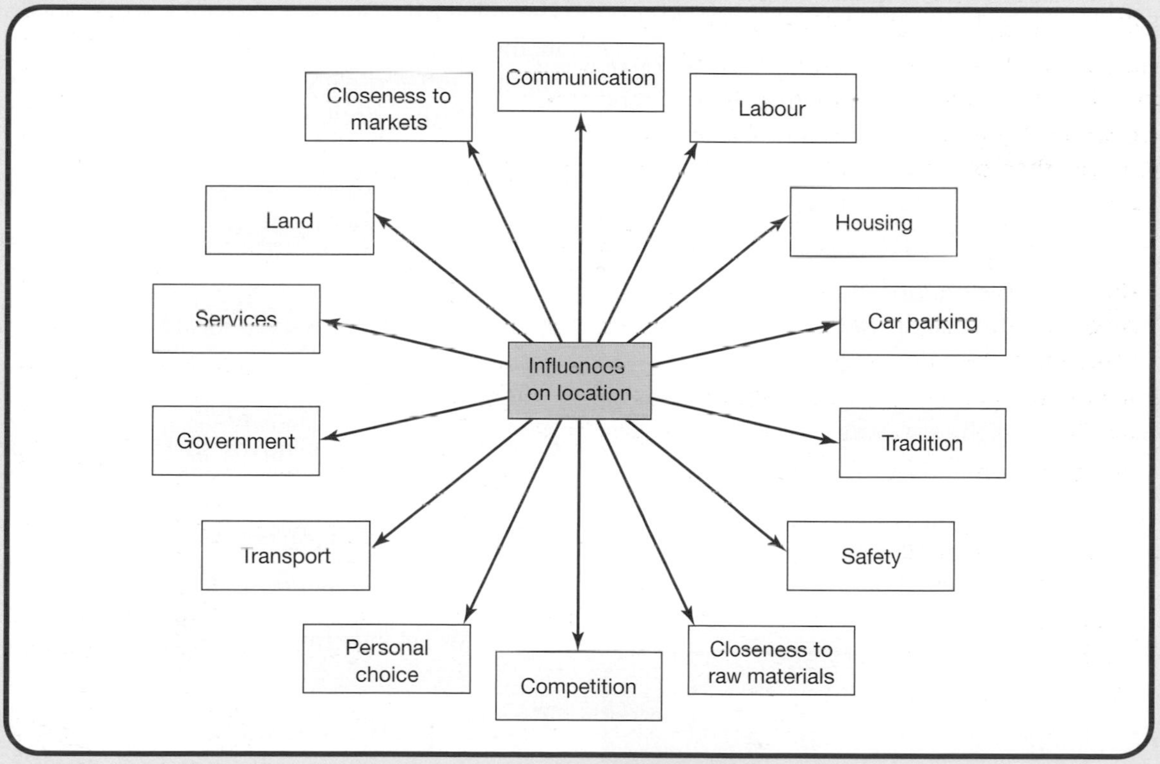

Services

All businesses need to have available the basic services of:

- electricity
- water
- waste disposal
- telephone
- drainage.

In the case of manufacturing businesses, other ancillary services are also required such as technological back-up for machinery and computers. If these services are already available, the firm considering locating to that area will save time and money, and will consider that site before one which does not have the basic services.

Different types of business require services in different proportions. For example, firms engaged in food production usually require a large quantity of water, while waste disposal would be extremely important in the case of an abattoir.

Land

A major consideration is the price of land. The cost of land varies greatly from area to area, and the success of the new business could be seriously affected by this capital cost. The cost depends on:

- how central the site is. Sites in the centre of towns are the most expensive to buy or rent and also have a higher rates valuation. In addition, they are usually smaller so are suitable for use by retailers rather than manufacturers
- the area of the country in which it is situated. As a general rule, land becomes more expensive near large towns or cities. It is cheaper to buy or rent in more remote areas or in areas which are considered to be less prosperous
- the competition for the site. Having a number of parties interested in the site will increase its price considerably

- the availability of land. Land is a very scarce resource and planning restrictions are rigid.

However, other factors also have to be considered regarding the suitability of the land:

1. At some time in the future the business may wish to expand, so the business has to be sure that there is available land for future expansion.
2. Whether the land must be purchased or is available for renting is also relevant.
3. The amount of the rates payable to the local authority will also influence new businesses.

Government influences

The influence of the government is very significant in the location of industries. Some parts of the country suffer greatly from unemployment as a result of the decline of traditional industries. Government policy is to try to cure employment black spots and to even out wealth and resources throughout Northern Ireland.

In order to do this the government:

- encourages businesses to locate in certain areas by providing advance factories at reduced rates in those areas
- offers financial incentives such as grants and tax relief
- sets up industrial estates
- attracts foreign investment
- bids for EU investment.

Transport costs

The cost of transport is a major consideration. If the business is a manufacturing business requiring heavy and bulky raw materials from another country, it is more economical to locate the business near a seaport in order to reduce costs of transporting over land. Similarly, if the finished product is a heavy one and is mostly exported, a location near the port would further reduce costs.

However, Northern Ireland is a very small country and therefore the distance to be travelled overland is relatively small to any part of the province. The consideration of transport overland in Northern Ireland is much less important for this reason, than it would be in a large country such as Canada, for example.

Communications

A sound infrastructure of good roads or a reliable rail network encourages firms to choose to move to an area. Having these in place would assist the business to deliver goods more quickly to its customers and would also help it to receive its deliveries more easily.

Closeness to a seaport or airport may also be important, depending on the type of product being made, and on whether or not raw materials have to be imported.

Large sums have been invested in roads in Northern Ireland

Labour

Skilled labour is an important element in any business. If a supply of skilled labour already exists in an area, that area immediately becomes more attractive to new businesses. This might occur, for example, in an area where a business has closed down and left skilled labour redundant.

Businesses are also attracted to areas where there is an available labour supply of people who can be trained.

Businesses sometimes choose to establish in areas of high unemployment because wages there are likely to be lower than in areas where competition for workers is strong. However, the introduction of the minimum wage has narrowed the difference in the wage levels to a large degree.

Housing

New businesses frequently have to bring a number of key workers with them – workers who have been trained by the firm in some of their other plants. This practice means that those key workers can be used to provide on-the-job training for local employees.

Some areas provide housing for key workers

If houses are easily available for the key workers coming into the area, it is a positive feature of the area for the business locating there.

Closeness to raw materials

In examples of manufacturing firms where the raw material is heavy, it makes economic sense to place the business near the source of the raw materials. For instance, timber firms frequently locate in heavily forested areas.

Some of Northern Ireland's traditional industries were originally started in places where a supply of the required raw materials were available. However, in some cases, the supply of those raw materials has been exhausted for many years and the industries continue with imported materials. (See the case study on Belleek Pottery in this theme.)

It is therefore true to say that closeness to raw materials was more important in past centuries than at present because transport systems are more developed now.

Closeness to markets

As in the case of closeness to raw materials above, closeness to markets is now less important than it once was for manufacturing businesses.

However, this factor is of great importance in the case of retail businesses. They need to be located centrally in areas which are popular with shoppers and where they are obviously going to get customers.

Shopping centres usually have one major retail store as the anchor shop and a series of other smaller outlets and boutiques. The large store attracts large numbers of shoppers and all the other retail outlets in the centre benefit from the passing trade.

For example Marks and Spencer is the anchor shop in the Foyleside Shopping Centre in Londonderry but all the other shops and restaurants in Foyleside are also busy because of the large numbers of visitors to the Centre.

Competition from other businesses

If the new business is a retail business, it will decide to locate where there is not a lot of competition and where its market will be strongest. For example a chemist would choose to open a shop in a village or an area of town where there are no existing chemist shops.

Safety

Business activity which causes health risks would not be permitted to be located in an area where it would provide a danger. This would be particularly important in the case of nuclear power stations, petrol refineries or chemical plants.

In examples such as these, it is important that the business is sited far away from houses and public places.

Car parking

Available car parking facilities are very important for retail businesses, but most particularly for those selling groceries or goods such as DIY materials. These goods are heavy and difficult to carry so customers need to be able to park near the shop.

There is also the added fact that town centre parking is expensive and limited. These are the main reasons why large out-of-town retail centres such as Sprucefield outside Lisburn are so popular.

Car parking facilities are also important for manufacturing businesses in order to accommodate employees, delivery vehicles, visitors and trade representatives.

Personal choice

For small family-owned businesses the decision about location is very often based on where the family wants to live. Family-owned businesses are sometimes passed down through the generations of one family and therefore the business is located in the area where the family has always lived.

Tradition

Frequently we find the continuation of an industry in an area after the original reason for being there has disappeared. The case study on Belleek China is also an example of tradition. The china clay is no longer available locally but the industry remains in Belleek because there is a supply of very skilled labour in the area and a tradition of china making.

Activity

Details of fourteen influences on location are given in this unit. In the spaces provided below, state the three most important influences for each of the businesses named.

A supermarket

....

....

....

A meat processing factory

....

....

....

A garden centre

....

....

....

An old people's home

....

....

....

The world famous Belleek China is manufactured in the small village of Belleek which is situated on the banks of the River Erne and on the border between Counties Fermanagh and Donegal.

In 1849 John Caldwell Bloomfield inherited the Castlecaldwell estate which included the village of Belleek. This was shortly after the potato famine in Ireland and the new landlord, concerned about his tenants, was anxious to find work for them. A geological survey of the area revealed the presence of feldspar, kaolin, flint, clay and shale – the necessary raw materials for the production of pottery.

In 1858, using his own capital plus that of two wealthy friends who were interested in the project, John Caldwell Bloomfield opened a pottery on a site at the side of the village where the river would provide power to drive a mill wheel. He used his influence to get the Railway Service to build a railway to Belleek so that coal could be brought in to fire the kilns and also provide a method of transport for the finished product to be taken to markets.

The new pottery provided a much needed source of employment for local people. However, experienced potters were also required and they were brought to Belleek from Stoke-on-Trent – one of the most famous and established pottery areas.

The Belleek Pottery became very prosperous and by 1865 it had established a steady market throughout Ireland and England as well as America, Canada and Australia.

Belleek Pottery continues to operate on the same site although obviously its structure and methods have had to be up-dated. A major capital investment, partly funded by the Industrial Development Board in 1983, made this possible. The building has been modernised, all the kilns are now powered by electricity and the water wheel is no longer in use.

Activity

Read the case study on Belleek Pottery Ltd and answer the following questions:

1 What was the major reason for opening the pottery in Belleek?

2 Name three other influences for choosing the site in Belleek.

3 Give details of two reasons why china is still manufactured in Belleek.

Social and environmental considerations in production and its location

Businesses must consider social and environmental issues. These issues are very individual to the type of business and to the nature of the area it is in.

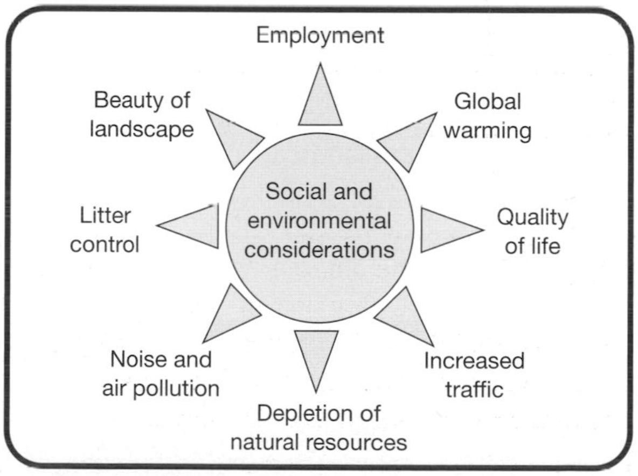

Employment

The most important social issue is the effect on the employment of the area. Positive effects occur when a business establishes in a district by the new jobs it creates for production workers and clerical workers, as well as catering, cleaning and security staff. In addition, employment may be created in other subsidiary businesses by the need for extra components for the main business. This increased employment has wider spin-off benefits for the shops, hotels and places of entertainment in the area which are all positively affected by the increased wealth and higher standard of living in the district. This general improvement in the area encourages other businesses to locate there and the benefits continue to grow.

All these effects are reversed if a business decides to relocate away from the area and redundancies occur as a result of the move of the business to another place.

Quality of life and beauty of the landscape

Environmental issues must also be considered in order not to damage the quality of life for the people of the area by ruining the surrounding landscape. Consideration is being given to the environment in recent times because of the evidence of environmental damage of past generations in some parts of the British Isles.

Northern Ireland was never as heavily industrialised as parts of England and Wales, so fortunately it escaped most industrial damage. We have a beautiful country and the vast majority of businesses take their responsibility for it very seriously.

Global warming and pollution

People today are concerned about global warming, about the depletion of natural resources, about holes in the ozone layer and about modern farming methods. It is important to protect:

- the beauty of the landscape
- natural habitat for wildlife
- the quality of the air

- the quality of the water in rivers and lakes
- the beauty of the coastline.

In addition, it is important to control:

- noise
- litter
- smell.

Planning is strictly controlled by the government and local authorities. No building development is permitted in areas of natural beauty or in green belts of the countryside, and plans must be submitted for all building work to ensure that it fits in with the surrounding area.

Further strict legislation protects the environment from air and water pollution and also controls litter. Emissions into the air of smoke and fumes from factories are monitored so that further damage to the ozone layer would not be caused. A business's waste disposal policy must ensure that no chemicals or other dangerous substances are released into the drainage system where they eventually would find their way to the rivers and lakes.

Increased traffic

Nevertheless, there would be increased traffic in the area as a result of the location of manufacturing businesses there. This creates congestion on the roads, the heightened possibility of accidents, damage to the road surface and fuel emissions from vehicles.

Restrictions are put on the noise levels from factories and on the night hours when goods may be transported through residential areas.

Depletion of natural resources

Farmers are given encouragement to delay hedge and grass cutting until young birds have been reared and not to use chemicals on their land which would be injurious to wildlife. They are also prohibited from cutting down trees for the same reason.

Most businesses have environmental policies which show their commitment to the environment.

The following case study gives details of the work done by Phoenix Natural Gas in respect of the environment.

Phoenix Natural Gas is highly aware of its environmental responsibilities. Its product, natural gas, has huge environmental benefits to the consumer by improving air quality. Since coming to Northern Ireland, the company has connected over 45,000 customers which it estimates has caused a 2.3% reduction in the carbon dioxide in the atmosphere. The use of gas has also reduced the level of sulphur dioxide by 42%.

Other steps which Phoenix has taken to protect the environment are:

- The company has undertaken a major recycling project. Where possible it has used new polyethylene pipes inside the old gas network in Belfast. This has been done in order to cut down excavation in the area
- The main Phoenix building makes maximum use of natural light and natural ventilation cutting down costs of heating and lighting
- The company recycles paper, batteries, printer cartridges and toners. It also recycles old mobile telephones and IT equipment
- It uses only environmentally friendly products.

SuperValu run a 'Best Kept' Award which is a competition aimed at getting more young people involved in environmental projects. The scheme rewards young people and schools for a commitment to our natural and built heritage. The competition offers prize money for winning schools of £300 with £120 prize money for runners-up.

Activity

Match the businesses named on the left with their most suitable locations. The first has been done for you to start you off.

BUSINESS	LOCATION
A chemical factory	At the entrance to a hospital
A toy shop	In the centre of population near several large towns
A leisure centre	In a remote area but convenient to farms
A newspaper and confectionery shop	In an area far away from houses
An abattoir	Attached to a hotel
A hospital	In the middle of the orchard country
An apple juice factory	In a high street shop
A flower shop	Beside a bus station

Checklist

At the end of this theme you should be able to:

- understand the factors which influence the location of production
- evaluate the social and environmental considerations in production and its location.

Quality assurance

Quality is defined as 'the constant achievement of all that customers require'.

Importance of quality assurance

Modern firms – whether they produce goods or services – are extremely conscious of the need to maintain high standards of quality if they are to retain their places in the market. They need to produce goods or services which are reliable and perform well. Competition is fierce, and consumers demand that business organisations will meet their expectations for excellence. Otherwise, they will go to another producer who offers higher quality items or a better service.

For this reason, most businesses undertake the process to obtain recognised quality standards. Being awarded a recognised standard is an assurance to members of the public that the business organisation has met the high standards required and this gives consumers confidence in dealing with that firm.

Charter Mark

Up until March 2008 a Charter Mark was awarded to public service organisations which provided the highest possible quality services to their customers. The scheme is being phased out over a period of time. Since a Charter Mark certificate lasts for three years, the scheme will officially close in June 2011. The Charter Mark is being replaced by the Customer Service Excellence Standard.

Customer Service Excellence Standard

The government has developed the Customer Service Excellence Standard for public service organisations to improve their effectiveness and efficiency. This Standard places importance on members of the public and ensures that they are top-priority in public service provision. To achieve this aim, emphasis is placed on:

- delivery of the service
- whether the service is delivered on time
- level of information available to the customer
- professionalism of the service
- staff attitude
- understanding the customer's experience of the service
- constant measurement of the service.

The aims of the Customer Service Excellence Standard are to:

- encourage continuous improvement in the delivery of public service
- encourage individuals and teams to learn new skills when dealing with customers
- reward organisations which deliver good services based on customers' needs.

Activity

Answer the following questions.

1 Why did the government introduce the Customer Service Excellence Standard?

2 As a member of the public, what would you expect of the service in an organisation which had been awarded the Customer Service Excellence Standard?

3 What would your reaction be if you were an employee in an organisation which had been awarded the Customer Service Excellence Standard?

ISO 9001

ISO 9001 is a Business Management Standard award designed to help organisations to manage their processes and is subject to regular validation by external assessors. It concentrates on process management, checks that documented systems are in place and that everyone is sure of his/her role in the organisation.

ISO 9001 looks at how the business:

- trains its staff
- checks that its products or services are correct
- handles mistakes
- tries to improve its products or services
- uses its resources.

Before being given the award, the business has to go through external assessment procedures.

Having this award enables the business to:

- meet its customers' requirements
- have low levels of customer dissatisfaction
- continually improve its working practices
- be confident in markets where high quality is essential.

Customers of an ISO 9001 business have confidence that its products have successfully passed rigorous standards and that the risk of failure is greatly reduced.

The Northern Ireland Council for the Curriculum, Examinations and Assessment (CCEA) has been awarded an ISO 9001. Look at some of the comments which two CCEA employees made about this:

Involvement in working for ISO 9001 has given me renewed interest in my work. It gives us renewed confidence in what we do in our day-to-day work.

What we had to do to achieve this award touched all staff to a greater or lesser degree. We now have documented and reliable systems in place which assure the quality of our operations. We'll also be reviewing and updating these on a regular basis as we're retested for the award every six months.

Activity

Answer the following questions in your notebook.

1 What is the main difference between the Customer Service Excellence Standard and the ISO 9001 award?

2 What is the guarantee of continued high standards in the ISO 9001 award?

3 One of the CCEA employees said that the award gave her renewed confidence in her day-to-day work. Why would this be so?

European Foundation for Quality Management (EFQM)

The European Foundation for Quality Management (EFQM) was created in order to encourage European business organisations to improve their standards so that European businesses would be world leaders and achieve total advantage over their competitors.

The EFQM model has nine criteria which look at what the business does and what it achieves:

- leadership
- policy and strategy
- people
- people results
- partnership and resources
- processes
- customer results
- society results
- key performance results.

Investors in People

At the very centre of the award 'Investors in People (IIP)' is the importance of the people who work in the business and the need to invest in their training and development.

IIP establishes a level of good training practice so that the people in the business can help the firm to achieve its goals. Employees feel motivated by the process resulting in all-round and continuous improvement.

The idea behind the Investors in People award is that if the people who work in an organisation are improved, they will improve the organisation's systems which, in turn, will improve the performance of the entire organisation.

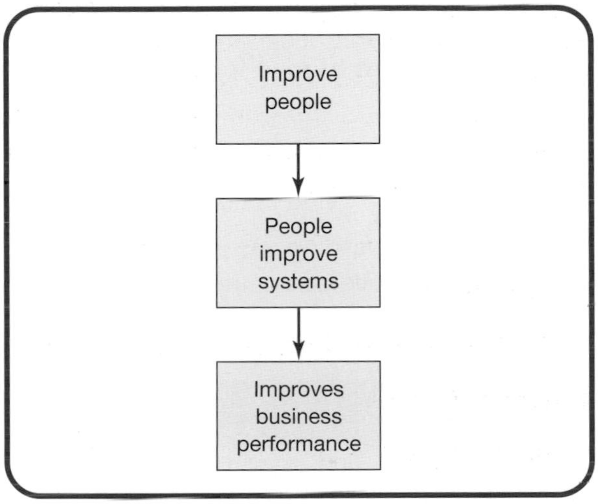

The Investors in People scheme is also externally assessed and is about:

- resolving all the people issues in the organisation
- improving the skill levels of all staff
- supporting the development of everyone working in the organisation
- getting people to take responsibility for their own development
- encouraging people to improve their own performance
- getting everyone to understand the firm's aims.

Activity

Answer the following questions:

1. **What effect might an Investors In People award have on the careers of employees in the business?**
2. **Getting employees to understand the firm's aims is an important part of the Investors in People award. What benefit would this be to the firm?**

Why do businesses apply for quality awards?

Businesses experience the following advantages for their organisations.

- Having an award is good for the image of the business
- Having an award assures the public that the firm's product or service is good
- Having an award gives the business an advantage over its competitors
- Having an award should improve the profitability of the business
- Having an award motivates the employees as they feel they are part of a good organisation
- Working for an award encourages team spirit in the organisation.

Activity

You should do some research in businesses in your area. Find out if they have been awarded any recognised quality standard or are working for one at the present time.

1 Find out the details of their award(s).

2 Analyse the reasons why those businesses have applied for the awards.

Checklist

At this stage you should understand:

- the meaning and importance of quality assurance
- outline details of the principal awards
- the reasons why businesses apply for quality standards.

Theme 2.5

Health and safety

Employers have a general duty to ensure, so far as is reasonably practicable, the health, safety and welfare of their employees at work. They also have a duty towards people who are not their employees but use their premises.

The main piece of legislation covering occupational health and safety in the United Kingdom is the Health and Safety at Work Act, 1974 (often referred to as HASAWA). In Northern Ireland, this legislation is known as the Health and Safety (N Ireland) Order, 1978.

The Health and Safety at Work Act, 1974 and the Health and Safety (N Ireland) Order, 1978

These laws apply to all places of work and set out the responsibilities of both employers and employees to ensure that the work environment is safe.

Rights and responsibilities of employers in the area of health and safety

Employers are expected to:

- ensure the safe use of articles and substances
- provide health and safety training for employees
- appoint a Health and Safety Officer
- carry out regular fire drills
- provide protective clothing, such as goggles, where necessary
- maintain all machinery and systems in efficient working order
- provide safe premises with clear signs and enough space for people to move around with ease
- ensure safe practices in the workplace
- have the premises adequately ventilated and well lit
- provide suitable workstations with supportive seating for office-type work
- maintain an indoor temperature of at least 16 degrees Celsius (or 13 degrees Celsius if the work involves physical activity)
- carry out cleaning and the removal of waste regularly
- equip the premises with drinking water, clean washing facilities and toilets
- provide storage space for employees' clothing
- provide facilities for rest periods and to eat meals.

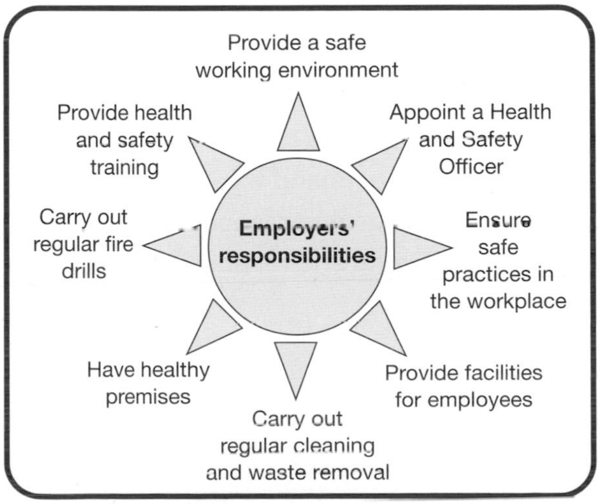

Rights and responsibilities of employees in the area of health and safety

Employees have a duty to support the health and safety procedures in their workplace and to take reasonable care of their own health and safety as well as the health and safety of other people.

Employees are expected to:

- take all reasonable care for their own health and safety as well as the safety of others
- co-operate in meeting the firm's health and safety requirements
- use all equipment carefully to keep it in good working order
- wear the protective clothing and equipment provided
- undergo health and safety training
- report all faults and dangers.

Activity

Study your school's health and safety policy and use it to write notes on your own health and safety responsibilities as a pupil in that school.

Checklist

At this stage you should:

- know and understand the implications of health and safety legislation
- know the rights and responsibilities of employers for health and safety
- know the rights and responsibilities of employees for health and safety.

3

MARKETING

Theme 3.1

Market research

Market research is the collection of information from consumers and people who may become consumers, finding out whether they like or will buy the firm's products. Such research may be about existing products or new products.

What do we mean by 'market research'?

Businesses are market-driven – they need to sell their products – and therefore consumers' opinions are most important to them.

Businesses spend large sums of money finding out about their market because:

- the information ensures that they are providing the products which consumers are most likely to buy
- it enables them to price the products at an acceptable level for consumers
- it can show if the packaging is attractive to consumers
- it indicates the type of people who would be their target market
- it shows the area in which sales are likely to be more successful
- sometimes it gives information about competitors
- it makes firms aware of any changes in consumers' tastes or requirements
- having all this information gives the firm confidence to develop the most appropriate marketing strategy
- it can also prevent the firm from making expensive mistakes.

Activity

Rory is a Year 12 student who will be leaving school in June after he has finished his GCSE examinations. He is planning to set up a window cleaning business in his home town.

Make a list of the information Rory would need about the market before he establishes the business.

Methods of market research – primary and secondary

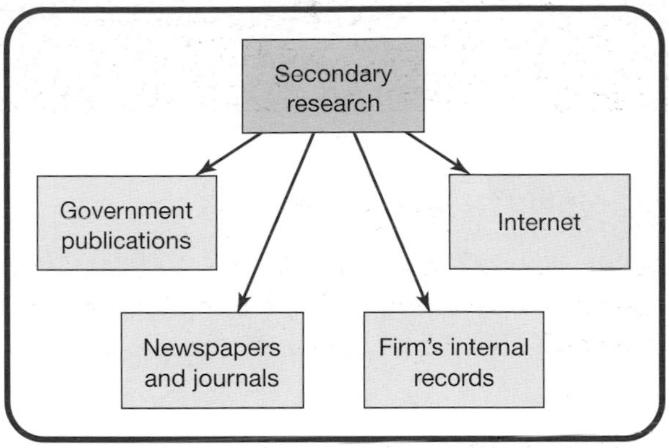

Secondary research/desk research

Secondary research is also known as 'desk research' which gives a clue how it is worked. Secondary research is done by using published statistics, data and other information which had been collected previously. This makes secondary research very suitable for use by smaller firms.

This information may come from government publications, from external sources such as newspapers, trade journals, government publications or the internet. Information may also come from the firm's internal sources such as its own sales and financial records.

This figure shows the various ways in which secondary research can be done.

Advantages of secondary research

- The information is cheap to obtain
- The information is available immediately
- The information will have been well researched and will be accurate
- The data available covers a wide range of sources.

Disadvantages of secondary research

- The data is unlikely to have been collected for exactly the same purpose as the business requires so may not meet the firm's needs exactly
- The information may be out-of-date
- The information is available to every other firm in the market.

Activity

Copy the following table and complete it to show the advantages, disadvantages and uses of internal and external secondary research.

Method	Advantages	Disadvantages	Suitable for:
Internal sources			
External sources			

Primary research/field research

Primary research is also known as 'field research' which gives a clue about how it is carried out. Primary research is the collection of original information and is carried out by making direct contact with consumers and members of the public who may become consumers.

Advantages of primary research

- The business can design the research in the best way to discover the particular information it needs
- The business can be sure that the information gathered is up-to-date.

Disadvantages of primary research

- Designing the research, gathering the information and analysing it can be slow
- For this reason businesses often employ specialist researchers but this can be expensive.

This figure shows the various ways in which primary research can be done.

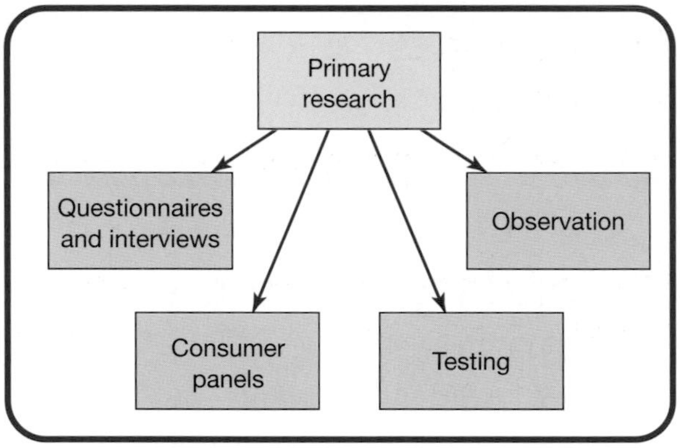

Questionnaires and interviews

This is probably the most common method of primary research. You may have been stopped on the street or in a shop yourself and asked questions about a certain product. Questionnaires can be conducted by telephone or by post as well as face-to-face.

Advantages of questionnaires and interviews

- Information is taken directly from the people who are, or will be, the firm's consumers
- The questioner can help the member of the public to understand the questions.

Disadvantages of questionnaires and interviews

- Some people resent being stopped and questioned
- Sometimes people misunderstand the questions and give misleading responses which makes the results less accurate
- It is a slow method
- Postal questionnaires are not always returned.

Observation

As its name suggests, this method of primary research involves watching or observing the reactions of people to products. For example people may be observed making their selection of goods in supermarkets.

Advantages of observation

- It is not costly for the business
- Consumers need not even be aware it is happening.

Disadvantages of observation

- It is less accurate and is open to interpretation
- It is not suitable for all products.

Consumer panels

The use of consumer panels involves taking responses from people who regularly sit on panels and give their opinions on given products or other consumer information. Panel members are paid and have been selected for their expertise or knowledge in this area.

Advantages of consumer panels

- Very detailed information can be gathered
- The panel members are skilled and impartial.

Disadvantage of consumer panels

- It is an expensive method.

Testing

Testing involves members of the public being given samples of the product and being asked for their opinion of it. This is frequently used in supermarkets when a new variety of a food such as cheese is being launched on the market.

Advantages of testing

- Tests are straightforward to organise
- Consumers' first-hand opinions are given.

Disadvantages of testing

- It may not test a cross-section of the public
- It is not suitable for all products.

Activity

Let's return to Rory who plans to set up a window cleaning business. He now needs you to advise him how he might find the information he needs about the window cleaning market in his home area.

Write down the names of the methods he should use and tell him how to find the information he needs.

Activity

Copy and complete the following list to show the best method of primary research to use to collect information in each example:

1 A new flavour of cheese ....
2 Detergent ....
3 Television programmes watched ....
4 A new soft drink ....
5 Trainers ....
6 Golf balls ....
7 Baby wipes ....
8 Computer software ....
9 Bathroom tiles ....
10 Cars ....

Sampling

Sampling is a part of primary research. Instead of asking opinions from a large number of people, this method questions a selection – or sample – of people. For accuracy of results, it is estimated that any sample should consist of approximately 2,000 people. The people questioned would be chosen as being representative of the population as a whole.

Sampling has the advantage of being manageable for the firm which would find it impossible to survey everyone. It is also within its financial means and time limitations.

Methods of sampling

There are several methods by which sampling can be done. The most commonly used are shown in the following figure.

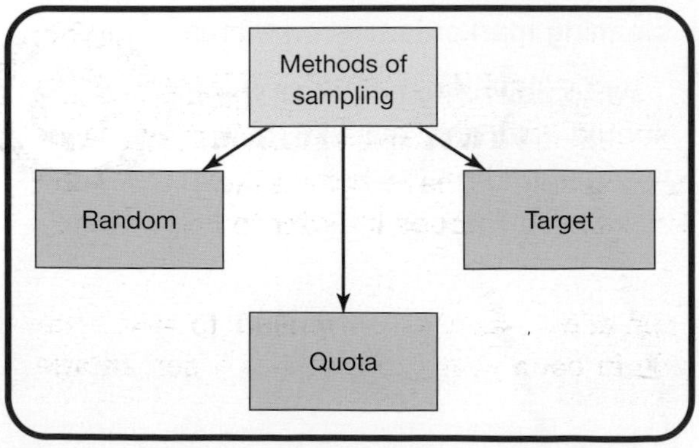

Random sampling

A random sample is where people are randomly selected and asked for their opinions. The random sample may be taken as every tenth person who walks down the street or every fiftieth name in the telephone directory for example.

There is a possibility that some of the people questioned may not be familiar with the product or even be interested in it. For instance, there is not much point in questioning a very elderly gentleman about trainers! Therefore the results of random sampling are of most use where the product is one which nearly everyone uses.

Advantages of random sampling

- Personal opinions are given by those surveyed
- Everyone has a chance of being chosen.

Disadvantages of random sampling

- Results are not very accurate unless a very large sample is used
- Random surveys are the most expensive type of survey

- The method is unsuitable for some products
- It does not necessarily reach the most appropriate people.

Quota sampling

Quota sampling is where interviews are held with a set number of people who fall into pre-determined categories. For example, a quota sample might consist of 50% males and 50% females or one-third teenagers, one-third middle aged people and one-third elderly people.

As in random sampling, these people's views are taken to reflect the views of everyone in their gender or age group.

It is important that the sample also reflects the composition of the people in the area, so, if there were more elderly people living in the area than teenagers, then the sample should contain more elderly people than teenagers.

Advantages of quota sampling

- Results are more accurate than in random sampling
- It is more likely to reach the appropriate people
- Personal opinions are given by those surveyed
- Everyone in the particular category has a chance of being chosen
- Quota surveys are considerably cheaper than random surveys.

Disadvantages of quota sampling

- The composition of the population must be known in order for the correct proportions to be interviewed
- The method is unsuitable for some products.

Target sampling

Target sampling is where people from only a particular market segment are questioned. This narrows down the people questioned to include only those who are really going to be interested in the particular product being researched. There is little point, for example, in questioning teenagers about walking sticks or non-drivers about cars.

The survey might be limited for example, to a particular area, or to people who work in a particular profession, or share a particular sport or hobby. Target sampling would be carried out wherever and whenever these people are likely to be present.

For example, people who fish for a hobby could be targeted by a firm producing fishing rods while everyone living in a certain town could be sampled to get their views on the proposed opening of a casino in that town. If the researchers were gathering information about sportswear they might question people in leisure centres, or they might question people at a motor show for their views on a new car.

Advantages of target sampling

- Results are more accurate than in other methods of sampling
- It is more likely to reach the appropriate people.

Disadvantage of target sampling

- Target samples may be small.

Activity

Your school is considering the formation of a chess club. You have been asked to undertake a quota sample of both boys and girls from all year groups in order to find out their level of interest in the new club.

The following information about the school population has been supplied to you. The information gives the total number of boys and girls in each year group and the percentage which that represents of the total school population of 500 pupils. It has been decided to exclude Year 14.

Whole school population

YEAR	BOYS	% BOYS	GIRLS	% GIRLS	% TOTAL
8	45	9	48	9.6	18.6
9	35	7	40	8	15
10	40	8	30	6	14
11	45	9	45	9	18
12	50	10	50	10	20
13	35	7	37	7.4	14.4
TOTAL	250	50	250	50	100

Activity

1 Make a copy of the table leaving out the figures for the numbers and percentages of the pupils.

2 Complete your table to show the numbers and percentages of pupils in each year group you plan to interview.

3 Write a first draft of the questions you plan to ask the pupils.

4 State whether you agree or disagree with excluding Year 14, and give your reasons.

5 How would you have carried out this survey if you had been allowed to conduct it?

Market segmentation

Market segmentation is a very useful method by which businesses may study the market for their products. Market segmentation is the selection of the groups of people who would be most interested in a particular product so that the product may be targeted at them. Targeting the correct segment of the market is vital to the business if it is to achieve sales.

This method involves dividing the market for a product into different groups and types of consumers. Examples of the groups are given in the list below. While all groups differ from one another, members of groups are seen to share tastes and to have similar spending patterns. For example, most teenagers share tastes in clothes and music while the majority of wealthy people tend to go to the same restaurants and drive similar cars.

Markets are commonly segmented according to:

Age. Each age group has its own choice of product. Think of the differences in preferences in music and clothes as examples. Do your parents like the music you listen to? Does your granny like your clothes?

Gender. In some products males and females choose differently. For example, research has shown that males and females have different tastes in the cars they buy. Females are more influenced by the shape and appearance of the car while males tend to be more influenced by its performance.

Ethnic/cultural background. Each race or ethnic grouping of people has its own taste in food, music and clothes. Their religions also may have different requirements which they will want to observe.

Geography. Consumers living in different areas of the country, or in different countries, like different foods and often have different hobbies.

Socio-economic class. This classification looks at the occupation of the head of the household and places the occupations in different bands. Obviously the occupation will determine the level of income of the household which, in turn, will determine the type of spending of the family.

Activity

Copy and complete the following list to indicate the market segment which should be targeted in each example.

1 A top-of-the-range car ....

2 Naan bread ....

3 Farming equipment ....

4 Rock music ....

5 Trainers ....

6 Caviar ....

7 Toys ....

8 Computer software ....

9 Tickets for a city fashion show ....

10 Walking sticks ....

Checklist

At this stage you should be able to:

- understand the different methods of market research
- interpret the results of market research
- understand the different methods of sampling
- explain market segmentation.

Introduction to the marketing mix – price

Marketing is the process which identifies, anticipates and satisfies customers' requirements profitably.

Marketing

Before you can understand the marketing mix you should be sure that you understand what marketing is. The word 'marketing' is used frequently but could you define what marketing really is?

Let's take the definition used by the Chartered Institute of Marketing, above. In other words, marketing finds out what products or services customers want either now or in the future and provides those products or services to them at a price which leaves a profit for the business. You should be aware that marketing is about much more than simply selling.

Modern marketing focuses very clearly on the customers and always looks at the business from their point of view. It asks what customers really need and if the business is meeting that need. Market-driven businesses will change the product or service to suit the customer.

The marketing mix

The marketing mix describes all the key activities which are used in marketing a firm's products. This is frequently referred to as the four Ps – Price, Promotion, Place and Product.

Some people argue that two other Ps should be added to the marketing mix. P for People who are, as we have seen, such an important part of marketing. The final P is for Packaging but packaging is really part of Promotion.

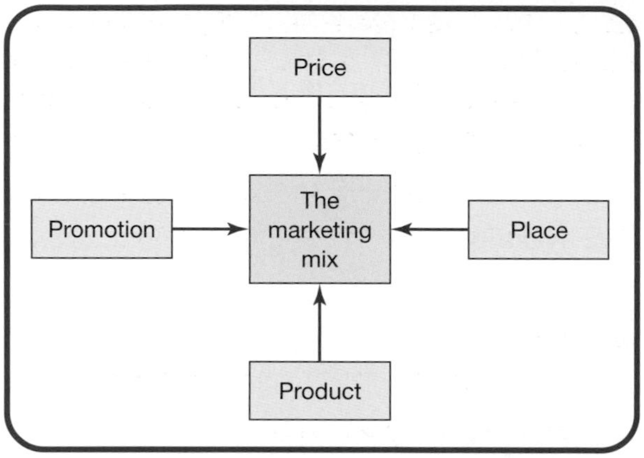

The idea of the marketing mix is the same idea as when mixing a cake. A baker will alter the proportions of ingredients in a cake depending on the type of cake he/she wishes to bake. The proportions in the marketing mix can be altered in the same way and differ from product to product.

A new brand of detergent, for example, would be marketed very differently from a new range of expensive jewellery. The new detergent would be advertised widely in newspapers and on television, possibly with introductory offers and demonstrating how clean it makes the washing. Expensive jewellery will be advertised in expensive glossy magazines in a way which portrays luxury.

The mix will also vary at different times throughout the life of a product. The price would be lowered or advertising might be increased at times when sales are falling off. A business will manipulate the four elements of the marketing mix in whatever way it has to in order to keep ahead of its competition.

The next four sections study each of the elements of the marketing mix in turn.

Price

Pricing policies

There are a number of pricing policies which a business may adopt. The choice of policy depends on:

- the type of product being marketed
- the competition in that market
- the price which people would be willing to pay
- the costs of production which must be covered.

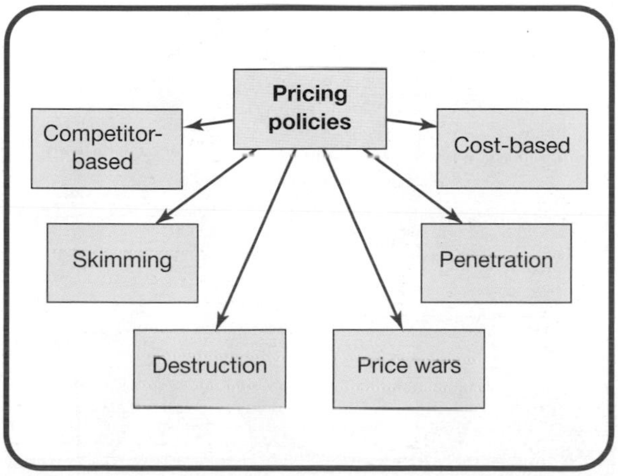

Competitor-based pricing

Competitor-based pricing simply accepts the price which competitors are charging for a product and then prices its product at the same level or slightly lower in order to gain some advantage over the competitors.

Competitor-based pricing would operate in a market where there is strong competition and involves close monitoring of competitors and any changes they make to their prices. This strategy is operated for products such as washing powder where customers will buy their favourite brand in whichever shop offers it at the lowest price.

Cost-based pricing

Cost-based pricing, also sometimes referred to as 'cost-plus pricing' involves working out the firm's total fixed and variable costs and then adding on a percentage profit. The firm also has to consider the total number of items which it plans to produce and sell.

The calculation is simple:

$$\textbf{Cost-based Price} = \frac{\textbf{Total Costs}}{\textbf{Total Sales}} + \textbf{Profit}$$

The big advantage of cost-based pricing is that the firm is guaranteed to make a profit on its sales since it has covered its costs. However, the danger is that the firm may not be able to sell the expected quantity of the product perhaps because competitors are offering the same goods at a lower price. Therefore, in operating cost-based pricing it is vital to be aware of competitors' prices and what the market will bear.

Skimming

Skimming is most often used in the case of new products when there is little competition in the market. This strategy sets a relatively high price initially in an attempt to 'skim' the market – like skimming the cream off the milk! Some people would be willing to pay the higher price because the product is new and unique and few other people would own it. Later on, other firms will enter the market setting up competition so, in order to maintain sales, the price would be reduced.

The high initial price gives the impression of high quality and is justified by the manufacturers because the product usually would have had high costs in research and development. The danger of skimming is that some people will be deterred by the high price and prefer to wait until the price falls.

Pricing of mobile phones is an excellent example of skimming. When mobile phones were first produced they were expensive and few people owned them. Initially they were something of a status symbol. Later they were produced in large numbers by a variety of manufacturers and the price fell to such an extent that today most people own a mobile phone.

Penetration pricing

Penetration pricing is where a low price is set at the beginning in order to gain entry to an existing market, and where the price increases when the place in the market has been secured.

Penetration pricing would be used by a new business trying to break into – or penetrate – a market where other competitors already are well established. Obviously this pricing strategy is suitable for a competitive market.

In order to attract customers to the new store, and away from the competitors, they have to be lured by low prices. The basic idea is that, once the customers have been lured by the lower prices, they will become regular customers. It is at that stage that prices would be raised.

This method of price setting ensures sales, at least in the short term. It is possible, however, that the price has to be set so low that profits may be minimal.

Destruction pricing

Destruction pricing is also known as 'destroyer pricing'. It is a ruthless strategy which is designed to destroy competitors' sales or even drive them out of business altogether.

This method operates by reducing the price of an existing product or selling a new product at an artificially low price. Sometimes this new low price may be below cost level so the firm would be sustaining a loss for a period of time. Once the competitors have been driven out of the market, the prices would be raised again.

If the competitor is a small business it would be unable to reduce its prices in this way and may be forced to close. This has been the fate of so many of our corner shops and village stores in Northern Ireland.

Price wars

In very competitive markets such as the grocery market, businesses sometimes engage in price wars in which prices of some goods are cut to a very low level in order to secure sales. The idea is to attract customers to their particular supermarket to buy the marked-down goods and encourage them to buy other goods while they are there.

Price wars are not popular with businesses, however, even though they often happen. They are risky because advantages gained over other firms are short-lived and rival firms tend to respond by slashing prices even further.

If pursued long enough, price wars would cut profits seriously and, in the end, only the customer benefits by the low prices.

Activity

Study the following situations and name the pricing strategy which is being described in each example.

1 A new hardback book is published at £20. Two months later it is sold in paperback for £10.

....

2 A new supermarket in Lisburn opens selling a particular chocolate bar at 50p. Existing supermarkets in the town lower their prices of the chocolate bar to 40p.

....

3 Several stationery companies in Belfast keep lowering their prices for computer paper to take sales away from each other.

....

4 A bicycle manufacturer introduces a new model at a low price in order to attract sales.

....

5 A chemist shop in Lurgan researches the price of particular brands of toothpaste in all local outlets and then charges the same prices as they are charging.

....

6 A florist in Lisnaskea sets her prices to cover her total costs plus a little profit.

....

Activity

Six pricing policies are described in the column on the left. You should link each one to the appropriate name in the column on the right. The first one is done for you.

Description	Pricing policy
This policy is based on the prices charged by competitors	Destruction pricing
This policy charges a high price at the beginning and reduces it later	Market-led pricing
This policy cuts prices very low in order to take sales away from competitors	Cost-based pricing
This policy tries to put other firms out of business	Penetration pricing
This policy sets a low price at the beginning and increases it later	Skimming
This policy is based on the costs incurred in making and selling the goods	Price wars

Factors which affect price

Price has to be carefully worked out for every item put on the market. Several factors have to be considered.

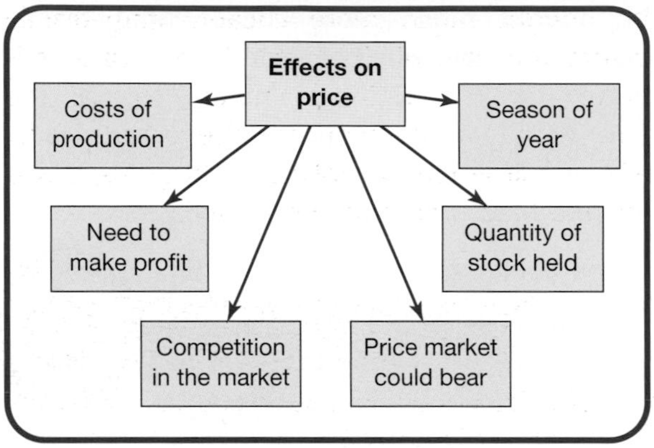

Costs of production

The producer has to calculate the total costs incurred in manufacturing the goods. These costs would include factory overheads and raw materials.

The retailer has to calculate the costs incurred in offering the goods for sale such as transport charges, wages to sales staff and shop overheads.

The price charged to the consumer has to be set at a level which would cover all these costs.

Need to make a profit

The overall aim of any business owner is to make a profit from the business, so the goods must be priced at a level which not only covers the total costs but also leaves a margin of profit for both the manufacturer and the retailer.

The owners would expect the level of profit on their investment in the business to be at least as much as the interest they could have earned if they had left their money in the bank. A healthy profit margin also encourages other investors to buy into the business.

The highest level of profit, however, will not necessarily be made by charging the highest prices since this could discourage sales.

Competition in the market

We have already seen in this theme how competitors' prices are monitored in order to increase sales. The aim in business is to set the price at a level which would encourage customers away from competitors.

To do this, the price has to be slightly lower than that charged by the competition if the goods are exactly the same.

Price which the market could bear

It is most important that the business is sensitive to the price which customers can afford and are willing to pay. This is also linked to the type of product.

If the goods being sold are luxury items they would be targeted at a wealthier market so that particular market could bear a higher price. Goods being sold in a shop in a less well-off area will have to be priced at a level which the customers there could afford.

Whatever the circumstances, the price charged has to be the one at which the highest level of sales would be made.

Season of the year

The demand for certain items rises at particular times of the year. The highest sales of toys are made in November and December for example, for the Christmas market. At these times of greatest demand the price is at its highest and falls immediately after the event. This is why it is possible to buy Christmas cards very cheaply in January.

The red rose you bought for your girl friend or boy friend for St Valentine's Day was very expensive, but the next day the price would have been considerably lower!

Quantity of stock in hand

At times when there is a surplus of goods in stock a retailer will hold a sale in order to reduce stocks. The price charged to the consumer obviously is affected.

This also happens with airline tickets which can be bought much more cheaply immediately before the date of the flight. In this case, it is better for the airline company to sell the remaining seats at a reduced price rather than fly with a half empty aeroplane. In business, this is referred to as 'under-used capacity'.

Activity

Six factors which affect prices are described on the left. You should link each one to the appropriate name in the column on the right. The first one is done for you.

Description	Pricing policy
The price charged has to cover all costs of production and selling the goods	Season of the year
The price is set so that the owners make some money for themselves	Price the market could bear
The price depends on the time of the year	Cost of production
The price depends on how much people can afford to pay	Need to make a profit
The price depends on what other firms are charging for the same goods	Quantity of stock in hand
The price is determined by how much of the goods the firm has	Competition in the market

Relationship between price and demand

Before exploring the relationship between price and demand, you should be sure that you understand the business meaning of 'demand' and how it differs from 'needs'.

We all have needs and wants. We NEED food, basic clothing and shelter in order to survive. We WANT a range of fashionable clothes, a more luxurious house or a bigger car but these items are not essential for our survival.

The total of our wants become 'demand' when those wants are backed up by money or when we are able to pay for them. So we can now define demand:

Demand is the quantity of goods which will be bought at a given price.

Successful businesses are those which can satisfy consumer demand and can get:

the right goods
to
the right place
at
the right time
and at
the right price

Activity

Read the text above and then comment on each of the following businesses:

1 A fashion store was unable to buy its summer clothes until August.
2 A filling station is charging 20p per litre more for petrol than other filling stations. However, its nearest filling station is fifty miles away.
3 A supermarket is charging 10p per litre extra for milk but all the other shops are closed.
4 A high class antique shop has opened in a working class area of the city.

There are many factors which cause a change in the demand for particular goods:

- **The price being charged for the goods**. Usually the higher the price being charged, the lower the demand for the goods
- **Customers' tastes**. People buy what they like or according to the prevailing fashion. For example, if alcohol were free some people would still not buy it because they are teetotal
- **Level of income**. Customers usually buy what they can afford. As income increases people would not necessarily buy more goods but they probably would buy better quality goods
- **Price of other goods**. Some goods act as substitutes and can be bought instead. For example, if potatoes were very expensive, people might eat pasta instead. Other goods are complementary goods which means they are often used together. For example, if the price of fish fell, people would eat more fish. This might cause extra demand for potatoes because we often eat fish and chips together.
- **Advertising**. Increased advertising, if successful, would cause an increase in demand
- **Credit rates**. At times when the lending rate is low, people will be able to borrow more from banks and building societies and demand for goods will increase as they buy more goods.

Activity

Damien is a butcher who has a large stock of beef in his shop. Unfortunately there has been a recent health scare which has put some people off buying beef.

1 Advise Damien on ways to increase demand for beef.

2 What else might Damien do in order to increase trade generally in his shop?

The relationship between price and demand is best illustrated graphically with price on the vertical axis and quantity demanded on the horizontal axis.

As price falls, demand rises. This fact can be shown on a demand line which always slopes downward to the right.

This graph illustrates demand for a certain item:

50 kilos are demanded at 50p per kilo

300 kilos are demanded at 10p per kilo.

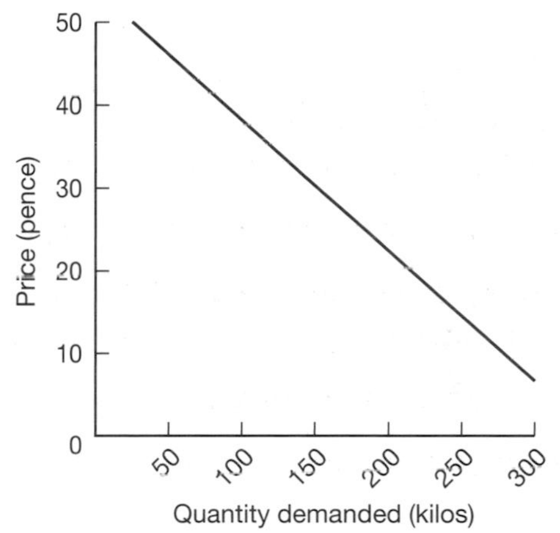

Activity

Study the above graph showing demand.

1 Read off the number of kilos which would be demanded if they were priced at 40p per kilo.

2 Find out how many kilos would be demanded if the goods were priced at 30p per kilo.

3 What do your answers prove about the relationship between price and demand?

4 Name the goods for which the above figures would be true.

Checklist

At this stage you should be able to:

- understand the term 'marketing'
- identify and discuss a range of pricing policies and their use in different circumstances
- investigate the factors which affect price
- analyse the relationship between price and demand
- evaluate pricing policies for given circumstances.

Theme 3.3

The marketing mix – promotion

The second part of the marketing mix is promotion. This is another commonly used term but could you define it?

Promotion is the process by which businesses inform customers about their products and encourage them to buy those products.

Promotion is a very important element of the marketing mix because even the best products will not be sold if consumers do not know about them.

Promotion is important not only at the introduction of a new product, but as an on-going process throughout its life, because customers need to be reminded about it if sales levels are to be maintained.

Promotion also keeps the name of the company and the name of its product(s) at the forefront of customers' minds. This creates an image for the company and also helps to keep it ahead of its competitors.

Activity

Study the above information, then copy and complete the following statements to show what effective promotion does for a company.

1 Promotion is important at the .... of a .... product

2 Promotion makes .... aware of .... products

3 Promotion keeps customers .... about products

4 Promotion maintains .... for the company

5 Promotion creates an .... for the company

6 Promotion helps to keep the company ....

Methods of promotion

There are many methods of promotion but the two most usual are advertising and sales promotion.

Advertising

Advertising is an important aspect of promotion and one in which companies invest large sums of money. They do this in order to:

- introduce a new product to the public and encourage sales
- remind the public about an existing product and boost its sales
- target a new segment of the market thereby increasing their market share
- provide information about products or events.

Types of advertising

There are three types of advertising and each one has a different function:

1. Informative advertising. This type of advertising is purely factual and its intention is to give information. Advertisements about forthcoming events, advertisements giving technical information or advertisements recalling products because of faults are all examples of informative advertising.

ANTIQUE FURNITURE AUCTIONS

BALNAMORE HOTEL,
BALLYMONEY
FRI 10TH APRIL, 8 PM

COLLEGE HALL,
OLD DUNDONALD ROAD, BELFAST
THUR 16TH APRIL, 8 PM

Both auctions to include:
TABLES, CHAIRS, BEDS
BATHS, SINKS, CARPETS
Viewing from 6.30 pm on day of sale

FOR DETAILS OF BOTH AUCTIONS, CONTACT:
SAINTFIELD ANTIQUES CENTRE
CROSSGAR

Informative advertising giving details of an auction

2. Persuasive advertising. As its name suggests, the intention of persuasive advertising is to persuade members of the public to purchase the advertised product. This type of advertising aims to convince people that the product being advertised should be selected in preference to the goods produced by the rival firms. It also aims to convince them that the quality of their lives would be improved if they were to buy that particular product.

3. Generic advertising. The word 'generic' means 'applied to a large group or class; general not specific'. Generic advertising is, therefore, advertising for a whole industry or a particular type of goods regardless of where the product is sold. Advertising by the Milk Marketing Board encouraging people to drink more milk is an example of generic advertising.

Activity

Which type of advertising is described in the following examples?

1 A doctor is telling everyone about the new opening hours at his surgery

2 Advertising which encourages members of the public that potatoes are good for them

3 A new perfume is being advertised in the glossy magazines.

The diagram on the next page illustrates the various methods of advertising.

Hoardings and posters

Hoardings are large boards situated at the side of the road. Hoardings have an immediate visual impact on passing traffic and can be seen at a distance. To be effective, they must be large, and therefore are limited to short messages which can be read quickly. This advertising method has no control over its audience so it must be designed to appeal to all tastes and age groups. It is most suitable for advertising goods which are bought by the majority of the population.

In cities, large, brightly-lit neon signs are commonly found as modern replacements of hoardings. These neon signs are expensive to maintain and therefore are used only by large multi-nationals such as Coca-Cola. Neon signs on point-of-sale fridges now frequently replace posters and are also used by companies such as Coca-Cola.

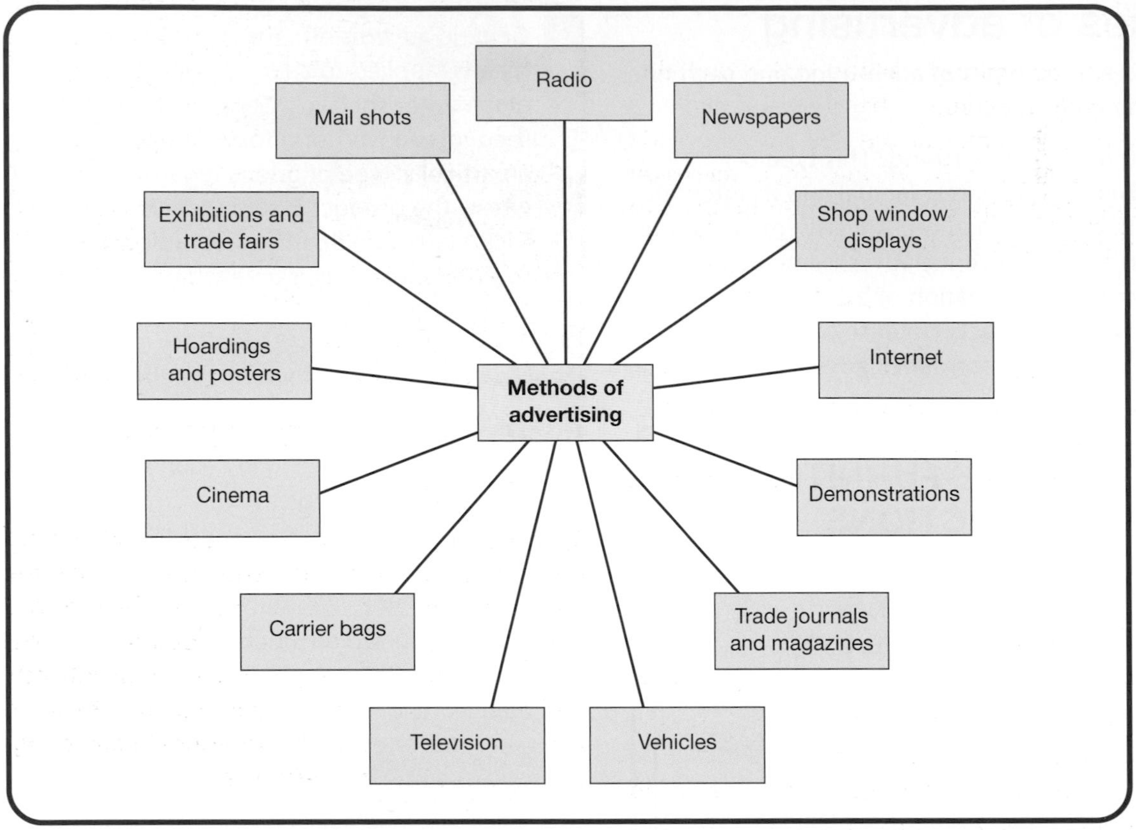

Hoardings

Television

This is the most expensive type of advertising costing approximately £1,000 per viewing second according to the time of day. It reaches a wide audience and is highly effective because it can be glamorous and entertaining.

Seeing the product on television has an important visual impact. Times of advertising are altered to suit the audience so toys, for example, are advertised during the day or early evening to target children.

Radio

Radio is the advertising method which probably has the widest audience because the radio is listened to at all times of the day and in a wide variety of places. It is cheaper than television advertising and different stations can be used to target different sectors of the market.

Cinema

This type of advertising can reach only those members of the public who visit the cinema. It is therefore more restricted than either radio or television advertising. Cinema advertising is frequently locally based and is often used by shops in the area.

Internet

The internet is the fastest growing and most recent form of advertising. Advertisements on the internet have a world-wide audience and can be reached at any time. They are capable of giving vast amounts of information which can then be saved or printed by the customer. It is possible for the customer to link with the advertisers in order to get further information. On the other hand, the internet cannot be accessed by anyone who does not have the necessary equipment.

Newspapers

Newspapers are bought by the majority of the population so this form of advertising is capable of reaching a wide audience. All newspaper advertising is expensive however. It is important that the advertisers choose the appropriate newspaper to reach their target market because different sectors of the public read different newspapers. For example, readers of the *News of the World* would have no interest in *The Times* or vice versa.

Newspapers can also cater for small classified advertisements about items for private sale. They may cover a local area – such as the *Portadown Times* – or have a province-wide readership – like the *Irish News*, the *News Letter* or *Belfast Telegraph*.

Magazines and trade journals

Specialist trade journals are good for advertising items such as specialist equipment since the target market for that equipment is likely to read the journals. Magazines are bought by most people and their vast range caters for all interests and age groups. Advertising in magazines can be accurately targeted at the appropriate age group and is, therefore, very effective.

Exhibitions

Exhibitions are attended by large numbers of visitors and are aimed at a certain sector of the market. For example, the Ideal Home Exhibition is held every September in the King's Hall, Belfast and attracts a large number of exhibitors showing household furniture, materials and equipment. People visit the exhibition to view the latest trends in house design.

The annual motor show, at the same venue, shows the latest models of cars and encourages the motoring public of Northern Ireland to order them.

Demonstrations by experts

This is a very effective method of advertising and is favoured by food manufacturers or manufacturers of kitchen utensils for example. An expert is employed to give demonstrations using the product. The idea is then got across to the public that the product must be excellent if the expert uses it. In the following picture, Jenny Bristow is using Denny products and giving the public ideas of how those products may be used.

Mail shots

The term 'mail shot' covers all leaflets sent to people's homes. Mail shots are often used to inform people within a targeted area about the opening of a new store or about local special sale events. There is no guarantee that the mail shots will be read, and some people resent being sent what they consider to be junk mail.

Vehicles

Advertising on the sides of vehicles can be very effective because it may be seen by a large number of people in different parts of the country. This method is cheap if the firm's own vehicles are used.

Advertising on public transport vehicles – such as buses – is popular but this must be limited to matters of interest in the area serviced by the public transport vehicle. As with hoardings, the message must be limited to a few words.

Shop window displays

These displays are very effective in attracting the passing public to enter the shop and make purchases. If the window display is good it will give the impression that the goods inside the shop are also good. One advantage of this method of advertising is that customers are likely to act immediately. On the other hand, the display is limited to people who are in that immediate area.

Carrier bags

Advertising on carrier bags is very cheap but effective because it is seen by large numbers of shoppers in the area of the shop. Very often carrier bags are recycled so the audience may be doubled.

Activity

Identify and write down the most appropriate methods of advertising to use in these particular circumstances.

1 A small shop, with very little money to spend on advertising, has a very attractive range of new clothes in stock. Few people know about the new range.

2 A village grocery shop has decided to remain open to 10 pm on six days per week.

3 A new household gadget is being launched on the market by a large company.

4 Your family has bought new furniture and wishes to advertise your old furniture for sale.

5 A large well-known ice-cream manufacturer wishes to improve sales of all types of ice-cream throughout the country.

6 A local jewellery business wants to tell the public about its excellent stock.

7 A craftsman, who makes wood carvings, is famous locally for his original designs and excellent workmanship. He would like to expand his market.

8 Organisers of a charity dance would like to make people aware of the event.

9 The government wants to encourage people to travel by train.

10 A school is advertising the dates of its open nights.

Sales promotion

Sales promotion is an overall term covering all methods which are used to persuade the customer to purchase the product. The diagram on the next page illustrates the various types of sales promotion.

Sales promotion methods

Special offers

These are very commonly used. Examples are buy two get one free, or get 10% extra free. The customer is attracted by the low price and sales for the shop would be increased.

Discounts

This is where 10% or half price for example, is given off the total price. Again the customer is attracted by the low price and buys the product.

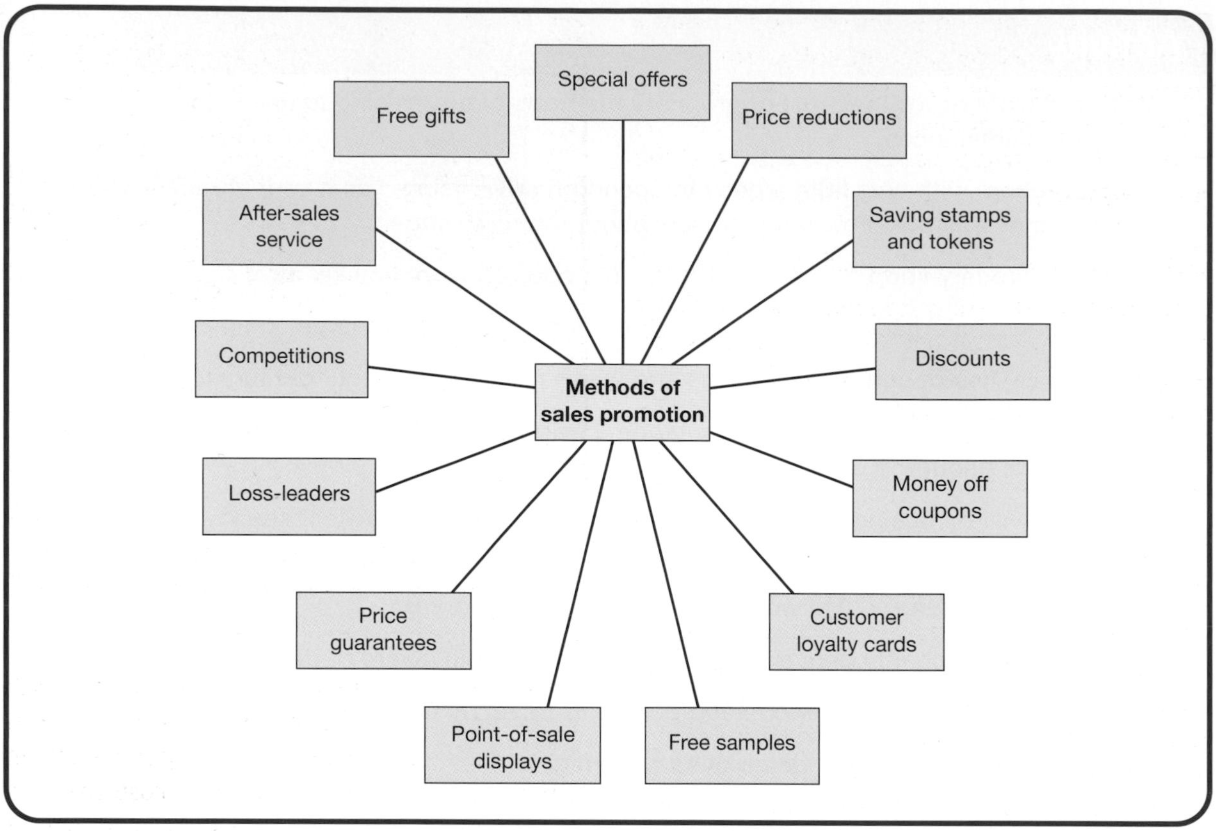

Loss-leaders

This is another form of price reduction found in larger shops. The price of one or two items is reduced to a very low level (even to the level of making no profit on those items). These low price goods attract customers in, and the shop hopes to encourage them to buy other, full-price goods while there. Bread is often offered as a loss-leader in supermarkets.

Price reductions

In this case the price of the product is reduced for a short period of time. The low price encourages people to buy that particular product which improves its sales.

Money-off coupons

Sometimes coupons are printed on the packaging of a product offering the next purchase of the product at a lower price. Coupons sometimes are sent in the post or can be cut out of newspapers. Customers save the coupons and have to buy the product again to take advantage of the offer. In this way, sales of the product are doubled for the company.

Competitions

Customers are sometimes encouraged to buy a particular product by printing entry forms for a competition on the packaging or including a leaflet at the point of sale. The prize is usually very worthwhile – a luxury holiday or a car – and this encourages people to buy the product.

Customer loyalty cards

Customers' cards are swiped at the check-out point and the totals of their purchases are recorded electronically. Each purchase earns points and the points can later be exchanged for cash or air miles. Such cards encourage customers to return to the same store in order to build up their points.

Free samples

Free samples of some products are given of items such as food, cleaning materials or make-up. Customers are sometimes asked to sample foods in shops. Some products occasionally have free samples of another product attached, and sometimes magazines have free samples of make-up attached to their front covers. All these samples are designed to introduce the product and encourage people to buy it.

Free gifts

Some products contain small free gifts enclosed in their packaging. For example, Kellogg's gave small toys in their cereals at one time but were criticised because of the safety factor. Other free gifts are obtained by collecting a certain number of tokens printed on the packaging. Sales are improved because customers have to buy more of the product in order to collect the tokens and get the gift.

Point-of-sale displays

Special displays are sometimes mounted in the shop to encourage shoppers to buy that particular product in that shop. An area is allocated to the product and special display stands erected to draw attention to the product. For some products such as small kitchen appliances, the display may also include a demonstration showing the benefits of those particular appliances.

Price guarantees

Customers are encouraged to shop with companies which offer price guarantees such as 'our prices cannot be beaten'. Computer World in Lisburn, for example, challenges customers to find its goods in other shops for less money. If they can find the same goods at a cheaper price, Computer World will refund the difference in the two prices.

After-sales service

Offering an excellent after-sales service is usually an encouragement for customers to choose a particular company when buying an expensive item such as a computer. This gives the customer confidence that assistance would be available if required. For this reason, customers are willing to pay a higher price rather than take advantage of special offer prices in large shops which do not have an after-sales service.

Savings stamps and tokens

In this type of promotion, stamps or tokens are given with purchases and saved. They can then be exchanged for goods which have been displayed in a catalogue or in the store. These are less popular than previously because they take time and can be mislaid.

Activity

Name the sales promotional method which you would recommend in each of the following examples and explain your choice of method.

1 Sales of fish have fallen off since a recent health scare about chemicals being dumped at sea.

2 Sales of mobile phones need some help because nearly everyone has already bought a phone.

3 A new cereal is being launched on the market by a well-known company which already markets many varieties of cereal.

4 A new luxury car is being launched. The car is very expensive.

5 A cheese manufacturer wishes to improve sales of all types of cheese in order to beat the competition.

6 A small computer retailer is generally having difficulties because people are buying from the large retailers which have a larger variety and can sell at cheaper prices.

7 New tights are being introduced to the market.

8 A firm of soup manufacturers has found that sales of its new soup flavours are not popular.

Two other very popular methods of promotion are the use of sponsorship and public relations.

Sponsorship

It is quite common for businesses to sponsor sporting events, charity events or school events. All of these activities portray the business as being public spirited and interested in its local community. The business donates the funds necessary to run the event, and, in return, the players wear kit displaying the company logo. The company name also is usually emblazoned around the sports field. This provides wide publicity for the business especially if the event is being televised.

You will notice, for example, on television that the programme 'Who Wants to be a Millionaire' is sponsored by Pukka Pies. This programme has a large following so, by association, the name of the sponsor is linked with success and popularity.

Public relations

Any activity under the heading of public relations is one where the public's awareness of the company is raised and the company is seen to be generous. Creating a good impression in this way creates a loyalty with members of the public who will then be more likely to buy from the business.

Examples of public relations activities are where companies donate sizeable sums of money to charity or perhaps contribute cash or products towards famine relief or a war-torn area.

SuperValu stores across Northern Ireland have helped their community partner Action Cancer during a recent week-long fundraising drive organised to keep the charity's Big Bus service on the road.

Legal constraints on promotion

The government aims to protect consumers and to ensure that there is fair and honest trading in our fast-changing society. One area in which protection is needed is the area of promotion, so that consumers are not deliberately misled by false advertising and promotional offers which are not genuinely value for money. A number of laws have been passed for these purposes, and they control the framework in which promotional activity may operate.

It is interesting that the most common areas of consumer fraud investigated today are car clocking and trademark infringement. In these cases, cars offered for re-sale are described as having low mileage, and, in the second type of fraud, counterfeit goods – mainly perfumes and cassettes – are described as being expensive brands.

Legal constraints on promotion states that:

- goods or services supplied must be accurately described, giving full information about the item being sold
- prices charged for goods or services must be genuine. If products are described as 'reduced' in a sale, they must have been on sale at the higher price in that shop for at least twenty-eight consecutive days in the previous six months
- all prices displayed must also include VAT
- the country of origin must appear on the packaging of all imported goods
- dangerous products such as poisons, medicines or solvents must show on the packaging that they are dangerous and must also include first aid procedures to follow if necessary.

The level of detail given in the above summary is all that is required for GCSE (CCEA) Business Studies. However, some students may require more detail for other purposes, or may simply be interested in further reading. For those reasons, the following notes on individual laws and other constraints on promotion are included.

Trade Descriptions Acts, 1968 and 1972

These Acts were among the earliest pieces of legislation and still are the major tools used to guarantee fair practice in promotional activities.

The Trade Descriptions Acts prohibit the giving of false descriptions or the supplying of goods or services with false descriptions. This covers all information given on the goods about:

- their quantity or size
- their method of manufacture or testing
- the place and date of their manufacture
- the people who manufactured them.

The scope of the Trade Descriptions Acts is very wide and includes all forms of services as well as all types of goods. For example, some farmers were prosecuted for falsely describing their cattle as coming from a BSE-free herd.

In addition, these laws ensure that prices are genuine. If products are described as 'reduced' in a sale, they must have been on sale at the higher price in that shop for at least twenty-eight consecutive days in the previous six months. Otherwise, sale bargains may only be described as 'special purchases' which indicates that those products were bought specially to offer to customers at a lower price. Sometimes the quality of special purchases is less high than that of the regular stock, and the law ensures that consumers are made aware of this possibility.

The Trade Descriptions Acts also state that the country of origin must appear on the packaging of all imported goods. Descriptions may either be written, pictorial or oral, and any breaches of the Trade Descriptions Acts may incur fines of up to £5,000 or imprisonment of up to two years.

Consumer Protection Act, 1987

The Consumer Protection Act, 1987 covers more than promotional activities but it is not appropriate, in this section on Promotion, to examine any other aspect. The Consumer Protection Act, 1987 lays down rules to govern the use of such terms as 'sales price', 'reduced price' and 'bargain offer'. The point of the Act is to ensure that prices advertised in any of these ways are genuine reductions.

According to the terms of the Consumer Protection Act, 1987 it is an offence to give misleading information regarding the pricing of any goods or services. All prices displayed must also include VAT.

The Consumer Protection Act also ensures that dangerous products such as poisons, medicines or solvents must show on the packaging that they are dangerous and must also include first aid procedures to follow if necessary.

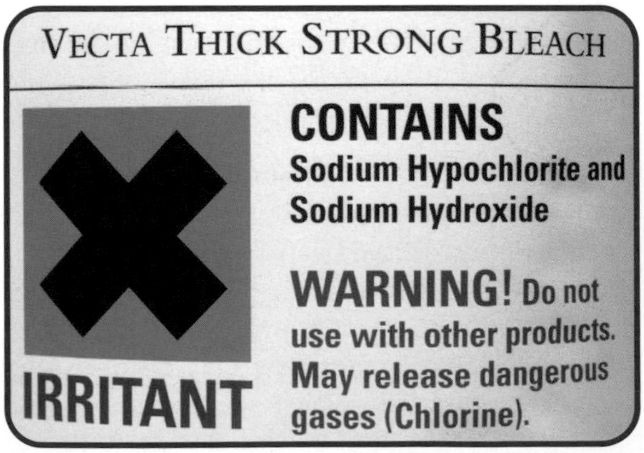

Other constraints on promotion

In addition to the legal constraints on promotion, several bodies have been established to give further protection to consumers in this area. In some cases these bodies have been set up by the government, while in other instances, they are independent.

Advertising Standards Authority (ASA)

The Advertising Standards Authority is an independent body set up to monitor all advertisements which are not broadcast.

The basic principles of the Advertising Standards Authority are to make sure that all advertisements are:

- legal, decent, honest and truthful
- prepared with a sense of responsibility to consumers and to society
- in line with the principles of fair competition.

The basic function of the Advertising Standards Authority is to ensure that the public is not misled or offended by advertisements. In order to fulfil this function, the ASA carries out spot checks on approximately ten thousand advertisements every week and will ask the company either to withdraw or amend any advertisement which does not comply with its principles.

The majority of advertisers are so anxious not to offend the ASA's principles that many of them seek the Authority's advice before publication, which saves them the possible expense and bad reputation caused by having to withdraw an advertisement later.

If a company does not withdraw or amend its advertisement, the ASA does not have any legal power to make it do so. The ASA's main sanction is to ask publishers to refuse more space for an advertisement until its terms have been upheld. In the case of continued offences, the ASA will refer an advertiser to the Office of Fair Trading who can legally prevent similar advertisements being published in the future.

The Advertising Standards Authority also deals with complaints from members of the public who have felt misled or offended by an advertisement. On average the Authority deals with 12,000 complaints per year.

The Advertising Standards Authority regulates all advertising in non-broadcast media which includes everything shown in the diagram below.

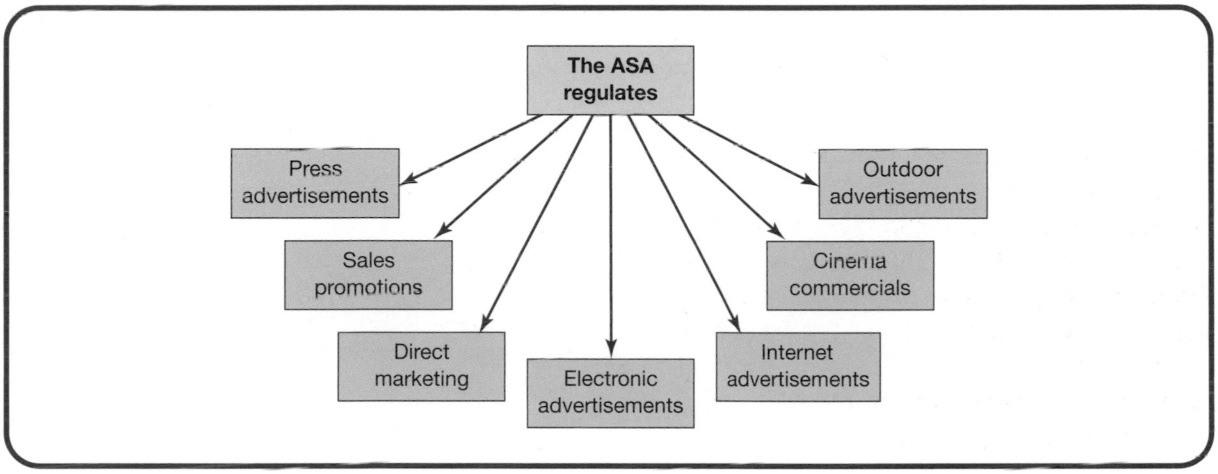

Ofcom

Ofcom (Office of Communication) is an independent organisation which regulates the communication industries in the United Kingdom. Ofcom was formed in 2003 and took over the previous duties of the former Independent Television Commission. Its duty is to protect consumers from harmful or offensive material.

Its basic principles are to make sure that all communication:

- adheres to rules on taste and decency
- is impartial
- does not give offence or cause harm
- supports market growth and competition
- sets high technical standards.

So, broadly speaking, its function for broadcast communication is very similar to the function which the Advertising Standards Authority has for advertising media.

Office of Fair Trading (OFT)

The Office of Fair Trading is an independent body which was set up in 1973 as a result of the Fair Trading Act although its powers changed with the Enterprise Act, 2002. Its basic function is to promote and protect the interests of consumers. To do this, the OFT ensures that businesses act fairly towards consumers and operate openly and in a competitive way. This includes making sure that consumers have as much choice as possible.

The Office of Fair Trading has two major aims:

1. To protect consumers and explain their rights.
2. To ensure that businesses compete and operate fairly.

The main activities of the Office of Fair Trading are to:

- give advice to members of the public on consumer affairs
- enforce consumer protection laws, taking court action if necessary against firms which do not behave properly

- investigate how markets are working
- explain and improve awareness and understanding
- fight against the abuse of market power
- investigate mergers that might lessen competition and cause monopolies.

Activity

Answer the following questions:

1. What are the major principles of the Advertising Standards Authority?
2. How does the Advertising Standards Authority carry out its function?
3. Why do companies often seek the advice of the Advertising Standards Authority before they publish an advertisement?
4. What is the major difference between the work of the Advertising Standards Authority and the work of Ofcom?
5. What are the major principles of Ofcom?
6. What do the initials OFT stand for?
7. Describe the function of the OFT.

Ethical and moral issues relating to promotion

The word 'moral' concerns the difference between right and wrong and concerns identifying the right thing to do. The word 'ethical' is similar and refers to the rules of conduct which should be applied.

In the area of promotion, the moral and ethical issues have largely been covered by legislation. Advertisers are legally prevented from acting immorally. They are not allowed to make false claims about their goods in advertisements and other promotional material. They must be truthful in their descriptions of the price, size, weight and all other details of their products.

The Trade Descriptions Act also states that the country of origin must appear on the packaging of all types of imported goods. Some people do not wish to buy the products of countries which perpetuate practices they dislike. For example, at one time many people here refused to buy South African fruit because they were strongly opposed to the practice of apartheid in South Africa. Labelling the goods with the country of origin allows customers to make up their own minds on the issue and gives them the information to do so.

Some products such as cigarettes are proven to be health hazards. Morally it is wrong to

encourage people to purchase products which may ultimately affect their health. For this reason, the packaging of cigarettes must carry a health warning and advertising of cigarettes is not allowed on television.

The consumption of alcohol makes some people act in an unsocial way and is positively dangerous when driving. Expensive advertising campaigns by the government have been mounted to inform drivers of the risks, and to discourage the practice. This is an aspect of promotion which is beneficial to the well-being of the community.

Checklist

At this stage you should be able to:

- **understand the most commonly used methods of promotion**
- **evaluate the most commonly used methods of promotion**
- **identify the most appropriate methods of promotion in particular circumstances**
- **show awareness of the legal constraints on promotion.**

Theme 3.4

The marketing mix – place

You will recall that, in the introduction to this section, you learned that successful businesses are those who can get:

the right goods
to
the right place
at
the right time
and at
the right price

Theme 3.4 is about getting the goods to the place where they are going to sell most successfully. This means that manufacturers must study carefully where to sell their products as well as how to get them, in good condition, to that place. To do this, the business must consider:

- the most appropriate sales outlets for that product
- the most appropriate channel of distribution to use
- the most appropriate method of transport for that particular product.

Decisions about the type of sales outlet to use will depend on the type and value of the goods being sold and the socio-economic or cultural class of the area. The skill is in placing the appropriate goods in the most appropriate area.

There is no point in placing very expensive goods in a poor area where people could not afford to buy them, nor is there any point in placing cheap goods in a wealthy area where people would not be interested in them.

Activity

State where you would place the following goods, giving reasons.

Pitchforks
Children's buckets and spades
Wallpaper
Jewish newspapers
Coffee
Expensive designer clothes
Shampoo
Secondhand furniture

Parties involved in distribution

The following four parties are involved in distribution, and it is important to make sure that you understand the roles of all four before you study the various channels of distribution.

Manufacturer/producer

The manufacturer or producer is the creator of goods in large quantities. In the case of goods such as furniture, cars etc. the manufacturer would be a factory owner. A farmer is also a producer – producing goods such as fruit, vegetables and meat. Similarly a fisherman is also a producer.

Wholesaler

The wholesaler is the link between the manufacturer and the retailer. The wholesaler purchases goods in bulk from the manufacturer, and transports them to warehouses where they are stored. The goods are then available for sale to retailers in smaller quantities. This process is often referred to as 'breaking bulk'.

The wholesaler provides a useful service for small retailers especially. Because of this service, retailers do not have to provide very large storage facilities nor do they have to buy and pay for large quantities of goods at one time. Instead they can visit the local wholesaler on a regular basis and restock when necessary. In some cases the wholesaler offers a delivery service and often credit facilities are given to the retailer.

Wholesalers also provide important services for manufacturers, saving them the numerous transactions which they would have if they had to deal directly with retailers.

The diagrams below illustrate this point, using only four manufacturers, one wholesaler and six retailers. Imagine the number of transactions throughout Northern Ireland if manufacturers had to deal with every retailer!

The Holmes Group, with warehouses at present in Ballymena, Belfast, Derriaghy, Enniskillen and Lurgan, is one example of a Northern Ireland wholesaler.

Retailer

The retailer is the final seller of the goods to the customer. Retailing is most frequently done in shops and they may range in size from very large supermarkets to very small village shops.

Whatever the scale on which they operate, they all provide a similar service to the customer. The retailer makes the goods available for the customer at a convenient place and also further breaks bulk of the products so that the customer is able to buy small amounts.

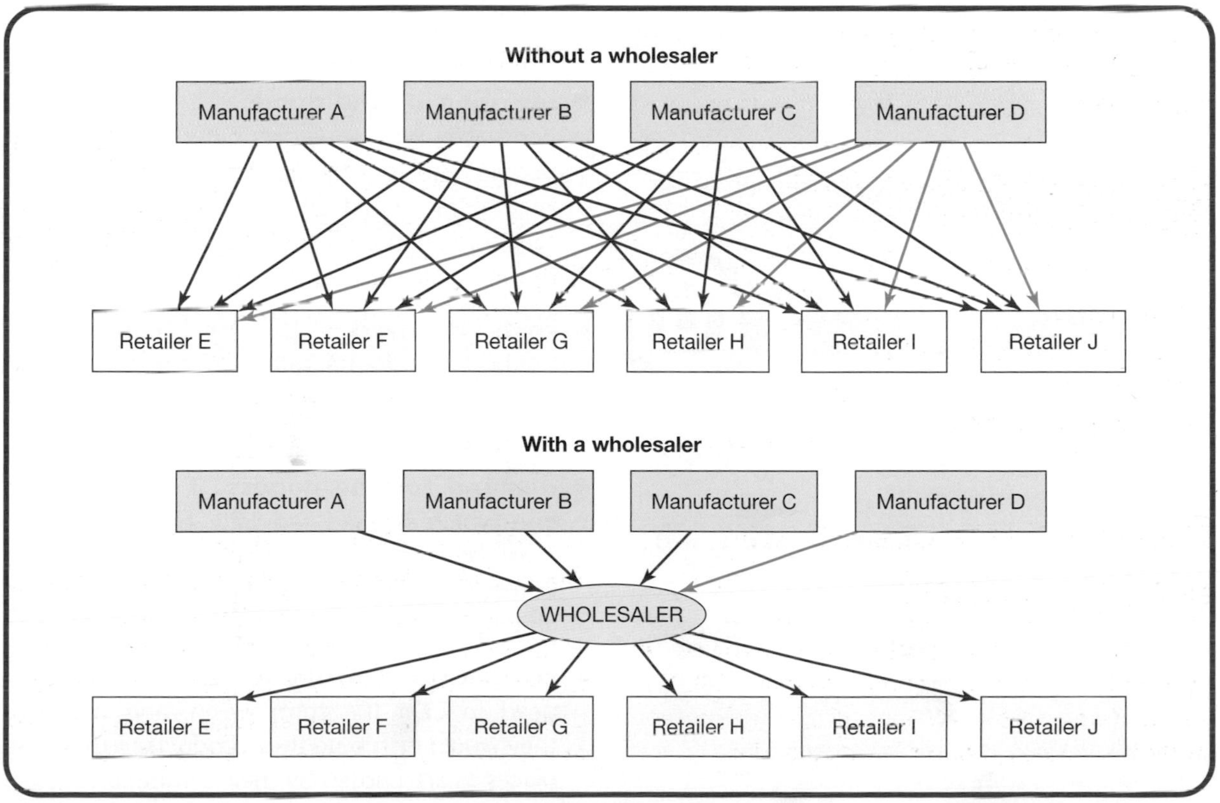

Consumer

The consumer is the final user of the product. The consumer would buy small, usable amounts of the product and replace them frequently.

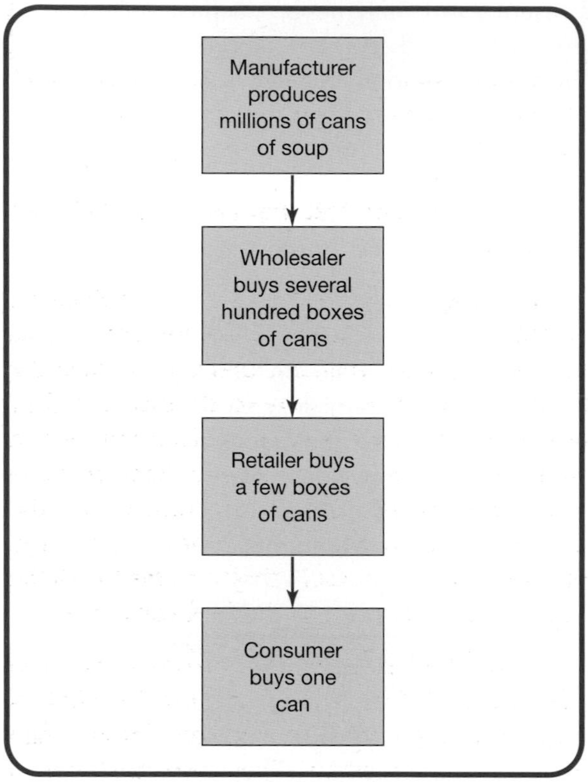

How bulk is broken (using canned soup as an example)

Activity

Refer back to the diagrams on the previous page which illustrate the number of transactions which would be made with and without a wholesaler.

1 What environmental advantages would there be in having fewer transactions?

2 Name one social cost of closing wholesalers.

Channels of distribution of goods and services

Channel of distribution is the way in which the goods are passed from the manufacturer to the consumer.

The choice of channel of distribution depends on the:

- **type of goods** – if the product is a very specialised one, the manufacturer and consumer are likely to want to be directly in contact with each other. For example a shipping company would be in direct contact with its ship-builders
- **value of the goods** – generally the rule is that the more expensive the product is, the fewer the places which sell it. This maintains the expensive and elite image of the product. For example, it would be unusual to be able to buy a Rolex watch in very small towns
- **life span of the goods** – if the product is perishable, it must be distributed widely so that people can get it quickly. Fresh fruit and vegetables would be in this category, and therefore are usually sold directly from producer to the retailer or even to the consumer
- **costs involved** – the most cost-effective method has to be found. If the channel of distribution involves high costs it would be unsuitable for low-cost goods
- **demand for the goods** – if the product is one which is used regularly by everyone, it must be distributed widely and be available immediately. For example, people expect to be able to buy shampoo almost anywhere
- **competition for the goods** – manufacturers need to beat the competition, and therefore they would distribute their products to the same places as are chosen by their competitors.

There are three channels of distribution in common use:

1. From the manufacturer to the consumer via the wholesaler and the retailer.
2. From the manufacturer to the consumer via the retailer.
3. From the manufacturer directly to the consumer.

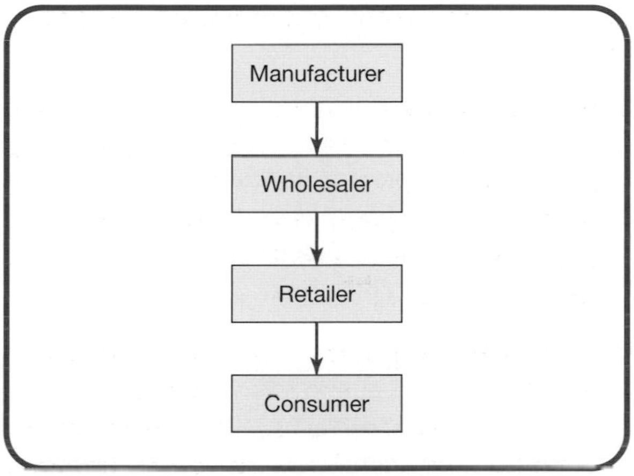

Channel 1 – From the manufacturer to the consumer via the wholesaler and the retailer

Channel 1 is the traditional channel of distribution and involves the product being passed through two middlemen before it finally gets to the consumer. The product is first sold by the manufacturer to the wholesaler, then it is sold by the wholesaler to the retailer, and lastly, it is sold by the retailer to the consumer.

This channel of distribution is still widely used, particularly by small retailers who avail of the storage, bulk-breaking, credit and delivery services of the wholesaler. However this method is being replaced in the case of large retailers as we shall see in our study of Channel 2.

Channel 2 distributes the goods from the manufacturer to the retailer who then sells the product to the consumer. This method is becoming more common and has been made possible for two reasons. Firstly, the growth of pre-packed goods makes distribution easier and secondly, some

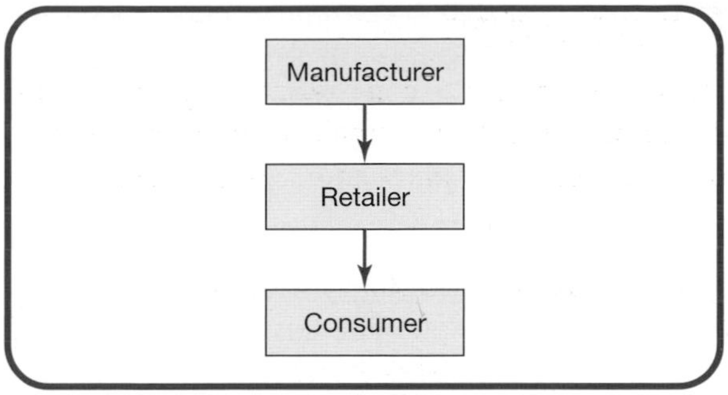

Channel 2 – From the manufacturer to the consumer via the retailer

retailers are so large that they can act as their own wholesalers.

Large companies such as Marks and Spencer, Sainsbury's, Tesco, Currys or Computer World all buy directly from manufacturers. They have the financial reserves necessary to do this, and their orders are so large that manufacturers find it easier to deal with them directly. Because these firms deal with the manufacturers directly, placing very large orders, they earn large discounts and, as a result, they are able to sell the goods at a lower price to the final consumer.

Manufacturers feel that sometimes they can push sales of their products more forcefully if they deal directly with retailers rather than through a middleman. They also are now in more direct contact with retailers because they see the retailer as being close to the consumer, and this puts them in a better position to hear the views of consumers.

Finally, it is believed that direct contact between manufacturer and retailer – Channel 3 – builds up loyalty to the company and to its products.

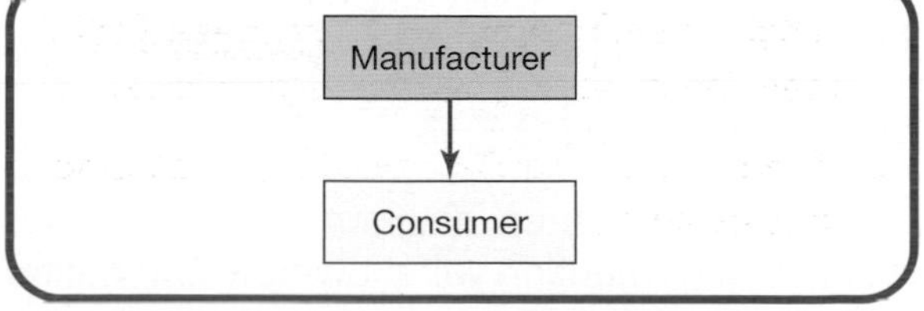

Channel 3 – From the manufacturer directly to the consumer

This channel distributes goods directly from the producer to the end-user. It is suitable for certain types of business – for example, businesses selling fresh produce, and businesses selling very exclusive, and therefore very expensive, goods.

Small craft industries often receive orders for items such as individually designed pieces of furniture, for example. The customer would have designed the item and then would liaise directly with the craftsman who has the skill to produce it.

Farmers often sell fresh fruit and vegetables at market stalls directly to their customers, and garden centres also sell their plants and flowers using this method. Exclusive dress designers, such as Dior, also work in this way, directly consulting with their clients who are often film stars or royalty.

It is also possible to visit factory shops which are established by factories as outlets for their goods. One example of this practice is at Tyrone Crystal Ltd in Dungannon where the Visitors' Centre sells the factory's products. This factory also accepts orders for specially designed and engraved presentation pieces of crystal which is a further example of a direct transaction between manufacturer and consumer.

Activity

Maureen runs a restaurant in Tandragee. She has added a successful sideline to her restaurant by selling ready-made meals in shops in Tandragee, Richhill, Armagh and Portadown.

Maureen has carried out some market research and is certain that there would be a very good market for her ready-made meals among the elderly people in the area. Her plan is to sell complete dinners each day to the elderly people living in the local folds and sheltered accommodation.

Her accountant is unsure about cutting out the retailer and starting into direct selling to the consumer.

Maureen needs your help to persuade her accountant about the benefits of her plan, and asks you to word process the arguments she should use.

Changing trends in the distribution of goods and services

Looking at the three diagrams illustrating the channels of distribution will show how distribution has been simplified. Three stages in Channel 1 may be reduced to a single stage in Channel 3.

The present trend in home shopping is likely to continue because of the fact that the majority of women continue with their careers and have less time to shop. Long-established mail order catalogue companies such as Freemans remain popular for their convenience of home shopping and credit facilities. Many of the high street shops such as Next or Debenhams also have mail order services.

Shopping via the internet is growing enormously in popularity, especially with its increased security of payment methods.

Increasingly, the trend is for large retailers to act as their own wholesalers and buy their goods directly from the manufacturers. Price savings made in this way allow the supermarkets to pass on these benefits to consumers in the form of lower prices. This stimulates trade even further for the retailing giants but causes greater difficulties for small retailers who cannot compete with the price reductions offered by the supermarkets.

Nevertheless, there will probably always be a place for small shops because of their long opening times, the convenience of their location and their personal service.

Implications of the internet for distribution

The internet offers businesses of all sizes the possibility of worldwide trading. For the first time, traders can now be connected to customers in over 100 different countries, allowing them the chance to be literally in more than one place at the same time.

Recent surveys have estimated that there are 544 million people online worldwide. Just think of the vast opportunities all those people give businesses to expand their markets! The internet enables everyone to sell directly to the public, bypassing all the middlemen.

The most suitable products for sale via the internet are small items such as books and videos, low-cost items which people will take a risk on buying, or hard-to-find, unique items such as crafts products.

While the overall trading opportunities are immense, distribution of products to a worldwide market can be a problem.

Implications for distribution of internet sales are as follows:

- Products have to be delivered in safe condition, cheaply and on time. Small items can be posted using either surface mail or air mail. Larger items must be shipped to their destination. International trade is therefore dependent on existing carrier and postal services
- Matters involving customs and excise, import and export regulations and shipping laws must all be observed
- Internet sales service must be accompanied by a fleet of delivery vehicles. The use of the internet should not be seen as being only for international trade. Local marketing is also one of its features. More and more large supermarkets are offering online shopping with a delivery service.

Activity

Norman is a retired gentleman and an excellent craftsman. As a hobby, he makes wooden items such as ornaments, picture frames, small pieces of furniture, carved boxes and wooden bowls. Although this work started off as a hobby, people regularly ask him to supply goods for them to give as presents. His work is so good and his designs so original that you are sure they would sell very well to a wider market.

Norman has never had to use a computer in his life and does not understand how the internet would help him.

Write, or word process, a short account of how the internet could help his business.

Methods of transport used to distribute goods

Distribution involves transporting the goods to their final destination. The choice of transport method depends on the answers to the following questions:

- Is the product valuable?
- Is the product perishable or breakable?
- What is the weight of the product?
- How quickly is the product required?
- How much does the method of transport cost?

Various methods of transport are available:

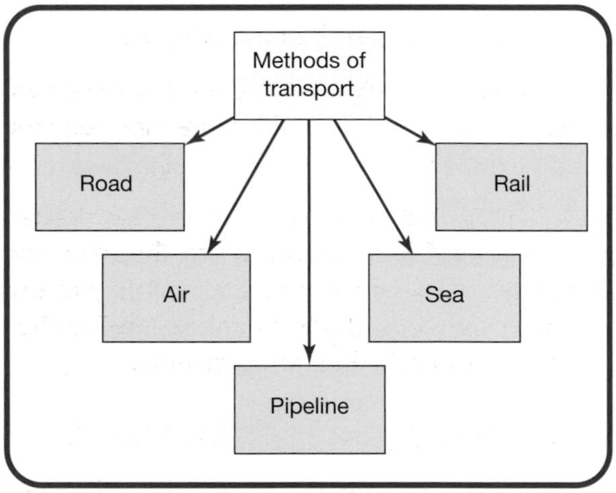

Lorries are most frequently used in Northern Ireland

Advantages of road transport

- It is a very adaptable system and permits door-to-door delivery
- It can be used at any time of the day or night, and is not dependent on timetables
- In some circumstances, return loads can be organised which reduces the cost
- Road transport is more secure than some methods of transport because the goods are always accompanied by a driver.

Disadvantages of road transport

- Buying and maintaining the vehicles, and paying fuel costs and drivers' wages are all very expensive
- Congestion on the roads can sometimes lead to delays.

Road transport

In Northern Ireland, road is the most commonly used method of transport and we depend on it for our supplies. Road transportation is mainly by lorries and vans which are generally owned by the traders and manufacturers themselves. Containerisation is a feature of road transport which allows lorries to make excellent use of their space.

Road transport is suitable for all types of goods and is used for bringing new stock to businesses in Northern Ireland as well as for transporting its exports to the ports.

Rail transport

Northern Ireland is poorly serviced by railways and many areas are too far from the existing lines to make any use of them.

Altogether, Northern Ireland has 210 miles of railway. This operates from Belfast to Dublin, from Belfast to Coleraine and Londonderry with a branch line from Coleraine to Portrush, and suburban routes from Belfast to Portadown, Bangor and Larne.

Advantages of rail transport

- Rail transport is cheaper than road transport
- It is also faster in larger countries where long distances may be travelled.

Disadvantages of rail transport

- Rail transport needs road transport to take the goods to the railway station and from the station to their final destination
- The goods are handled by more people which has implications for their safety and security.

Air transport

Northern Ireland is served by two main airports – Aldergrove International Airport and George Best Belfast City Airport. In Northern Ireland, many business travellers and other people depend on air transport in order to attend meetings in England.

Advantages of air transport

- It is very fast which makes it most suitable for small, light products especially if speed is important
- It is a very secure method of transport.

Disadvantage of air transport

- Air transport is very expensive and those costs are then passed on to the consumer.

Sea transport

Sea transport is the principal method of transport used for international trade.

Advantages of sea transport

- It is much cheaper than air transport
- Its economy makes it suitable for heavy goods and large quantities which are not required very quickly
- Using the roll-on roll-off system, fully loaded lorries are driven straight on to the ships and straight off again at the end of the journey. This allows the goods to remain undisturbed and their good condition is assured.

Disadvantage of sea transport

- Sea transport really only works in conjunction with road transport which is essential to continue the journey of the goods to their final destination.

Pipeline transport

This method of transport is associated with the transportation of oil and gas over long distances. For example, oil from the oilfields in the Middle East is piped hundreds of miles to the docks for export. Using road transport for this purpose would be extremely expensive and inconvenient.

In Northern Ireland, Phoenix Natural Gas has laid 600 kilometres of natural gas pipeline to distribute gas around the greater Belfast area. In addition, the company has installed 500 kilometres of 24 inch sub-sea pipelines across Belfast and Larne Loughs to bring gas from England to the province.

Phoenix Gas pipes being laid in Belfast area

Activity

Complete the boxes on the right hand side to show the type of transport which is most suitable in each situation.

Product	Appropriate method of transport
Fresh flowers coming from Jersey to Northern Ireland	
Jam being distributed from a warehouse in Belfast to a shop in Islandmagee	
Petrol being distributed to filling stations throughout Northern Ireland from Belfast	
Daily newspapers coming from England to Northern Ireland	
A human heart needed for a transplant operation in London from Templepatrick	
Oil from oilfields in the Middle East to the nearest port	
Twice weekly supplies to Tesco in Northern Ireland from its central stores in England	
Taking live sheep from a farm near Newtownhamilton to the local market	

Checklist

At this stage, you should understand:

- the most commonly used channels of distribution
- changing trends in distribution
- implications of the internet for distribution
- Details of the methods of transport used to distribute goods.

Theme 3.5

The marketing mix – product

The final part of the marketing mix is the product – possibly the most important element of all. After all, if there is no product there is nothing to market.

Let's be clear, before we go any further, what exactly 'product' is. Products are not only goods but may also be services. A product may be defined as the commodity which the business is offering for sale.

A car is obviously the product of a company such as Ford, a holiday is the product of any hotel or travel agency, a band's product is a concert, an operation or other treatment would be a hospital's product while legal advice from a solicitor is also a product.

A product is the commodity which the business is offering for sale.

Product life cycle

All products have a lifespan. Some products, such as mustard, seem to have a very long lifespan while other items are crazes for a period of time but tend to go out of fashion equally quickly.

However, even products such as mustard have had to change over the years in order to maintain their places in the market. For example, originally mustard was manufactured in powder form. Later it was developed in its ready-made form and, even later, a variety of flavours were added to give us the range of mustards we can buy today.

The concept of the lifespan of a product is illustrated by the product life cycle which shows the path of a product from the very beginning through to its withdrawal from the market. This identifies six separate stages in the life cycle of a typical product:

1. Research and development
2. Introduction or launch
3. Growth
4. Maturity
5. Saturation
6. Decline.

Activity

Use a dictionary to look up the meaning of these six terms. Complete the following table with the definitions you have found. It is important that you apply the definitions to a market situation.

Life cycle stage	Definition
Development	
Introduction	
Growth	
Maturity	
Saturation	
Decline	

Stage 1 – Research and development

This stage takes place before the product is put on the market at all. During the research and development stage, market research would be carried out on the product and it would also be tested, particularly in the case of mechanical or scientific products.

This stage would be very lengthy for expensive products such as cars, and could last as long as ten years. By contrast, this stage would last a very short time in the case of fashion items where the producer would be anxious to get the product ready for the market as quickly as possible while the fashion lasted.

Stage 1 is an expensive stage for the producer. Research is expensive and no income is being received, so the product is in a loss-making position at the research and development stage.

Stage 2 – Introduction or launch

In the introductory stage of the life of a product, emphasis is placed on marketing and promotion in order to make the public aware of the product and to create a desire to buy it.

At this point, sales would be slow at the beginning for all goods but would increase rapidly for low cost goods such as detergents if the marketing activity had been successful. In the case of high-fashion goods, sales would also be fast because people would want to have the item as quickly as possible. Sales would be slower for expensive products such as cars, because most people would not spend so much money on a product which had not proved its reliability.

The product would still not be in a profit-making position at this introductory stage because sales would not yet be great enough to cover the costs incurred in the first research and development stage.

Stage 3 – Growth

At this stage, sales grow rapidly as most people would be aware of the product by now, many would have tried it and it would be starting to achieve a degree of customer loyalty.

At the growth stage, sometimes prices can be reduced especially if other producers start to provide competition by putting similar products on the market.

The increased sales will put the product into a profit-making position at this stage as the income from sales covers the initial costs of research and development.

Stage 4 – Maturity

At the maturity stage, sales levels are maintained and the product has an established place in the market. However, the competition becomes very intense at this stage and it is more difficult to increase the volume of the product's sales any further. In an attempt to do so, the product will be advertised intensively once again.

The maturity stage is usually a lengthy one in household products but would last for a very short time in fashion items as the next new craze takes over.

Profits at this stage are at their highest because sales have stabilised. Nevertheless, an astute business would realise at this stage that it needs to begin to research and develop a second product to have ready to replace its first product when it reaches the later stages in the cycle.

Stage 5 – Saturation

The saturation stage is the highest point in the life of the product. Although competition is intense, there are unlikely to be any new competitors at this stage.

Sales have been pushed as far as possible and new customers cannot be found. Some may be attracted to the product because of decreased prices or extra advertising. At this stage the weakest products will drop out of the market which may prolong the saturation stage of the others for a period of time.

Profits would still be good at the maturity stage but not growing.

Stage 6 – Decline

The decline stage is the final stage in the life of a product. Sales have fallen to such an extent that they are not covering the manufacturing costs and the product is therefore unprofitable.

Further advertising or price reductions would not be successful and the product should be withdrawn from the market when this stage is reached. However, this decline stage can be lengthy for some products. For example, Horlicks appears to be less widely used now than previously and less advertising is done. However, the product still has a good place on the market because there is still a sufficient number of customers to sustain it.

Other, short-life products – like last year's high fashion – simply cannot be sold at any price, and so their decline stage is exceptionally short. The business which has prepared for this stage will have a second product ready for introduction to the market to replace the declining product.

Activity

Think of any five products which are at the following stages of the product life cycle at the present time, and write their names in the table below.

Product	Stage
	is at the introduction stage
	is at the growth stage
	is at the maturity stage
	is at the saturation stage
	is at the decline stage

Illustration of the product life cycle

The product life cycle is illustrated on a graph. By now, you will have realised that the length of the different stages will vary according to the type of product being manufactured and sold. For this reason, the shape of the graph will be different for various products.

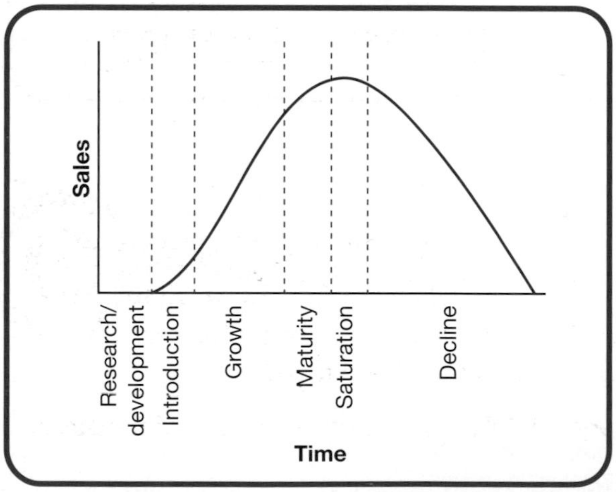

Typical product life cycle of detergent

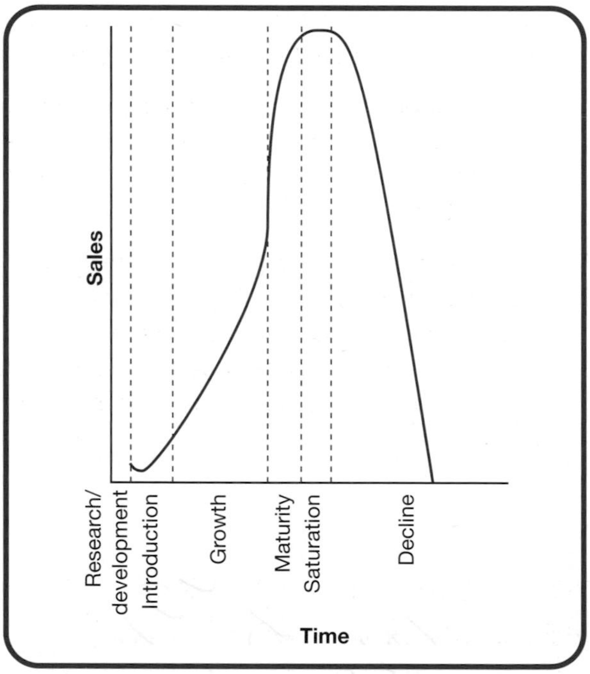

Typical product life cycle of a high-fashion item

Activity

Place the following products on the product life cycle (right) at the stage you think is most appropriate:

Computers
Pencils
Ovaltine.
Ice cream
Mobile telephones

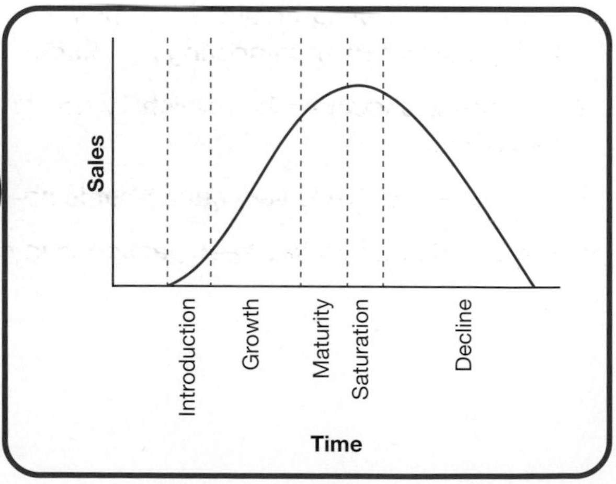

Strategies used to extend the product life cycle

Businesses aim to prolong the life of their products as long as possible in order to maximise profits. This is frequently done by making minor alterations to the product which makes people want to have the latest variety or model. For example:

- Sales of Flash cleaners have been expanded by introducing a variety of Flash for the bathroom, for the kitchen, etc.
- Popular drinks such as Coca-Cola, Club Orange and Lilt have introduced 'lite' varieties so that people on diets would continue to buy them
- New, updated editions of books are introduced to maintain sales when previous editions are becoming out-of-date and sinking into the decline stage
- Car manufacturers bring out new designs to their cars on an annual basis, sometimes only involving minor modifications. In each of these cases, the new model or 'improved formula' product is re-launched to persuade consumers to buy it.

In other cases packaging of the product is altered to give an updated appearance to the product while promotion and advertising are obvious methods by which to extend the product's life cycle. This is done at stages in the product's life when sales need to be stimulated.

A price reduction is another strategy frequently used to encourage sales and combat competition. In other cases manufacturers may reconsider the place in which they are selling the product and may decide to introduce it to the export market in order to improve sales.

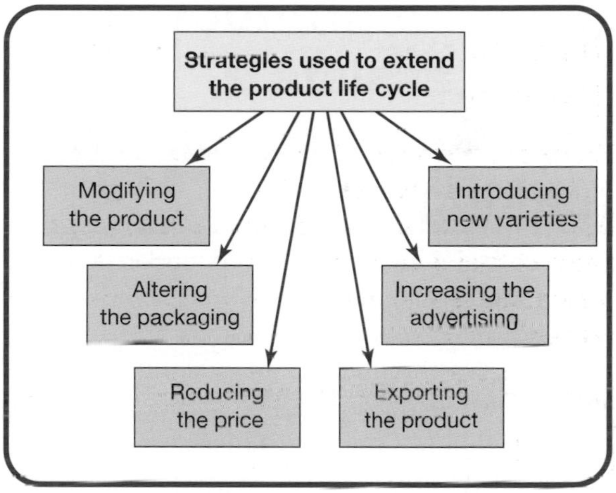

Activity

The following products have reached the saturation level of the product life cycle. How would you extend their lives and prevent them going into the decline stage?

1. **A window cleaning cream which has had a very reliable reputation for a long time but is losing out to newer competing products.**
2. **A high-fat chocolate bar which is no longer popular because of a recent healthy living campaign.**
3. **A computer which is very cheap but is not suitable for e-mailing or using the internet.**
4. **A fizzy drink which has been packaged in the same way for fifty years.**

Activity

Complete the following table to show the level and type of each element of the marketing mix which it is appropriate to use at each stage of a product's life.

	Price	Promotion	Place	Product
Introduction				
Growth				
Maturity				
Saturation				
Decline				

How the product life cycle assists a business in decision making

A successful business needs to understand the stage in the life cycle which its product has reached. If it does, it will then be able to make decisions which either might prolong the life of the product or have another product ready for the market at just the right time.

The product life cycle informs the business of the stage its product has reached. The business can then react by readjusting its use of the elements of the marketing mix. A successful business applies the elements of the marketing mix in exactly the most appropriate proportions.

- **If the product is in the introduction stage**: the business needs to make sure that it is being offered for sale in the most appropriate place and using the most appropriate pricing policy which would be either skimming or penetration pricing. At this stage, the business will also decide to advertise widely to create an awareness of the product. The product will be made in low quantities at this stage until sales have improved.
- **If the business is in the growth stage**: less advertising would be required because sales are growing, but the business would decide to produce in greater quantities in order to meet the demand. Competitive pricing would also have to be introduced if other producers had brought similar products to the market. At this growth stage, a forward looking business would consider marketing abroad and would be exploring opportunities through the internet.
- **If the product has reached the maturity stage of the life cycle**: sales would not be increasing so the business would stabilise production levels because it would not want to have excessive stock. The business would also decide to increase its advertising and change the style of advertising to persuasive advertising in order to encourage the public to buy the product. Although profits at this maturity stage would be very high, a successful business would realise that it should begin to research and develop a second product. Alternatively, it might take the opportunity to slightly alter minor aspects of the product and re-launch it as 'new' or 'improved'.
- **If the product is at the saturation stage**: intensive advertising would be continued and the business might decide to reduce the price of the product or to engage in sales promotions such as offering free gifts or 'buy one get one free'.
- **If the product has reached the decline stage**: the business would try to extend this stage as long as possible but at least until the remaining stock had been sold. The appeal of

the product at this stage is only either to those who have a loyalty to the product, or to those who are slow to try new ideas. If the product is one which is likely to have a short decline stage, an immediate decision to stop production would be made, and no further advertising would be undertaken. Price reductions or other sales promotions would be offered only if large stocks remained, in which case strategies such as 'buy three for the price of two' would be used to clear them. At this decline stage, the business would decide to introduce its new product to the market.

It can be seen therefore, that information obtained from the product life cycle does assist a business in its decision making.

Depending on the type of product, and on its stage in the cycle, the business would decide to change the balance of its marketing mix by making alterations to:

- the product itself
- the price of the product
- the place in which it is sold
- the style of promotion.

Legal constraints on products

The government has imposed a number of legal constraints which are designed mainly to protect consumers from faulty or unsafe products. However, it is recognised that the law also acts as a useful framework for business and, in the vast majority of cases, businesses are anxious to treat customers fairly and to produce goods which are of high quality. They want to deal with complaints in a proper manner because poor quality goods or poor service gives the business a poor reputation and ultimately affects sales.

Nevertheless, it is impossible for the law to cover every eventuality. Consumers still need to exercise common sense and caution when buying goods. If a stranger offers you a brand new, very modern car with luxurious extras for £1,000, your common sense should tell you to walk away from what is obviously an illegal deal.

This is summed up in the Latin words 'caveat emptor' which means 'let the buyer beware'. This is exactly what the buyer should do by taking time to read the small print on packaging for example.

? Let the Buyer Beware!

Summary of the provisions of legislation in relation to products

Legal constraints on products state that:

- goods and services supplied by a business must be 'of satisfactory quality'. This means that goods must be properly and safely manufactured and comply with safety regulations

- goods must be fit for the purpose for which they were sold, e.g. a waterproof coat must keep out the rain

- goods must be exactly as they are described on the packaging, e.g. the contents of a tin of biscuits, must be like the illustration on the outside of the tin

These tins should contain the type of biscuits illustrated

- any person injured by a defective product is entitled to sue the producer or manufacturer for damages
- goods must not be sold which are under weight or in short measure
- it is an offence for caterers to sell food that is unfit for human consumption, is contaminated, or is falsely or misleadingly presented.
- all premises used by food businesses must be registered with their local district council. This includes vehicles selling hot dogs or ice-cream
- people who handle food must have received practical hygiene training appropriate to their job. This is to ensure that people have the practical skills and knowledge they need.

All food businesses need to be registered

The level of detail given in the above summary on legislation on products is all that is required for GCSE (CCEA) Business Studies. However, some students may require more detail for other purposes, or may simply be interested in further reading. For those reasons, the following notes on individual laws and other constraints on products are included.

Sale and Supply of Goods and Services Act, 1994 (amended by the Sale and Supply of Goods to Consumers Regulations, 2002)

This Act ensures that goods and services supplied by a business are 'of satisfactory quality'. This means that goods must be:

- properly and safely manufactured and of satisfactory quality
- as they are described on the packaging
- fit for the purpose for which they were sold.

In order to comply with the Sale and Supply of Goods and Services Act, 1994, manufactured goods are expected to be made in a way which complies with safety regulations. For example, toys must not have small parts which a baby could easily remove and choke on. Satisfactory quality includes the state and condition of the goods including their appearance, finish, freedom from minor defects, safety and durability. Goods are also expected to be as they are described, so the contents of a tin of biscuits, for example, must be like the illustration on the outside of the tin.

Goods must also be fit for their purpose so a waterproof coat, for example, must keep out the rain. However, it is important that the customer looks at the labels carefully. In the example of the coat, if the label described the coat as being 'shower proof' the manufacturer intended it to withstand rain showers rather than downpours. The consumer would not have a justifiable complaint if he/she used it for any other purpose – such as going out in heavy rain.

If manufactured goods do not comply with the above details, the consumer is entitled to a full cash refund. An offer to repair the goods instead, does not have to be accepted.

The Sale and Supply of Goods and Services Act does not cover goods which have been bought privately.

Consumer Protection Act, 1987

The Consumer Protection Act, 1987 is designed to protect consumers from products that do not reach a reasonable level of safety. Any product not achieving the level of safety which consumers are entitled to expect is said to be defective.

Any person injured by a defective product is entitled to sue the producer or manufacturer for damages. However, if unsafe goods have been supplied, under the terms of this Act, an offence would also have been committed even if no one were injured by those goods.

In the case of foreign goods which were imported to this country, the consumer may take action against the importer, or against any firm which had branded the goods with its own name. Wholesalers or retailers are not liable under the terms of this Act.

The consumer is expected, as in the case of the previous Act, to use the product responsibly. Warnings and instructions given with the product should be obeyed, and the product should be used with reasonable care. Therefore, if the manufacturer could show that the product became defective because of the way in which the consumer used it, then the consumer would have no right to claim against the manufacturer. Any action against a manufacturer must be taken by a consumer within three years of the injury.

Certain products are not covered by the Consumer Protection Act, 1987. Those goods not covered are:

- growing crops
- water
- food
- aircraft

- motor vehicles
- medicinal products
- tobacco.

The Consumer Protection Act, 1987 is enforced by the Trading Standards officers of local authorities. They have the power to test products and suspend the sale of items which they believe contravene safety legislation.

In the case of imported goods, Customs Officers have the power to hold goods at the port for up to two days in order to make enquiries about their safety.

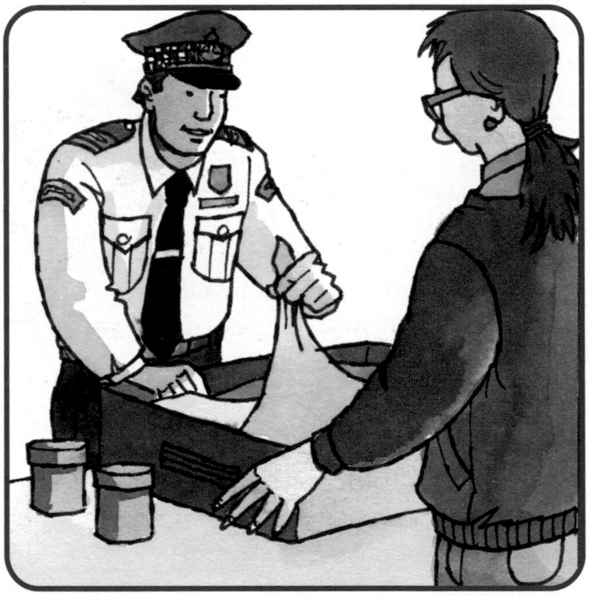

Food Safety (Northern Ireland) Order, 1991

The Food Safety (Northern Ireland) Order, 1991 is enforced by Environmental Health Officers, and aims to make sure all food offered to the public is safe to eat and is properly described. This Order makes it an offence for caterers to sell food that is unfit for human consumption, is contaminated, or is falsely or misleadingly presented.

All premises used by food businesses must be registered with their local district council. This includes vehicles selling hot dogs or ice-cream.

The Food Safety (Northern Ireland) Order, 1991 requires people who handle food to have received practical hygiene training appropriate to their job. This is to ensure that people have the practical skills and knowledge they need.

Weights and Measures (Northern Ireland) Order, 1981

Enforcement of the Weights and Measures (Northern Ireland) Order, 1981 is the responsibility of the Trading Standards Service in Northern Ireland, and is a major part of the work of the Trading Standards Officers.

The provisions of the Weights and Measures (Northern Ireland) Order, 1981 are:

- it protects goods from being sold which are under weight or in short measure
- it ensures that the scales or other equipment of measurement are accurate.

Other constraints on production

Consumer protection, in the area of production, is provided via a number of channels other than the law. In some cases, the government has established agencies for the purpose of consumer protection while, in other cases, local authorities provide this service and do regular checks on products. Some industries themselves have established voluntary codes in the interests of consumers, and there are also other independent organisations which take on this role.

The Consumers' Association

The Consumers' Association was set up in the 1960s to improve the standards of goods and services available to the public in the United Kingdom. It provides a valuable service giving advice and information to consumers on a wide range of products and services. The Association is the largest independent consumer organisation in Europe, and is totally funded by subscriptions from members.

The Association carries out testing of consumer products and reports on their findings. For example their work on washing machines put the machines of a large number of manufacturers through rigorous tests, compared the results, decided on the washing machine which was the best value in terms of money and performance, and reported the results in its magazine *Which?*.

Adverse reports in *Which?* are so disliked by manufacturers that they frequently modify the product and have it retested. Consumers are able to consult the magazine and get impartial information before making a purchase.

Activity

1. **Name any large product – such as a television or washing machine – your family is thinking of buying soon.**
2. **Then visit your nearest library and ask to see some past issues of the magazine *Which?*.**
3. **Use the magazines to research the price and make of the recommended model of whatever product you intend to purchase.**

The British Standards Institution

The British Standards Institution (BSI) is an entirely independent organisation which carries out tests on products in order to make sure that they meet the British, European or international standard or public specification for reliability, quality and safety.

The Institution awards its Kitemark to a product which passes its tests. The Kitemark is understood by the public to be a sign of good safety and quality, and therefore any product displaying it sells well in the shops. For this reason, manufacturers and service providers are eager to have the Kitemark awarded to their products. The Kitemark indicates that the product has been tested, audited and meets the required standards.

A Kitemark holder is audited regularly to ensure that their products continue to meet the standards and reliably deliver safety and quality. Kitemark and the Kitemark symbol are registered trademarks of BSI.

Activity

Visit as many DIY shops as you can, and make a note of the number of times you see the BSI Kitemark, and the types of products which have the Kitemark. Look to see if those products bearing the Kitemark are manufactured by a range of companies or just a few. Also note if those products bearing the Kitemark are more or less expensive than other competing products.

Use the following table to record your information.

Name of product	Name of manufacturer	Price

You may also like to explore the work of the following organisations:

- The British Electro-Technical Approvals Board (BEAB) – checks electrical items to make sure that they are safe for consumers to use
- The Association of British Travel Agents (ABTA) – provides safeguards against being sold a holiday which is below the expected standard and it is worth checking that your travel agent is a member of the Association
- The National House Building Council (NHBC) – provides similar safeguards in house building and it is advisable to check that your builder is a member of the Council
- The General Medical Council (GMC) – will listen to and investigate allegations of careless or incompetent treatment by doctors.

Environmental Health Officers

Environmental health is controlled by the local district councils in Northern Ireland. The work of Environmental Health Officers falls into four areas – Pollution and Environmental Protection, Food Control, Housing and Health and Safety at Work.

Environmental Health Officers are concerned with ensuring the safety of food, at all stages of production, storage, distribution and sale until it reaches the consumer. They monitor housing standards and can take action to ensure that repairs to properties are carried out in order to make houses suitable for human habitation.

Activity

What would you do if you were in the following situations?

1 I bought a shirt but when I arrived home I changed my mind. I took it back to the shop the next day but the staff would not give me a refund. Can they do this?

2 I had new taps supplied and fitted on my bath by a plumber but they drip all the time. What should I do?

3 My new toaster has never worked properly. The shop manager told me to send it back to the manufacturer as the fault had nothing to do with the shop. Is this correct?

4 Recently I bought an electric cooker privately from a neighbour. What are my rights?

Competition

Competition in business is rivalry between businesses. It is a situation where they are competing against one another for a share in the market, and where they employ all kinds of tactics to discourage their customers from going to other businesses while also encouraging the customers from other businesses to come to them instead. Competition in modern business is at a very high level and makes businesses monitor each other's activities closely.

Competition can be very healthy as it encourages businesses to keep improving their services in order to out-do their competitors. It results in greater efficiency which gives customers greater selection and better products. Greater competition causes prices to fall – if there were no competition at all, businesses could charge what they liked.

Businesses may use a variety of strategies to manage competition:

- They will keep their prices at the same level as, or slightly lower than, their competitors
- They will try to beat the competitors by providing a better service
- They will expand their range of goods
- They will make sure the quality of their products is as good as their competitors' products
- They will make sure that they have the required products in stock
- They will advertise widely
- They will use promotional offers such as special discounts.

Impact of competition on the marketing mix

	EFFECT
PRODUCT	• Quality of products may have to be improved to attract customers away from the competitors • Range of products has to be greater than that of the competitors
PRICE	• Prices cannot be higher than the competitors' prices
PROMOTION	• Constant advertising is required to attract customers • Promotional offers such as discounts and special offers are used • Good customer service is very important to retain existing customers and attract new ones
PLACE	• Products must be available in the store when required, otherwise the customer will go to the competitor for them

Checklist

At this stage you should:

- understand the stages of the product life cycle
- understand strategies used to extend the product life cycle
- be aware of the legislation which relates to production of goods and services
- understand the levels of competition in business
- recognise the indicators of competition
- be able to analyse strategies which may be used to manage competition
- be able to analyse the impact that competition has on the marketing mix.

4

FINANCE

Theme 4.1

Cash flow forecasts

Before you study cash flow forecasts, you should know the difference between cash and profit.

Difference between cash and profit

- Cash refers to the money in use in the business and is coming in and going out all the time. Not all of that cash will be profit
- Profit refers to the amount of money which is surplus at the end of the trading period when all the expenses have been paid.

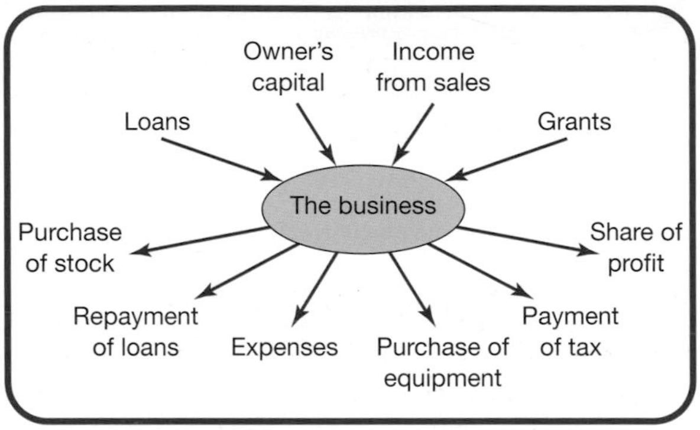

What is a forecast?

You are well used to hearing the weather forecast on the radio or television. It predicts what the weather will be like for the following few days and is very useful to people such as farmers who can then plan their outdoor work around those conditions.

A cash flow forecast acts in exactly the same way for a business. It predicts – or forecasts – the level of spending and level of income which the business will have during the following period of time. Always remember that a forecast is for the future.

The big difference is, of course, that no one can do anything to alter the weather, whereas the business owners and managers have some control over the timing of the flow of money in and out of the business.

So what is cash flow?

'Cash flow' is the term used to describe the flow of money into and out of a business.

Importance of cash flow to a business

It is important for a business to maintain an adequate level of cash flow. This is because:

- an even cash flow ensures that the business would never suffer from a shortage of ready money. This shortage would arise if the bills had to be paid at regular intervals but the income was coming in irregularly
- the business must ensure that there is a steady supply of money coming in so that it is able to pay its essential debts such as creditors and wages
- without adequate cash flow the business could be forced to close because suppliers would no longer trade with a firm which could not pay for its purchases
- employees would not continue to work for the firm if their wages were not being paid
- it would save the business from having to borrow money which would incur interest charges

- if the business has a good cash flow, it could take advantage of cheaper stock offers. Taking advantage of offers enables the business to re-sell the goods more cheaply and thus attract customers.

The following diagram illustrates the constancy of the flow of cash in and out of the business.

You can see that a cash flow problem would be created if the goods were not sold quickly and cash was not received in order to pay the expenses or pay the suppliers for the goods. That situation is known as a liquidity problem and many businesses have had to close for this reason.

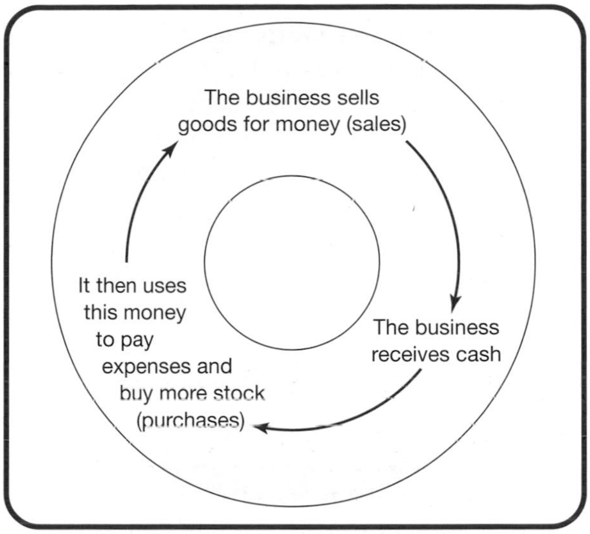

Activity

You are the Financial Director of The Plastic Products Company, a business which manufactures all forms of plastic containers. The factory is very well equipped with state-of-the-art machinery and has a highly trained workforce. Business has been very good for many years and The Plastic Products Company is well established in the market. One new firm has come into the plastics market recently and is keen to get new orders.

The Plastic Products Company has experienced some minor cash flow difficulties in the past, and a board meeting has been called to consider ways in which the firm might reduce the risk of future, larger cash flow problems.

As the Financial Director, you have been asked to explain at least four suggestions of how the risk might be reduced.

One of the ways to control cash flow is to prepare a cash flow forecast.

Purpose of a cash flow forecast

There are six main reasons for constructing a cash flow forecast:

1. **It enables the owner or manager to plan the firm's expenditure**. Perhaps a machine has to be replaced during the year while other expenses such as electricity always have to be paid at regular intervals. Recording all forecasted expenditure enables the business to see if these payments would result in cash shortages at certain times.

2. **It shows the amount required and when it is needed.** Any business wishing to borrow money will see from the cash flow forecast exactly how much needs to be borrowed and exactly when the extra cash is required. This prevents the payment of interest for longer than necessary.

3 **It shows when loans could be repaid.** Presentation of a cash flow forecast would show the bank or other lender if, and when, the business would be able to repay the loan. This would encourage the bank to give a loan.

4 **It inspires confidence and acts as a check on spending.** A cash flow forecast gives the owner confidence, and shows if the firm's financial plans are being maintained.

5 **It supports the firm's business plan**. A cash flow forecast is required as part of the firm's business plan and can be used to support it. (See Theme 7.1.)

6 **It sets targets for the business.** A cash flow forecast sets targets for the business to work towards and, at the end of the period, it shows what actually happened in the business. These actual results can then be compared with the forecast.

The difference between what actually happened in the business and the forecasted performance is known as the variance and owners would have to investigate the cause of large variances.

Consequences of incorrect forecasting

There are two main consequences:

1 **It would cause a shortage of working capital**. If a business failed to forecast its income and spending accurately it would experience a shortage of working capital.

Working capital is used to pay for the running expenses of the business. It follows therefore that if incorrect forecasting resulted in a shortage of working capital, the running expenses could not be paid.

2 **Some of the firm's assets may have to be sold.** If a firm forecasts incorrectly and runs short of cash, it may be forced to sell some of its assets. This could affect its production if, for example, machinery were sold.

Display of a cash flow forecast

A cash flow forecast records:

Receipts the total money received from sales or other means over the period – these are the receipts. These are recorded as separate items and the totals are also shown

Payments all payments made over the period of the forecast are recorded separately

Balances the opening and closing balances of cash each month.

The following cash flow forecast is displayed for six months for Mary Little who owns and runs a small hairdressing salon in Bangor. Mary set up her business on 1 January with her own capital of £8,000. She forecasts that for each of the first three months she will make £1,000 in cash sales which should rise to £2,000 per month in April when she has become established.

She will have to buy shampoo and other supplies of £500 per month during the first three months rising to £1,000 per month for the next three months. She will pay herself £600 per month and pay £400 per month to one assistant. During January she plans to buy extra equipment costing £3,000. Mary's rent has been agreed at £400 per month. Electricity costing £180 is due to be paid in March and June and telephone bills of £100 also have to be paid in March and June. £300 for insurance will be paid in January.

Cash flow forecast for Mary Little from 1 January to 30 June ....

	January	February	March	April	May	June	Total
RECEIPTS							
Sales	1,000	1,000	1,000	2,000	2,000	2,000	9,000
New Capital	8,000						8,000
Total Receipts	9,000	1,000	1,000	2,000	2,000	2,000	17,000
PAYMENTS							
Purchases	500	500	500	1,000	1,000	1,000	4,500
Salary	600	600	600	600	600	600	3,600
Wages	400	400	400	400	400	400	2,400
Equipment	3,000						3,000
Rent	400	400	400	400	400	400	2,400
Electricity			180			180	360
Telephone			100			100	200
Insurance	300						300
Total Payments	5,200	1,900	2,180	2,400	2,400	2,680	16,760
Opening Balance	0	3,800	2,900	1,720	1,320	920	10,660
+ Receipts	9,000	1,000	1,000	2,000	2,000	2,000	17,000
	9,000	4,800	3,900	3,720	3,320	2,920	27,660
– Payments	5,200	1,900	2,180	2,400	2,400	2,680	16,760
Closing Balance	3,800	2,900	1,720	1,320	920	240	10,900

Activity

RECEIPTS	Jan	Feb	March	April	May	June	Total
Sales	2,000	2,000	2,000	3,000	5,000	5,000	19,000
Total Receipts	2,000	2,000	2,000	3,000	5,000	5,000	19,000
Rent	300	300	300	300	300	300	1,800
Wages	500	500	500	500	1,000	1,000	4,000
Electricity			150				150
Advertising			500	500			1,000
Equipment	4,000						4,000
Total Payments	4,800	800	1,450	1,300	1,300	1,300	10,950
Opening Balance	0	–2,800	–1600	–1,050	650	4,350	–450
+ Receipts	2,000	2,000	2,000	3,000	5,000	5,000	19,000
	2,000	–800	400	1,950	5,650	9,350	18,550
– Payments	4,800	800	1,450	1,300	1,300	1,300	10,950
Closing Balance	–2,800	–1,600	–1,050	650	4,350	8,050	7,600

Study the cash flow forecast above, then answer these questions:

1 Choose one type of business from the following list which the cash flow forecast might be for: garden centre, toy shop, hairdresser.

2 Choose one type of business from the same list which the cash flow forecast would not be for.

3 Justify your choice of business in question 2.

4 How could the owner have prevented the low balances during the first three months?

5 State one disadvantage of that course of action.

6 What comment would you make about the overall performance of this business?

Activity

Roger put £17,400 into the bank as his own capital on 1 January to open a small café in Portrush. He forecasts that his sales will be £500 for each of the first two months, rising to £1,000 in March. Easter is in April and the day trippers start coming then so he anticipates his sales will be £3,000 in April and May and will rise again to £4,000 in June when the town has more visitors.

Roger has calculated that his purchases will be £300 in January and February, £500 in March, £700 in April and May and £1,000 in June. Roger plans to employ one part-time waitress in January, February and March. For April and May he will employ a second part-time waitress, and will take on a third part-time person for June. Each part-time employee will be paid £250 per month. Small items of new machinery are to be bought in January and April costing £400 each time. Roger's rent has been agreed at £400 per month. Electricity costing £150 is due to be paid in March and June and telephone bills of £100 will be paid in March and June.

You should now design a cash flow forecast for six months from January to June for Roger.

Activity

Complete the boxes marked A, B and C in the following cash flow forecast. Study the closing balance for March and advise the business on what action it should take.

Cash flow forecast – January to March

RECEIPTS	**January**	**February**	**March**
Opening balance	55,000	22,000	**A**
Sales	42,000	41,000	46,000
Total	97,000	63,000	**B**
EXPENSES			
Creditors	10,000	9,000	5,000
Purchases	22,000	11,000	10,000
Heat	3,000	0	0
Wages	40,000	41,000	38,000
Machinery	0	0	2,000
Total	75,000	61,000	55,000
Closing balance	22,000	2,000	**C**

Checklist

At this stage you should:

- know the importance of cash flow to a business
- understand the difference between cash and profit
- understand the purpose of cash flow forecasts
- be able to complete parts of a cash flow forecast from given information
- be able to interpret a simple cash flow forecast
- understand the consequences of incorrect forecasting.

Theme 4.2

Final accounts and balance sheet

Final accounts

Accounts can be described as a story in figures! The story which the final accounts tell is about the result of the year's work in the business and the amount of profit made.

There are two accounts which are collectively called the 'final accounts'. They are the trading account and the profit and loss account. As you can guess from their name, the final accounts are worked at the end of the trading year – which does not have to be at the end of the calendar year.

The purpose of the trading account is to find the gross profit (or gross loss), and the purpose of the profit and loss account is to calculate the net profit (or net loss) for the year.

These profits will be explained more fully later in the theme, so just remember their names for now.

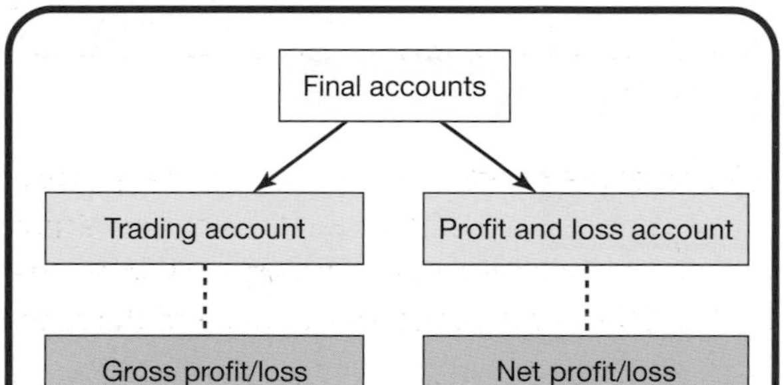

The trading account

As you have already learned, the purpose of the trading account is to find the gross profit.

How to find the gross profit

Gross profit is the difference between the money the firm makes from the sale of goods (sometimes called the turnover) and what the goods cost the firm to manufacture or buy as well as the expenses of selling them. These costs are known as the cost of sales.

Therefore, if a business has sales of £100,000 and the cost of sales is £75,000, the gross profit would be £25,000. However, if the sales are £100,000 and the cost of sales is £110,000 then the firm would make a gross loss of £10,000.

Gross Profit = Sales (or Turnover) – Cost of Sales

Activity

Using the details given, calculate the gross profit or gross loss for five different years for a carrier firm called Speedy Service. Answer the questions at the end.

	Year 1	Year 2	Year 3	Year 4	Year 5
Sales	£120,000	£140,000	£155,000	£160,000	£185,000
Cost of sales	£83,000	£ 97,000	£115,000	£165,000	£165,000
Gross profit					

1 In which year did Speedy Service have the worst trading result?

2 What do you think may have caused this poor result?

3 If you were the owner of Speedy Service, what would be your reaction to these results?

4 What would you advise the owner to do?

How to find the cost of sales

In order to sell goods, the firm has to purchase them. These new purchases will be added to the opening stock which is the stock of goods already in the business. At the end of the year some stock will be left unsold. The stock which is left is called the closing stock and will be kept for the next year.

Cost of Sales = Opening Stock + Purchases – Closing Stock

If a business has opening stock valued at £9,000, purchases of £15,000 and closing stock of £3,750 then its cost of sales would be £20,250.

In the trading account, this information is displayed in the following way:

	£	£
Opening Stock	9,000	
Add Purchases	15,000	24,000
Less Closing Stock		3,750
Cost of Sales		£20,250

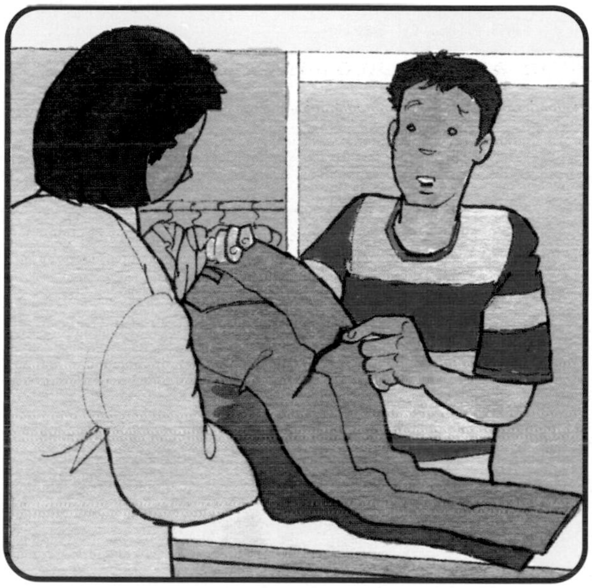

Returns inwards

Returns inwards and returns outwards

Some goods may have to be returned perhaps because they have been broken or the wrong goods have been delivered. Those returns are known as returns outwards (because they are going out from the firm) and they reduce the total amount of the purchases.

Some of the goods sold may have to be returned for similar reasons. Those are known as returns inwards (because they are coming back in to the firm) and they reduce the total amount of the sales.

Let us suppose that the above business had returns outwards of £500. In the trading account, the returns outward would be displayed like this:

	£	£
Opening Stock		9,000
Add Purchases	15,000	
Less Returns Outward	500	14,500
		23,500
Less Closing Stock		3,750
Cost of Sales		£19,750

Activity

Compare the first calculation of the cost of sales with the second calculation which included returns outwards.

1 What effect has returns outwards had on the cost of sales?

2 Why has the returns had this effect?

Now to summarise all the above information!

The trading account records:

1 The total earned from sales over the year – also known as the turnover.
2 The cost of sales.
3 Any expense incurred in selling the goods, e.g. wages of sales staff.

The title of the trading account must show the name of the firm and the end-of-year date.

Display of the complete trading account

The following trading account is displayed for Music Makers – a music shop.

Trading Account of Music Makers for the year ended 31 December ....

	£	£
Sales		27,500
Less Returns Inwards		1,000
		26,500
Less Cost of Sales:		
Opening Stock	9,000	
Add Purchases	15,000	
	24,000	
Less Returns Outward	500	
	23,500	
Less Closing Stock	3,750	
Cost of Sales		19,750
GROSS PROFIT		£6,750

Activity

Copy the following account and complete the spaces.

Trading account of Michael's Mechanics for the year ended 31 December ....

	£	£
Sales		35,000
Less Returns Inwards		[ ]
		33,000
Less Cost of Sales:		
Opening Stock	[ ]	
Add Purchases	18,000	
	25,000	
Less Returns Outward	350	
	24,650	
Less Closing Stock	4,750	
Cost of Sales		£19,900
GROSS PROFIT		£ [ ]

The profit and loss account

The purpose of the profit and loss account is to find the net profit which is the true profit of the business at the end of each trading year.

To find the net profit

Net profit takes into consideration all the overhead and running expenses which have to be paid by the business. Examples of a firm's expenses are rent, rates, electricity, telephone, salaries, depreciation and heating. Net profit is the amount of money remaining after these expenses have been paid out of the gross profit.

Therefore, if a business has a gross profit of £15,000 and its expenses are £9,000, the net profit would be £6,000. However, if the gross profit is £15,000 and its expenses are £19,000, the business would have a net loss of £4,000.

Net Profit = Gross Profit – Expenses

Activity

1 Using the details given, calculate the net profit for The Bookworm, a bookshop and The Fish Tank, a fish shop.

2 What advice would you give the owner of The Fish Tank?

	The Bookworm	The Fish Tank
Gross profit	£20,000	£14,000
Expenses	£14,505	£15,210
Net profit/loss		

Additional received income

Sometimes a business may receive small amounts of income which are not related to its main work. A shop, for example, may have unused rooms at the top of the building which it rents out as offices.

The profit and loss account records:

1 the gross profit (transferred from the trading account)

2 all overhead or running expenses

3 any additional income.

The title of the profit and loss account also must show the name of the firm and the end-of-year date.

The rent received from the offices would be additional income for the shopkeeper, and would be added on to the gross profit in the profit and loss account.

Now to summarise the above information on the profit and loss account.

Display of the complete profit and loss account

The following profit and loss account is displayed for Music Makers, a music shop.

Profit and loss account of Music Makers for the year ended 31 December ....

	£	£
Gross Profit		6,750
Add Rent Received		2,000
		8,750
Less Electricity	510	
Stationery	125	
Rates	756	
Interest on Loan	159	
Advertising	845	
Insurance	545	
Sundry Expenses	124	
Telephone	400	3,464
NET PROFIT		£5,286

Activity

Study the above account and answer the following questions:

1 Make a list of four other expenses which you think Music Makers might have.

2 Suggest two ways in which this business might improve its net profit.

3 Music Makers could reasonably expect to increase its net profit in the following year. State why this is so.

Activity

Copy the following account and complete the spaces.

Profit and loss account of Michael's Mechanics for the year ended 31 December ....

	£	£
Gross Profit		[ ]
Add Rent Received		2,500
		15,150
Less Electricity	630	
Stationery	190	
Rates	[ ]	
Advertising	500	
Insurance	700	
Postage	79	
Telephone	239	3,138
NET PROFIT		£ [ ]

Activity

Trading and profit and loss account for the year ended 31 December ....

	£	£
Sales		69,456
Opening Stock	450	
Add purchases	21,000	
	[ ]	
Less Closing Stock	461	
Cost of Goods Sold		[ ]
Gross Profit		[ ]
Administration	900	
Rent and Rates	3,600	
Wages	32,000	
Bad Debts	416	36,916
Net Profit		£ [ ]

Complete the spaces above.

The balance sheet

The balance sheet lists assets and liabilities. So what are assets and liabilities? Assets are items owned by the business and liabilities are items owed by the business.

The purpose of the balance sheet is to show the accurate value of the business on any given date. The balance sheet is not actually an account. It is a list showing all the assets and liabilities. It also shows the owners' original capital investment and any profits they are entitled to receive as well as their drawings (money they have taken out of the business for their own private use).

Activity

Decide whether each item in the following list is an asset or a liability.

Money in the bank ....

Money owing to suppliers ....

Machinery ....

Money owing by customers ....

Office equipment ....

Bank overdraft ....

Unpaid telephone bill ....

Premises ....

Assets are divided into fixed and current assets:

- Current assets – those assets which can quickly be exchanged for cash. An example is stock.
- Fixed assets – those assets which will be more permanent in the business. An example is machinery.

Liabilities are divided into long-term and current liabilities:

- Current liabilities – those liabilities which must be paid immediately. An example is creditors.
- Long-term liabilities – those liabilities which are borrowed for a longer time. An example is a bank loan.

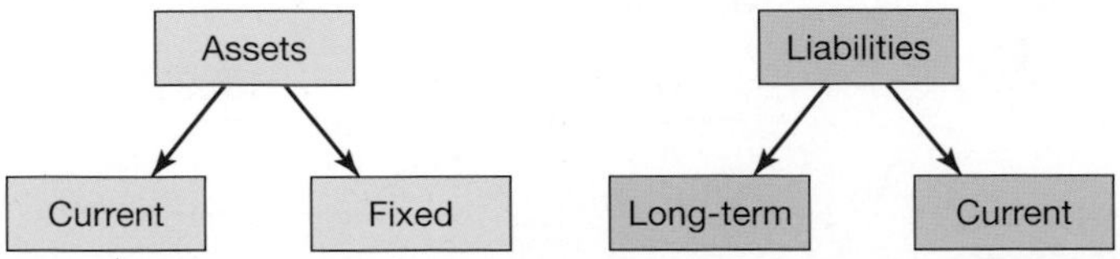

Working capital

Working capital is also displayed in the balance sheet. Working capital is the term given to the money which is available for the day-to-day running of the business. It is used to pay bills such as creditors and wages, as well as expenses like electricity or telephone. It is also used to buy goods for resale in a shop or raw materials in a factory.

It is important for a business to keep working capital at the correct level because, if it is too low, the firm will not be able to pay its debts and is said to have a cash flow problem. However, if the level of working capital is too high the business is not using its money in the most profitable way.

Working capital is calculated by subtracting the total of the current liabilities from the total of the current assets.

Working Capital = Current Assets – Current Liabilities

Now to summarise the above information on the balance sheet:

The balance sheet records:

1 The firm's assets – divided into current assets and fixed assets.
2 The firm's liabilities – divided into current and long-term liabilities.
3 The owner's capital and drawings.
4 The net profit (transferred from the profit and loss account).

The title of the balance sheet must show the name of the firm and the date it is being worked.

The following complete balance sheet is displayed for Music Makers.

Balance sheet of Music Makers as at 31 December ....

	£	£	£
FIXED ASSETS			
Premises		80,000	
Recording Equipment		13,200	
Motor Van		8,700	101,900
CURRENT ASSETS			
Cash in Hand	970		
Cash at Bank (Current Account)	10,050		
Stock	3,750		
Debtors	1,750	16,520	
CURRENT LIABILITIES			
Creditors		9,000	
Working Capital			7,520
			£109,420
LONG-TERM LIABILITIES			
Capital		80,000	
Add Net Profit		5,286	
		85,286	
Less Drawings		14,866	70,420
Bank Loan			9,000
Mortgage			30,000
			£109,420

In the above balance sheet you should note that:

1. The fixed assets are listed first, followed by the current assets.
2. The current liabilities are subtracted from the current assets to find the working capital.
3. The working capital is added to the total of the fixed assets.
4. The total of the long-term liabilities must equal the total found in step 3 above.

Activity

Complete the spaces in the following balance sheet.

Balance sheet of Michael's Mechanics as at 31 December ....

	£	£	£
FIXED ASSETS			
Premises		[ ]	
Machinery		4,300	45,300
CURRENT ASSETS			
Cash in Hand	[ ]		
Stock	4,750		
Debtors	750	6,020	
CURRENT LIABILITIES			
Creditors	800		
Bank Overdraft	1,200	2,000	
Working Capital			[ ]
			£49,320
LONG-TERM LIABILITIES			
Capital	35,848		
Add Net Profit	[ ]		
	47,810		
Less Drawings	2,490		45,320
Bank Loan			4,000
			£ [ ]

Activity

Answer the following questions.

1 Explain the difference between fixed and current assets.

2 Complete the following formula.

Working Capital = ... less ....

3 Why do you think that capital is classified as a long-term liability?

4 Define a current liability.

5 What do you understand by 'drawings'?

Activity

The following information has been extracted from Tim's balance sheet. Calculate Tim's working capital.

Current assets		Current liabilities	
Stock	600	Creditors	2,000
Debtors	800		
Cash	2,200		

Checklist

At this stage you should understand the basics of:

- a trading account
- a profit and loss account
- a vertical balance sheet.

Theme 4.3

Interpretation of accounts using ratios

Now that you understand the final accounts and balance sheet, you can start to interpret them and to extract information from them.

So who would be interested in this information? Obviously the owners and managers need to study the accounts. The firm's bank would also be interested. Tax authorities and the employees of the business all have their own reasons for watching its progress.

Activity

Copy the following list and put in one reason why each of these groups would be interested in the trading results of a business.

Owners ....

Managers ....

Tax authorities ....

Employees ....

By reading the final accounts and balance sheet it is easy to see the level of profit which the business has made and the size of its turnover. However, this does not tell us enough to enable us to assess the true performance of the business.

There are a number of ratios and percentages which help us to get an accurate calculation of the performance of the business and also enable us to compare its performance from year to year. All these calculations use figures which are shown in the Final Accounts and Balance Sheet.

Net profit percentage

This calculation shows the amount of net profit which is made on sales. It measures the firm's efficiency not only in trading but also in keeping its expenses down – the higher the percentage figure is, the better the overall performance.

The formula for finding the net profit percentage is:

$$\textbf{Net Profit Percentage} = \frac{\textbf{Net Profit}}{\textbf{Sales}} \times \textbf{100}$$

For example if a business has sales value £68,740 and its net profit is £13,500:

$$\text{Net Profit Percentage} = \frac{13{,}500}{68{,}740} \times 100$$

Net Profit Percentage = 19.6%

This means that for every £1 of sales, this firm makes 19.6p profit – an average result!

Activity

	Year 1	Year 2	Year 3
Sales	£54,706	£63,750	£70,322
Gross profit	£41,030	£45,900	£49,225
Net profit	£9,300	£10,200	£10,900
Net profit percentage			

Calculate the net profit percentage for each year.

Activity

Trading and profit and loss accounts for the year ended 31 March ....

	£	£
Sales		14,500
less Cost of Goods Sold		7,500
Gross Profit		7,000
Less: Rent	3,400	
Heat	120	
Sundry Expenses	880	4,400
Net Profit		£2,600

Using the above information, calculate the net profit percentage.

Stock turnover rate

This calculation shows the number of times in a year that the business is able to sell the value of its average stock. It is, therefore, another measure of the firm's trading efficiency – the higher the rate is, the better the business activity.

A firm's turnover rate depends on the type of goods it sells. If its goods are high value goods – jewellery, for example – it will make fewer sales but each sale is likely to be for a large amount of money. A jeweller may only replace stock once or twice a year. On the other hand, if the business deals in goods which are low value – vegetables,

for example – it will make a large number of sales but each sale would be for a small sum. Stock of perishable vegetables would be replaced every working day.

The formula for finding the stock turnover rate is:

$$\textbf{Stock Turnover Rate} = \frac{\textbf{Cost of Goods Sold}}{\textbf{Average Stock}}$$

For example if the Trading Account shows that a business's cost of sales is £13,800 and its average stock is £2,010. (Average stock is: opening stock plus closing stock divided by 2):

$$\text{Stock Turnover Rate} = \frac{13{,}800}{2{,}010}$$

Stock Turnover Rate = 6.9 times

This result means that the business sells its stock almost seven times each year.

Activity

Trading Account of Music Makers for the year ended 31 December ....

	£	£
Sales		27,500
Less Returns Inwards		1,000
		26,500
Less Cost of Sales:		
Opening Stock	9,000	
Add Purchases	15,000	
	24,000	
Less Returns Outward	500	
	23,500	
Less Closing Stock	3,750	
Cost of Sales		19,750
GROSS PROFIT		£6,750

Using the details in the above account, calculate the stock turnover rate for Music Makers.

Return on capital employed (ROCE)

This calculation shows the net profit which the owner has received on the capital invested. The owner should compare this result with the profit which would have been received if the money had been invested in shares in other businesses or deposited in the bank, for example.

The formula for finding return on capital employed is:

Return on Capital Employed

$$= \frac{\textbf{Net Profit}}{\textbf{Capital Employed}} \times \textbf{100}$$

For example if the capital invested in the business is £80,000 and the Net Profit is £13,500:

$$\text{Return on Capital Employed} = \frac{13{,}500}{80{,}000} \times 100$$

Return on Capital Employed = 16.8%

This result means that the owner is making almost 17% profit on his/her investment.

Working capital ratio

This ratio shows the relationship between a firm's current assets and current liabilities. The current working capital ratio measures the firm's ability to pay its current debts such as creditors.

The formula for finding the current working capital ratio is:

Current Working Capital Ratio

$$= \frac{\textbf{Current Assets}}{\textbf{Current Liabilities}}$$

For example if a business has current assets value £74,375 and its current liabilities are £36,200:

$$\text{Current Working Capital Ratio} = \frac{74{,}375}{36{,}200}$$

Current Working Capital Ratio = 2.05:1

Activity

Balance Sheet of Music Makers as at 31 December ....

	£	£	£
FIXED ASSETS			
Premises		80,000	
Recording Equipment		13,200	
Motor Van		8,700	101,900
CURRENT ASSETS			
Cash in Hand	970		
Cash at Bank (Current Account)	10,050		
Stock	3,750		
Debtors	1,750	16,520	
CURRENT LIABILITIES			
Creditors		9,000	
Working Capital			7,520
			£109,420
LONG TERM LIABILITIES			
Capital		80,000	
Add Net Profit		5,286	
		85,286	
Less Drawings		14,866	70,420
Bank Loan			9,000
Mortgage			30,000
			£109,420

Using the details in the above balance sheet, calculate the working capital ratio.

The above ratios are all which are required for GCSE (CCEA) Business Studies. However, you may be interested in two further ratios which may be worked from the final accounts.

Gross profit percentage

This calculation shows the amount of gross profit which a business has made on sales. It is a measure of the firm's trading efficiency – the higher the percentage figure is, the better the trading performance.

The formula for finding the gross profit percentage is:

$$\textbf{Gross Profit Percentage} = \frac{\textbf{Gross Profit}}{\textbf{Sales}} \times \textbf{100}$$

For example, if a business has sales value £68,740 and its Gross Profit is £29,500:

$$\text{Gross Profit Percentage} = \frac{29{,}500}{68{,}740} \times 100$$

Gross Profit Percentage = 42.9%

This result means that for every £1 of sales, this firm makes almost 50p gross profit – an excellent result!

Acid test ratio

This ratio measures if a business is able to pay its current debts without having to sell some of its stock. For this reason, the acid test ratio does not include stock in its calculation. It is agreed that an acid test ratio of 1:1 is safe.

The formula for finding the acid test ratio is:

$$\textbf{Acid Test Ratio} = \frac{\textbf{Current Assets} - \textbf{Value of Stock}}{\textbf{Current Liabilities}}$$

For example if a business has current assets value £34,900, if its stock value is £20,100 and its current liabilities amount to £18,000:

$$\text{Acid Test Ratio} = \frac{34{,}900 - 20{,}100}{18{,}000}$$

Acid Test Ratio = 0.82:1

Checklist

At this stage you should understand and be able to use the formula for:

- net profit percentage
- stock turnover rate
- return on capital employed (ROCE)
- working capital ratio.

Theme 4.4

Breakeven

Before attempting to work breakeven, it is necessary to understand costs. There are two types of costs – fixed and variable.

Fixed costs

Fixed costs are those costs which are not affected by the quantity of goods produced or sold or by the scale of services rendered. They are called 'fixed' because they do not alter regardless of the volume of work done in the business. For example, factory rent is a fixed cost because it will have to be paid in full whether the factory is manufacturing goods at full capacity or at a reduced level. Other examples of fixed costs are rates, administrative costs, cleaning and insurance. Sometimes fixed costs are referred to as 'overheads' or 'indirect costs'.

On a graph, fixed costs would be shown as a straight horizontal line as is shown here. You can see that the fixed costs stay on one level regardless of the number of units produced. You should also notice that the fixed costs are at that level even if there are no units being produced.

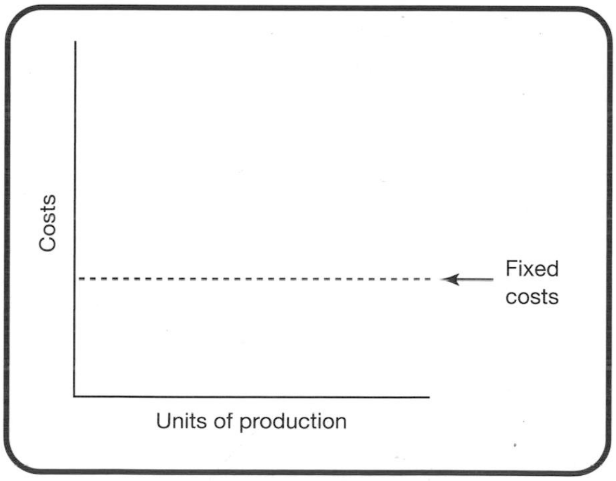

Variable costs

Variable costs are those costs which vary – or change – according to the level of work being done in the business. For example in a factory, wages will increase if the factory is working at full production level but will decrease if production is reduced and some employees have to be made redundant. Electricity usage will vary for the same reasons as will the purchase of raw materials.

On a graph, variable costs would be shown as a straight diagonal line because they rise in direct proportion to the rise in production. Notice that there are no variable costs at the point of no production.

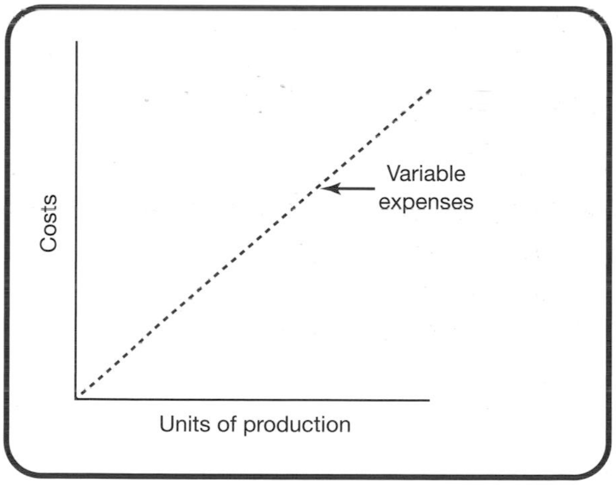

Total costs

The total cost of the business is found by adding together the variable and fixed costs.

Total Costs = Fixed Costs + Variable Costs

On a graph, total costs is shown as a diagonal line but notice that the total costs line starts at the level of fixed costs. This is because, even at the point of no production, the business has incurred total costs equal to the fixed costs.

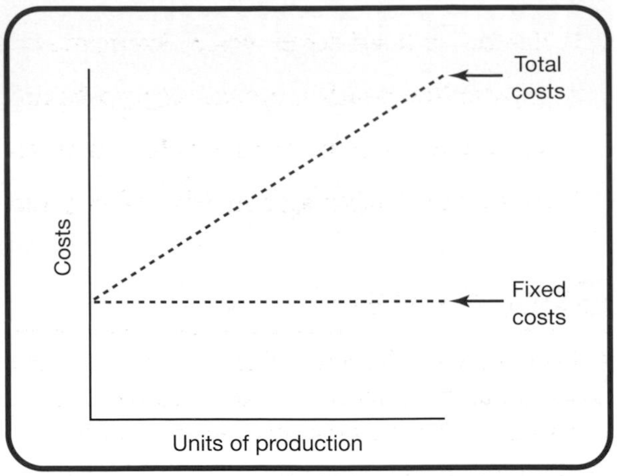

Drawing these graphs is an important element in learning about breakeven and you will get practice then in drawing them yourself.

Activity

Tick the appropriate spaces to show whether each cost listed is fixed or variable.

Cost	Fixed	Variable
Mortgage		
Depreciation		
Rates		
Transport of goods		
Machinery repairs		
Advertising		
Telephone		
Electricity		
Loan interest		
Postage of goods		

Activity

Complete the following table to show the missing amounts of costs in four different years' final accounts of Fivemiletown Flowers, a small florist shop.

Year	Fixed costs	Variable costs	Total costs
1	£8,000		£13,500
2		£6,000	£14,500
3	£9,000		£15,350
4	£9,500	£9,000	

1 Name two fixed costs which Fivemiletown Flowers might have.

2 Explain the steady increase in fixed costs over four years.

3 Name two variable costs which Fivemiletown Flowers might have.

4 Give one possible reason why the variable costs have risen sharply in Year 4.

Breakeven

A business's breakeven point is where its total costs equal the total of its sales income. It is the minimum point at which the business can survive. At this point the business is making neither a profit nor a loss – it is simply covering its costs.

If it can sell more goods than the level of breakeven it will make a profit. However, if its sales fall below the breakeven level, then the business would be in a loss-making situation.

Significance of the breakeven point

The concept of 'breakeven' is extremely important in business because it can show:

- the amount of goods which must be sold in order to make a profit
- the level of costs which can be borne
- the price which needs to be charged for goods
- how changes in the price would affect the firm's profits.

How is the breakeven point worked out?

The most usual method of finding the breakeven point is to work a graph. It is also possible to calculate the breakeven point using a formula. Both methods need to have information on both the firm's total costs and its revenue (income) from sales.

Calculating breakeven by formula

The formula for calculating breakeven is:

$$\textbf{Breakeven} = \frac{\textbf{Total Total Fixed Costs}}{\textbf{Selling Price Per Unit} - \textbf{Variable Cost Per Unit}}$$

Study the following example.

Desmond Cashel owns a bookshop in Omagh. Calculate his breakeven point if his total fixed costs are £4,000 per month, each book sells on average at £7 and his variable costs are £2 per book.

$$\text{Breakeven} = \frac{4{,}000}{7-2} = \frac{4{,}000}{5} = 800$$

This means that Desmond must sell 800 books every month in order to break even. He says that he would find this difficult to do so he decides to increase the price of his books from £7 to £9. The new calculation would be:

$$\text{Breakeven} = \frac{4{,}000}{9-2} = \frac{4{,}000}{7} = 571.4\ (572)$$

After the price increase, Desmond must sell 572 books every month in order to break even. He feels he can manage this level of sales but knows that he cannot increase his prices again or else his customers will begin to go to other bookshops.

Activity

1 Helen Dawson owns a bakery in Toomebridge. Her total fixed costs are £2,100 per month, her variable costs are £1 per unit on average and she sells each cake for £4 on average.

2 Calculate Helen's breakeven point by formula.

3 Helen gets the bad news that her rent is being increased by £100 per month. What is her new breakeven point?

4 Calculate Helen's breakeven point if:
  a she increased the average price of her cakes from £4 to £5
  b her rates increased by £50 per month
  c she employed a schoolgirl to help her on Saturdays. This would increase her variable expenses from £1 per unit to £1.10 per unit.

Activity

Complete the following table for Tom who is the manager of a toy factory in Magherafelt. The fixed costs of the factory amount to £500 per week and the variable costs are £2 per toy. Each toy is sold for £4. The table is started for you.

Number of toys sold	Total income from sales	Fixed costs	Variable costs	Total costs	Profit/ Loss
0	0	500	0	500	–500
25	100	500	50	550	–450
50					
75					
100					
125					
150					
175					
200					
225					
250					
275					
300					

Calculating breakeven graphically

A breakeven graph is used to illustrate the:

- profit or loss of a business
- relationship between total costs and sales
- relationship between fixed and variable costs.

Breakeven graphs do have some limitations which you should be aware of:

- Perhaps not all the goods will be sold
- Fixed costs are assumed to never change. This is not always the case. Some circumstances such as greatly increased production might mean taking on new premises which would increase the rates for example.
- Sales are not always made at a constant level. Businesses sometimes have to offer discounts to clear their stock.

Before beginning to draw a breakeven chart, it is essential to have details of the firm's sales, as well as details of its fixed and variable costs.

Worked example of a breakeven chart

This example works a breakeven graph for David Williams, the owner of a factory in Larne which manufactures small items of office equipment. He needs your help in finding the breakeven point for a new stapler which is just ready to be put on the market.

His fixed costs in the factory amount to £500 per week and his variable costs are £6 per stapler. Each stapler is going to be sold for £11.

It is easier to draw a graph if you first construct a table showing these details.

Number of staplers sold	Total income from sales	Fixed costs	Variable costs	Total costs	Profit/ Loss
0	0	500	0	500	–500
20	220	500	120	620	–400
40	440	500	240	740	–300
60	660	500	360	860	–200
80	880	500	480	980	–100
100	1,100	500	600	1,100	0
120	1,320	500	720	1,220	+100
140	1,540	500	840	1,340	+200
160	1,760	500	960	1,460	+300

We can then use the table to construct the graph and read off the breakeven point.

Note the following:

- The total income from sales and total costs may be read off the vertical axis
- It should show the total units of sales – staplers, in this case - on the horizontal axis
- The fixed costs should be plotted first
- Next plot the total costs
- Finally plot the income from sales
- Always remember to put on all labels
- The breakeven point should be shown with a broken line drawn to the horizontal axis.

The breakeven point is 100, therefore David Williams must sell 100 staplers per week in order to cover his costs of £1,100.

Activity

You should now return to the table which you completed for Tom.

1. **Use the information in the table to draw a breakeven graph for Tom's toy factory in Magherafelt, and indicate the breakeven point on the graph. It is important to label the graph fully.**
2. **Read the graph and answer the following questions.**
   i. **What would be the result if Tom sold 300 toys?**
   ii. **What would be the result if he sold 200 toys?**

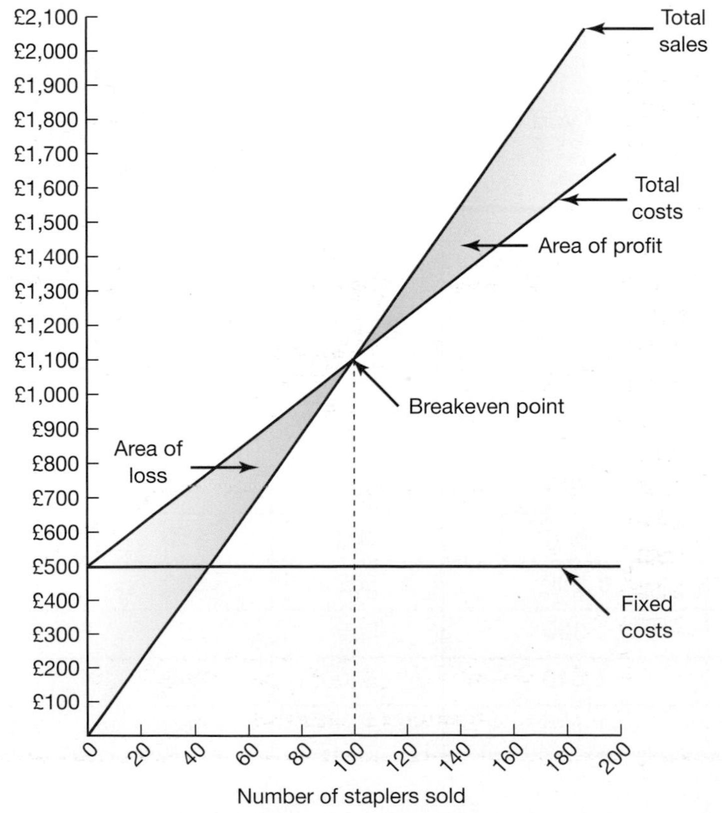

Breakeven chart to show sale of staplers by David Williams

The margin of safety

One of the main aims of a business is to make a profit and expand its market. No business therefore would be content to operate at the breakeven point for long, so once the business has found its breakeven level it then attempts to exceed it and plan for a higher level of sales. This higher level then becomes its 'selected operating point'.

The difference between the selected operating point and the breakeven point is known as the margin of safety. So:

The margin of safety is the amount which a business sells in excess of its breakeven point.

Let us return to the graph for the sale of staplers where the breakeven point was 100. David Williams now tells us that he plans to sell 140 staplers per week.

Study the following graph to see how the margin of safety is illustrated.

The margin of safety is 40 because David Williams plans to sell 140 staplers per week which is 40 more than the breakeven point.

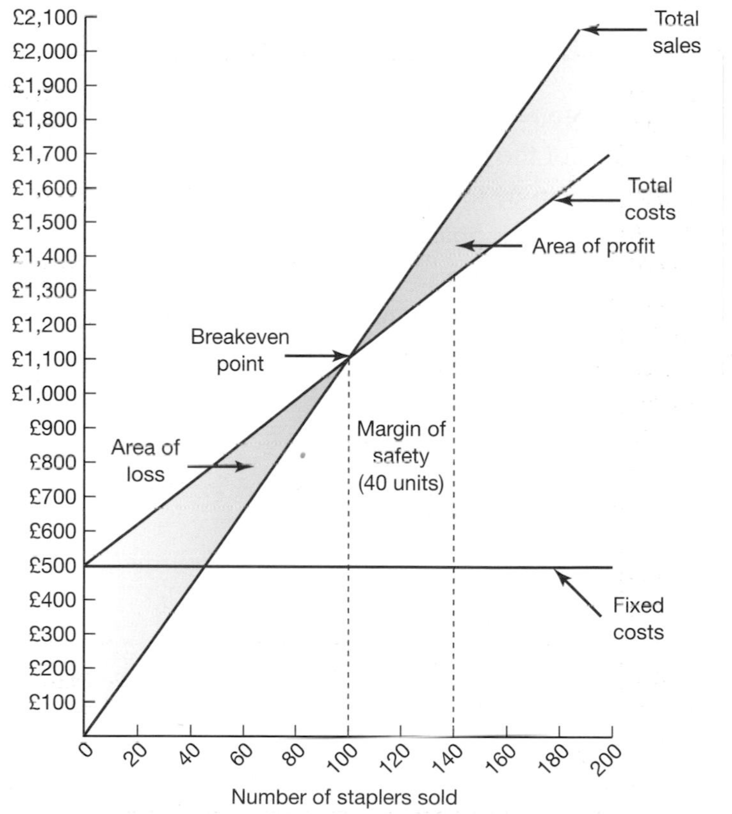

Activity

The following information was provided by RK Ltd. Study it and answer the questions which follow:

Monthly costs of production of a new toy	
Fixed costs	£2,000
Labour	£6 per unit
Materials	£4 per unit
Production capacity and expected sales	450 units
Selling price	£15

1 Explain why it is important for a business to calculate the breakeven point.

2 Calculate how many units RK Ltd need to sell in order to break even.

3 What do you understand by the term 'margin of safety'?

4 What margin of safety would RK Ltd have for this product?

5 What would it mean for RK Ltd if labour costs increased to £7 per unit?

Checklist

At this stage you should:

- be able to distinguish between fixed and variable costs
- understand the importance of the breakeven point
- be able to calculate breakeven by formula
- be able to calculate breakeven graphically showing all labels
- be able to analyse a breakeven graph
- understand the importance of the margin of safety
- be able to calculate the margin of safety.

5

MANAGING PEOPLE

Theme 5.1

Recruitment

Recruitment is the employment of new workers.

Good employers realise that the most important resource in any business is the people who work there. It is possible for a firm to have very modern technology and state-of-the-art premises but unless it employs the best possible work force it will never achieve its best results.

For this reason, employers put great emphasis on their recruitment procedures and on getting the best employees to suit their requirements.

Firms need to recruit new employees for several reasons. They may need to:

- employ extra workers because the business has grown
- bring in people who have skills they need, but do not have, in the business
- replace employees who have left because of retirement, resignation, promotion or dismissal.

Activity

Each of the following sentences describes either 'retirement, resignation, promotion or dismissal'. Match each one of these terms to the definitions given below:

1. This is when a person leaves because he has reached the end of his working life.
2. This is when a person has lost his job because of poor work or behaviour.
3. This is when a person leaves the post to move to a more senior post.
4. This is when a person leaves to go to another job.

Recruitment procedure

The stages in the procedure may vary from firm to firm but the following is typical.

Carry out a job analysis
↓
Draw up a job description
↓
Design a person specification
↓
Advertise the post and invite applicants
↓
Sort applications and draw up a shortlist
↓
Interview applicants who meet the criteria stated in the advertisement
↓
Select successful applicant and offer the job
↓
Complete the contract of employment

Before this procedure starts, the employer must decide exactly what the business needs. For example, the employer will have to be clear about the following:

- Which skills and qualifications are required in the firm?

- How many new employees are needed?
- Are the new employees required full time or part time?
- Should they be permanent or temporary?
- How soon would the new employee(s) need to start work?

DUNGANNON & SOUTH TYRONE Borough Council

Dungannon and South Tyrone Borough Council needs a person to work as a Tourist Information Receptionist in Killymaddy Tourist Information Centre, Ballygawley Road, Dungannon. The Human Resources Manager has decided on the following details. (This is known as a Needs Analysis.)

Duties Required	To carry out all receptionist duties
Skills and Qualifications Required	6 GCSEs at minimum Grade C (must include English Language)
Number of Employees Required	One
Terms of Employment	Full Time Permanent
Required Date of Employment	1 March ....

The best way to understand the documents used in the recruitment procedure is to work a set of documents through from beginning to end in a practical activity.

That would be a long activity to do all at once, so it has been broken down for you into stages throughout Theme 5.1. Since the information in the Job Analysis and the information in the Job Description overlap, you are not asked to work both of those documents.

You should proceed now through the activities in Theme 5.1 step by step.

Activity

Start by looking in the Job Finder section of either your local newspaper or one of the national newspapers – there may be more variety in the nationals. Choose any job advertisement which interests you, cut it out and file it safely.

Documents required in the recruitment procedure

1 Job analysis

Job analysis is a process to identify the particular duties and needs of a given post. Information might be collected on the tasks and duties of the post, the equipment needed, and the knowledge skills and abilities required for the work.

The analysis is conducted of the job – not the person. While it is possible that information about the job may be obtained from the employee, the reason for doing this is to find an analysis or description of the job – not the worker in the job.

The information gathered during job analysis is used in planning future training programmes, in setting wage and salary levels, as well as in recruitment and selection.

Several methods are used in job analysis. The most usual are interview, observation and questionnaires.

2 Job description

Purpose of a job description

The most important purpose of the job description is to define the main duties and responsibilities of the post. This is essential so that both the employee and the line manager are clear about what the employee might be expected to do.

A copy of the job description is sent to each applicant for the job so that he/she is clear what is required in the job.

Content of a job description

The job description should show:

- the title of the job
- the place where the job will be done
- a list of the main duties required in the job
- the person to whom the job holder reports (the line manager)
- names of any people who report to the job holder
- details of any equipment or parts of premises for which the job holder is responsible
- date of first issue of the job description and dates of any update.

Here is the Job Description for the Receptionist's post with Dungannon and South Tyrone Borough Council.

Killymaddy Tourist Information Centre

DUNGANNON AND SOUTH TYRONE BOROUGH COUNCIL

Receptionist	**Job Description**
Post	Tourist Information Receptionist
Place	Killymaddy Tourist Information Centre Ballygawley Road Dungannon
Job Purpose	To provide tourist information to members of the public visiting the Killymaddy Tourist Information Centre
Main duties	To meet the public in the Centre To answer questions and provide tourist information in person To answer telephone enquiries To handle sales in the tourist shop in the Centre To be responsible for cash and its safe deposit in the bank To provide monthly reports on the Centre's activities
Reports to	Information Officer
Date of issue	30 November 20—

Activity

You are now ready to draw up a job description for the post you have selected. Again, you should use the details in the advertisement to help you.

File your job description with your job advertisement.

3 Person specification

A person specification is drawn up after the job description has been prepared. Its purpose is to identify what an ideal applicant for the post should have in terms of:

- personal qualities
- knowledge
- qualifications
- skills
- previous work experience.

Usually the characteristics, achievements, qualifications, skills and previous work experience are listed, under three sub-headings, as Essential, Helpful or Optional.

The Person Specification for the Receptionist's post with Dungannon and South Tyrone Borough Council would look like this:

DUNGANNON AND SOUTH TYRONE BOROUGH COUNCIL

Receptionist Person Specification

	Essential	Helpful	Optional
PERSONAL QUALITIES:			
Good interpersonal skills	x		
Well groomed, tidy appearance	x		
Clear speaking voice	x		
KNOWLEDGE/SKILLS:			
Another European language		x	
QUALIFICATIONS:			
Minimum of GCSEs at Grade C			x
Word Processing Skills	x		
PREVIOUS EXPERIENCE:			
Experience in dealing with public	x		
SPECIAL REQUIREMENTS:			
Available to work unsocial hours	x		

Activity

Now go ahead and design a person specification for the post you have selected. Again, you may get some help from the details in the advertisement.

File your person specification with your other work.

4 Contract of employment

Purpose of a contract of employment

The main purpose of a contract of employment is to set out the rights and duties of both the employee and the employer. It is an agreement between the two parties and can be enforced by law. Therefore, it gives protection and security to both the employee and the employer. It begins when the employer makes an offer of work with payment of money and the employee accepts the offer at that rate and agrees to work. By law a full-time employee must be given a contract of employment within eight weeks of starting to work for that employer.

Content of a contract of employment

The following details must appear on the contract:

- Names of the employer and the employee
- Date of commencement of the job
- Title and description of the job
- Hours of work
- Agreed rates and method of payment
- Details of any pension schemes
- Arrangements for the payment of any commission, bonuses or overtime
- Length of paid holiday entitlement
- Level and duration of sickness, injury and maternity pay entitlement
- Length of period of notice to be given
- Details of grievance and disciplinary procedures
- Name, job title and location of the firm's grievance officer.

A typical contract of employment would look like this:

CONTRACT OF EMPLOYMENT

Between

Employer ....

Employee ....

Title of Position held ....

Date of Commencement ....

Hours of work ....

Payment rate (including commission, bonuses and overtime) ....

Method of payment ....

Pension schemes which apply ....

Holiday entitlement ....

Sickness, injury and maternity pay entitlement ....

Period of notice of employment termination ....

Details of grievance and disciplinary procedures including the details of the firm's grievance officer are set out in the Employee Handbook.

This Contract may be altered only after consultation between the two parties named.

Signed on behalf of the Employer	Employee's Signature
....	....
Date	Date ....

Activity

1 Use a computer to make a copy of the Contract of Employment shown above.

2 Assume that you have got the post you selected earlier from the newspaper. Call up your copy of the Contract and complete it as a Contract of Employment between yourself and the business named in the advertisement. File the Contract with your other documents.

Main methods of recruitment

When the employer has completed those four documents, the next step is to contact possible candidates and invite them to apply for the post. The employer may do this inside the firm – known as internal recruitment – or outside the firm, which is external recruitment.

Internal recruitment

The usual methods of internal recruitment are to advertise the post:

- on notice boards
- in internal news sheets
- by sending memos or e-mails to all employees.

Advantages of internal recruitment

1 The applicants are familiar with the business.

2 Existing employees are given the opportunity to gain promotion within the firm.

3 This improves staff morale and provides motivation.

4. It is a cheaper method than advertising externally.
5. The process should take shorter time to complete.
6. The procedure is much simpler.

Disadvantages of internal recruitment

1. The range of applicants is limited.
2. It does not bring new skills and ideas into the business.
3. It could lead to staff discontent if one colleague is promoted over the other employees.
4. Newly promoted employee may have to be trained for the new post.
5. The existing job of the newly promoted employee will have to be filled.

Activity

There is a vacancy for a sales assistant in your school tuck shop. The person appointed will be required to work in the shop Monday to Friday before classes in the morning, at break-time and at lunch-time, during term time. Anyone interested in the post should apply to the School Secretary for further details regarding duties and pay.

Using a computer, design an advertisement for the post. The advertisement should be eye-catching and suitable for display on the school's notice board.

External recruitment

External recruitment may have to be used. There are several reasons for the use of external recruitment:

- There may not be a suitable candidate within the business
- None of the present employees may be interested in the post
- Sometimes a business may wish to introduce 'new blood' who will bring in fresh ideas and up-to-date training.

Advantages of external recruitment

1. The range of applicants is very wide.
2. It brings new skills and ideas into the business.
3. It avoids jealousies among existing employees.
4. Fully trained staff may be appointed so expense may be saved on training programmes.
5. No other internal staff vacancies are created.

Disadvantages of external recruitment

1. The applicants are not familiar with the business.
2. Job opportunities are not created within the business for existing employees.
3. Existing staff may feel undervalued.
4. Some external recruitment methods are very expensive.
5. It is a slower process than internal recruitment.

Methods of external recruitment

The four main methods are shown below.

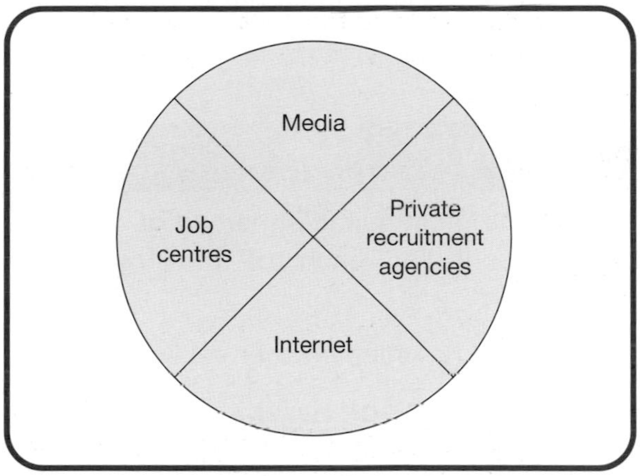

The media

The term 'media' includes a range of methods.

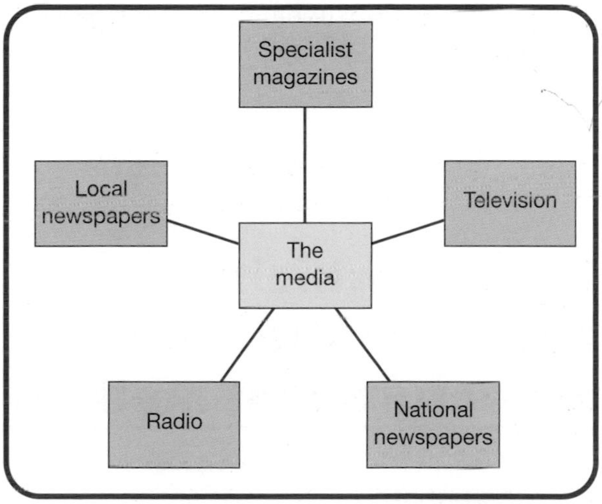

Advertising in local newspapers is less expensive but does not reach a wide audience. It would be suitable for jobs which are not very highly paid and for which people would not travel long distances.

Advertising in national newspapers is more expensive but is read by a greater number of people. Newspapers such as the *Belfast Telegraph* have special Job Finder sections. This method of advertising would be suitable for jobs which are more highly paid and for which people would be more willing to travel.

Specialist magazines are read by certain groups of workers and are used to recruit highly skilled or specialist workers. For example, *The Lancet* is a magazine for doctors, the *Nursing Times* is of interest to nurses and the *Times Educational Supplement* is read by teachers and other people working in the field of education.

From time to time some television and radio stations broadcast details of job vacancies. This is usually done on a local basis and would have similar features to advertising in local newspapers.

The internet

There are several websites on the internet which advertise a range of jobs and which firms may use. Many firms also have their own websites on which they advertise their vacancies. The main advantages of using the internet are that it:

- is not expensive
- has a wide audience
- attracts candidates who are up to date with the latest technology.

Activity

Imagine you are looking for a job. Name and give details of two disadvantages which using the internet would have for you when job hunting.

Job centres

Job Centres are run by the government and are found in towns throughout the country. They display notices about available work on behalf of employers on notice boards in the centres, via the internet, on local radio, and in newspapers. Job vacancies may also be viewed on www.jobcentreonline.com.

People who are unemployed, or are interested in a change of job, visit the Job Centres to find information and obtain advice about job vacancies and training courses. The Job Centres will help people to apply for suitable jobs and the big advantage is that the service is free. This method of recruitment is often used for finding workers who are skilled or semi-skilled such as factory workers, shop assistants and cleaners.

Activity

If you have access to the internet, search the Job Centre website (www.jobcentreonline.com) and make a list of any vacancies in your home area which would be of interest to you.

Private recruitment agencies

These are several private recruitment agencies in Northern Ireland which offer the service of finding suitable candidates for available positions. Two examples are Grafton Recruitment and Diamond Recruitment Employment Agency.

People looking for work register with the agency and employers contact the agency with details of available work. The agency matches the candidate with the most suitable work available. When a person is appointed, the firm pays the agency for the service.

The advantage is that time is saved by the employer which is very useful when a temporary worker is required quickly, for example to fill an absence due to illness in an office. However, the service is expensive.

Activity

Name the most suitable method of recruitment for each of the following positions:

1. **A part-time office cleaner in Limavady.**
2. **The Principal of Hazelwood Integrated College, Belfast.**
3. **A forklift operator in a hardware business in Enniskillen.**
4. **A qualified physiotherapist in Daisy Hill Hospital, Newry.**
5. **A sales assistant for a supermarket in Coleraine.**
6. **A clerical officer, needed for two weeks, in an office in Strabane.**

Factors which influence the choice of recruitment method

How a business recruits its employees will depend on several factors:

- The size of the firm
- The amount of money available for advertising
- The type of work being offered
- Where the firm is situated
- How many employees are required
- How quickly the new employee is needed.

How would a business know that its recruitment is effective?

Every business will examine how effective their method of recruitment is and will want to know if improvements might be made. They will probably look at:

- The response rate: did the method used attract a large number of applications?
- The type of response: did the method used attract applications from suitable candidates?
- Ease of operation: was the method used sufficiently quick and easy to carry out?
- Successful result: did the method used result in a good appointment?

Legal controls on recruitment

The overall aim of legal controls on recruitment is to prevent discrimination at work.

Legal controls have been created in order to protect minority groups such as women, the disabled, people from differing religions and people coming from other countries and cultures.

Controls on recruitment fall into four categories – race, religion, disability and gender. The provisions of each one are summarised here.

Legal controls on race state that:

- people of all races, colours, nationalities or ethnic origin must be treated equally during the recruitment and selection process

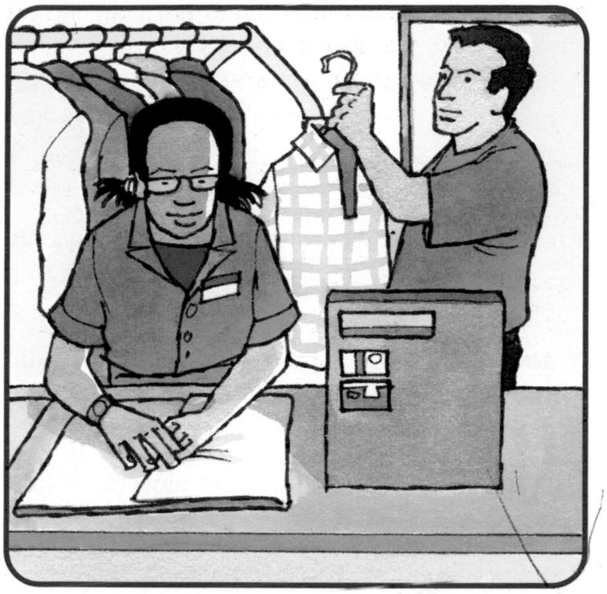

- people of all races, colours, nationalities or ethnic origin must be treated equally in all aspects of employment and in training
- in Northern Ireland such conditions also apply to Irish Travellers
- the employer would be liable if he/she allowed any of his/her employees to discriminate against other employees on racial grounds.

There are exceptions to these provisions. In each of the following circumstances the law would not have been broken where:

- a person of a particular racial group is required for a job – for example, in a dramatic performance or as a photographic model
- welfare services are being provided to a particular racial group and those services can best be provided by a person of the same racial group – social workers, for example.
- the employment is in a private household
- the employment is in a small business where there are fewer than six partners.

Legal controls on religion state that:

- people of all religious beliefs and political opinion should have equal opportunities in employment

- employers must create a 'neutral area' in the workplace. This means that they must prohibit the display of flags, emblems, posters and graffiti or the circulation of materials or the singing of songs which would give offence or cause fear
- employers must register with the Equality Commission if they employ more than ten people
- employers must annually submit information about the religious composition of their workforces – including part-time employees.

There are exceptions to these legal provisions on religion. Excluded are:

- any occupation where the nature of the job requires it to be done by a person holding a particular religious belief or political opinion – a minister of religion, for example.

Legal controls on disability state that:

- disabled people must have the same opportunities as other people in recruitment, training and selection for employment
- disabled people must not be treated less favourably than other people in their conditions of employment
- reasonable adjustments should be made to buildings to enable disabled people to work there – e.g. disabled toilets, ramps and lifts should be installed as well as car parking space provided.

Legal controls on gender state that:

- men and women should have equal treatment and opportunity in recruitment and selection and training
- men and women should have equal opportunities in promotion
- working conditions such as opportunities for retirement and pension provision must not discriminate on grounds of gender
- advertisements for jobs should not exclude either men or women
- men and women should have equal pay for equal value work. For this to apply, their work must be equally demanding or equally skilful and require equal levels of knowledge, decision making and responsibility
- it is unlawful to discriminate against someone because he/she is married
- women should not be discriminated against because of pregnancy or maternity leave
- sexual harassment is not condoned

- the employer would be liable if he/she allowed any of his/her employees to discriminate against other employees on gender grounds.

Activity

Fill in the spaces in the sentences below:

1 Legal controls aim to prevent .... at work. They are designed to protect groups such as ..... and the ....

2 Gender law forbids discrimination on the basis of a person's .... Or because he/she is ....

3 Employers are obliged to make adjustments to the work premises for .... employees.

4 Two exceptions to the Race laws are when .... services are being provided or the work is in a ....

5 The law states that women performing the same, or broadly similar, work as ... must be given the same ....

Activity

You have to decide which legal provision has been broken in each of the following situations:

1 No car parking spaces were reserved for disabled employees.

2 A woman was not given a job because she was married.

3 Irish Travellers were refused part-time jobs.

4 The pay structure in a company stated that male secretaries would be paid £1 per hour above the rate paid to female secretaries.

5 The firm's main building had no wheelchair access.

6 The firm refused to employ any Chinese workers.

7 Political slogans were allowed on factory walls.

8 A job advertisement stated that only women need apply.

The level of detail given in the above summary on racial, religious, disability and gender discrimination is all that is required for GCSE (CCEA) Business Studies. However, some students may require more detail for other purposes, or may simply be interested in reading further. For those reasons, the following notes on individual laws are included.

All recruitment is controlled by:

- The Sex Discrimination Act
- The Disability Discrimination Act
- Race Relations
- The Equal Pay Act
- The Fair Employment Act.

Sex Discrimination Act, 1976 and Sex Discrimination (Northern Ireland) Order 1976 (amended 1988)

The Sex Discrimination Act and its Northern Ireland equivalent forbid discrimination on the basis of a person's gender. It is also unlawful to discriminate against someone because he/she is married.

This Act states that men and women should have equal treatment and opportunity:

- when employers are advertising for applicants for jobs
- in the recruitment and selection of employees
- in the promotion of employees
- when employers are setting rates of pay and other conditions in jobs.

Other issues such as pregnancy and maternity rights, training, sexual harassment, terms and conditions of employment, retirement and pensions are also covered by this legislation.

The employer would also be breaking this law if he/she knowingly allowed employees to discriminate against other employees on the grounds of their gender.

Disability Discrimination Act, 1995

The Disability Discrimination Act, 1995 makes it unlawful to treat disabled people less favourably than other people in employment.

This Act defines disability as 'a physical or mental impairment which has a substantial and long-term adverse effect on a person's ability to carry out normal day-to-day activities'. Under the Disability Discrimination Act, 1995 discrimination occurs where:

- a disabled person is treated less favourably than someone else
- the treatment is for a reason relating to the person's disability
- the treatment cannot be justified.

Discrimination also occurs when there is a failure to make a reasonable adjustment for a disabled person and that failure cannot be justified.

Race Relations Act and (Northern Ireland) Order 1997

Under this legislation, people of all races, colours, nationalities or ethnic origin must be treated equally during the recruitment process, in employment and in training.

It is racial discrimination to treat a person less favourably on racial grounds than another person would be treated in the same circumstances. For example, if an employer set conditions or requirements which would be difficult for a person of another colour or race to meet then he/she would be guilty of racial discrimination.

The Race Relations (Northern Ireland) Order makes particular mention of Irish Travellers and makes it illegal to discriminate against them.

As with the Sex Discrimination legislation, the employer would be liable if he/she allowed any of his/her employees to discriminate against other employees in the business.

There are exceptions to the race relations laws. In each of the following circumstances the order would not have been broken where:

- a person of a particular racial group is required for a job – for example, in a dramatic performance or as a photographic model
- welfare services are being provided to a particular racial group and those services can best be provided by a person of the same racial group – social workers, for example
- the employment is in a private household
- the employment is in a small business where there are fewer than six partners

- the employment involves working outside Northern Ireland for most of the time.

Equal Pay Act (Northern Ireland), 1970 (amended 1984)

This Act states that women performing the same, or broadly similar, work to men must be treated in the same way as men. They must be paid the same, and must have the same conditions of service as men.

The Equal Pay Act applies to all full-time and part-time work and to all sizes of firm.

It is important to note that, to receive equal pay, the woman's work need not be exactly the same as the man's work. It must be of 'equal value'. This means that it must be equally demanding or equally skilful and require equal levels of knowledge, decision making and responsibility.

Fair Employment and Treatment (Northern Ireland) Order 1998

The Fair Employment and Treatment (Northern Ireland) Order 1998 updates the Fair Employment Acts of 1976 and 1989.

This Order was passed to ensure that people of all religious beliefs and political opinion in Northern Ireland have equal opportunities in employment.

In order to comply with fair employment rules, employers must:

- register with the Equality Commission if they employ more than ten people
- annually submit information about the religious composition of the workforce – including part-time employees
- submit information of people who have applied for jobs
- retain all information for three years so that their practices can be examined over a period
- review their practices at least once every three years
- create a 'neutral area' in the workplace. This means that they must prohibit the display of flags, emblems, posters and graffiti or the circulation of materials or the singing of songs which would give offence or cause fear.

Not all types of employment are covered by the Fair Employment Laws. The exceptions are:

- any occupation where the nature of the job requires it to be done by a person holding a particular religious belief or political opinion – a minister of religion, for example
- employment which is wholly outside Northern Ireland.

Moral and ethical issues underlying anti-discrimination legislation

All the laws you have just studied have been introduced so that proper rules of conduct are applied to recruitment, selection, training and employment and that discrimination, in all its forms, is prevented.

The moral foundation of the legislation is that the most vulnerable groups in society – women, the disabled, people belonging to differing religions, and foreigners – are protected and given their rights.

The government, in passing such laws, is making sure that employers behave in a moral and ethical way. They are obliged to treat all their employees equally and with respect. The underlying principle here is that everyone is equal in the eyes of the law, and therefore each one is entitled to equal treatment. In recruitment terms, the result should be that the best person is employed or given promotion regardless of that person's gender, religion, political opinion or physical ability.

The Sex Discrimination (Northern Ireland) Order makes sure that men and women are given equal opportunities in employment. A woman who has good qualifications and experience must be given the same chance to gain promotion as the men in the firm. She cannot be refused a job, for example, because she may have to take maternity leave.

The Equal Pay Act (Northern Ireland) makes sure that a woman is treated in a morally correct way, and is given pay equal to that of her male colleagues where the work she does is of equal value.

The Fair Employment and Treatment (Northern Ireland) Order was passed to make sure that people of all religions or political beliefs are given equal opportunities to get employment.

The Disability Discrimination Act was introduced to ensure that people who are disabled are given opportunities to work. Where their qualifications are adequate, disabled people must be treated equally with able-bodied people in the recruitment process. Employers are obliged to overcome any physical difficulties in their premises by installing ramps, lifts and special toilets. In this way, the legislation recognises the contribution which the disabled make to the business world and ensures that their disability does not prevent them from making that contribution.

The Race Relations (Northern Ireland) Order was designed to make sure that it would be possible for people from other cultures and races to get employment in Northern Ireland. As well as people from other cultures and races, this Act covers people of all skin colours and members of the Irish Travelling Community.

Role of the Equality Commission for Northern Ireland

The Equality Commission for Northern Ireland was established under the Northern Ireland Act, 1998. Its aim is to help build a more equal society in Northern Ireland.

The Commission's mission statement illustrates this aim:

> To value and promote respect for diversity, eliminate unlawful discrimination and achieve equality of opportunity for all.

How does the Equality Commission do this?

Its duties include:

- working to eliminate unlawful discrimination
- promoting equality of opportunity and encouraging good practice
- promoting good relations between people of different racial groups
- keeping the relevant laws under review.

The Commission's main work is to give advice and assistance to people who believe that they have been treated unfairly or discriminated against on grounds of their:

- colour
- race
- nationality
- ethnic or national origin (including being an Irish traveller)
- religious belief
- political opinion
- gender
- sexual orientation
- married status
- disability.

In cases where legal action is needed, the Commission will arrange legal representation. It can take legal action against individuals and organisations in some circumstances – for example, if they have published an advertisement which discriminates against someone from one of the groups shown in the above list.

The Commission also sees that the law on equality is enforced in order to bring about greater equality in the world of work and in society in general. The Commission has powers to ensure that employers monitor and review their employment practices as well as the composition of their workforce. For example, employers must show that they are willing to employ:

- both men and women
- both single and married workers
- people with different religious or political opinions
- people of any race or ethnic origin
- people with disabilities.

In addition, the Commission will:

- provide information, advisory and training services
- publish Codes of Practice which set standards for fairness and equality in employment, pay, housing and the provision of goods and services
- make sure that public sector organisations take equality into account
- undertake research into equality issues
- award grants for promotional and educational work
- carry out public education campaigns to raise awareness of equality issues.

Responsibility for implementing the fair employment legislation now rests with the Equality Commission. It is the duty of the Commission to:

- work to eliminate religious discrimination
- give advice to employers on their practices
- help anyone who has a complaint and requests advice.

The Equality Commission has powers to investigate any employer any time and, if necessary, to bring an employer before a Fair Employment Tribunal. The Commission may also issue directions on measures which must be taken by employers.

The Court to which the Equality Commission would bring its legal cases is called the Fair Employment Tribunal.

This Tribunal has two functions:

1. It decides on individual cases of discrimination. It has power to award damages for financial loss, for loss of opportunity or for injury to feelings.
2. It hears appeals against directions of the Equality Commission. The Tribunal has power to take steps to force employers to comply and can impose fines of them if necessary.

Activity

Fill in the spaces in the following sentences.

1 The Equality Commission works to eliminate .... discrimination. It has powers to bring an employer before a ....

2 In order to comply with the rules of the .... Commission, employers must register with the Commission if they employ more than ... people and must retain all information for ..... years.

3 Employers must create a .... in the workplace so they must not allow the display of ..... or the singing of ..... which would cause fear.

Activity

Study the following case and answer the questions at the end.

A woman was absent from her company on maternity leave. During her absence two promotion posts were advertised internally and filled without her being told about the positions.

She said that the company was guilty of discrimination against her because of her sex and pregnancy. She argued that because she was not told about the posts, she had not been able to apply for promotion.

1 In your opinion, is the woman's allegation of discrimination reasonable?

2 What action would you have advised the company to take when advertising the post?

Checklist

At this stage you should be able to:

- understand the purposes and content of a job analysis, job description, person specification and contract of employment
- discuss the advantages and disadvantages of internal recruitment
- discuss the advantages and disadvantages of external recruitment
- identify, describe and evaluate the main methods of recruitment
- explain the factors which influence the choice of recruitment method
- examine the effectiveness of methods of recruitment
- understand the legal controls on recruitment
- understand the moral and ethical issues underlining the legislation in relation to race, religion, disability and gender.

Theme 5.2

Selection

When you become involved in the selection process, remember that this is the first impression the employer will have of you, and first impressions do count. You never get a second chance to make a first impression!

Methods of selection

After the recruitment stage, the next step is for the employer to choose the new employee from the list of applicants who have applied for the position. That is known as the selection process.

In order to choose the most suitable applicant, it is important for the employer to find as much information as possible about all the applicants.

To do this, the following six methods of selection are most commonly used:

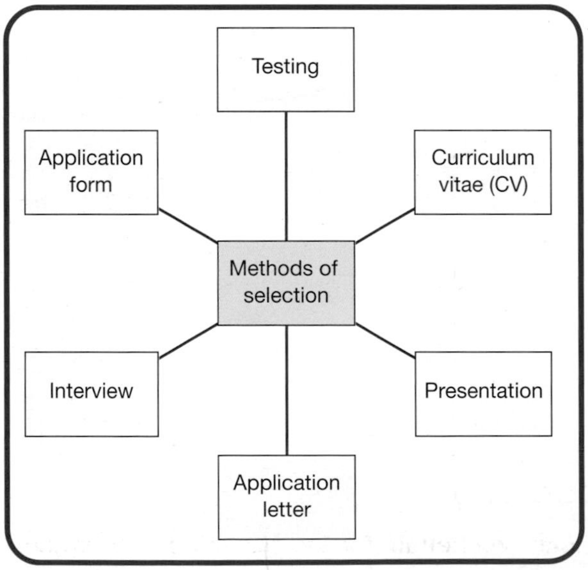

Application form

Sometimes an employer asks the applicants to complete a form on which they must answer all questions. An application form may be used because it has the advantage that the applicant is giving exactly the type of information which the employer needs, making it easy for the employer to compare applicants.

When completing an application form it is important to:

- work neatly and accurately
- complete all sections
- work in black or blue ink – NEVER in pencil
- sign and date the form
- check that all details are correct – untrue information would rule out your application.

Application letter

Sometimes the advertisement states that the applicant should reply by writing a letter of application. An employer may ask for an application letter because it shows the employer the level of the applicant's communication skills.

An applicant for a job has to show in the application letter that he/she is suitable for the post. The letter should make the employer want to meet the applicant.

To do this, an application letter should include the applicant's:

- personal details
- educational background
- qualifications and work experience
- names of previous employers
- names and addresses of two referees
- details of personal hobbies, interests and achievements.

Dungannon and South Tyrone Borough Council headquarters

All the rules for completing an application form also apply when writing a letter of application – work neatly and accurately, complete all sections, use black or blue ink and check all details.

Activity

DUNGANNON AND SOUTH TYRONE BOROUGH COUNCIL

Tourist Information Receptionist

Required for
Killymaddy Tourist Information Centre,
Ballygawley Road, Dungannon.

37 hours per week
Salary Scale £9,267–£12,390 per annum

Applicants for the above post should have a minimum of:
6 GCSEs (Grades A–C) including English Language
Ability to speak a foreign language desirable

Application by letter to be received by the Human Resources Section
Dungannon and South Tyrone Borough Council
Circular Road, Dungannon BT71 6DT
by 5 December.

You should now write a letter of application, on your own behalf, for the above position in the Tourist Information Centre.

Curriculum Vitae

Sometimes the advertisement asks the applicant to include a Curriculum Vitae (CV).

A Curriculum Vitae is simply a list of all the applicant's qualifications, work and achievements to that date. An employer may ask for a CV because it shows all the applicant's details and it also shows how well the applicant can organise and display information.

There is a standard format for a curriculum vitae and it includes the applicant's:

- personal details – name, address, telephone number, nationality, marital status and date of birth
- educational background
- qualifications
- work experience
- positions of responsibility
- previous employers
- details of two referees
- personal hobbies and interests
- other achievements.

Activity

You are now ready to design your own Curriculum Vitae. Begin by listing all the results of examinations you have sat, sports awards you have achieved, trips you have gone on, details of your work experience and any school positions you hold or have held such as prefect, sports captain or librarian.

Use a computer to arrange all that information, plus your personal details, under the headings given above. Later you can add to the CV as you pass more examinations etc.

When the employers receive all the application forms, letters and CVs they will sort them into two groups – suitable and unsuitable applicants. The 'suitable' group will include those who meet all the criteria in the advertisement, and the 'unsuitable' group will include those who do not meet the criteria.

Unsuitable applicants are then informed by letter that they have been unsuccessful and suitable applicants are invited to undertake a test or an interview or give a presentation.

Testing

Two types of tests are frequently used – practical tests and psychometric tests.

Practical tests are more usual in the selection process for manual, practical jobs. In a practical test the applicant would be asked to undertake a piece of work which would test skills required in the business. For example an applicant for the job of a computer operator may be asked to key in a letter or construct a database. This shows the employer whether the applicant's computer skills reach the level required in the business.

Psychometric tests are usually used when management level positions are being filled. Psychometric tests provide a description of the personality of the applicant, and the results are compared with the person specification. The applicants have to answer multiple choice questions about themselves which are designed to show what they like or dislike and how they would react in certain situations.

Interview

Interviews are very frequently used in the selection process. The applicants who have been short-listed are invited to an interview where they meet representatives of the firm to answer questions and discuss the post.

At the interview, all interviewees are asked the same questions and given the same time so that the employer can later compare the answers given.

Interviews are useful because they give employers the opportunity to meet applicants and to judge how suitable they would be in that particular job.

It is important for the applicant to:

- prepare thoroughly for an interview
- do research on the company
- dress suitably
- act naturally in the interview
- show a genuine interest in the firm
- arrive in good time.

Activity

Refer back to the position in the Tourist Information Centre for which you wrote an Application Letter. You have just heard that you are being interviewed for the job.

1 Draft three questions which you think you may be asked

2 Draft one question which would be appropriate for you to ask at the interview

3 What else might you do to prepare for the interview?

Presentation

It is now common for applicants for management positions to be asked to give a presentation as well as be interviewed. In this situation, the applicant would be given a title in advance and told the length of time the presentation should last.

The applicant would be expected to talk on the prepared subject which would be related to the work of the particular post. For example, applicants for a shop manager's post may be asked to speak on their ideas for motivating staff or increasing turnover.

Presentations are used by employers because they show the personality of the applicants as well as their communication skills, level of preparation and ideas about the job.

Activity

You have been asked to make a presentation when you attend the interview for the position in the Tourist Information Centre. You have been given the topic in advance and the title is 'The importance of the role of the Tourist Information Receptionist'. You have to speak for a maximum of five minutes and may use PowerPoint or an overhead projector if you wish.

Prepare your presentation for use at the interview.

Responsibilities of employers and employees in the selection process

Both employers and employees have the same responsibilities in the selection process. There are four main obligations which are expected from all parties. They are honesty, objectivity, fairness and confidentiality.

Honesty

It is expected that both employer and employee would be totally honest with each other. For example, documents provided by the employer, such as the job description or advertisement, must be accurate and clear. All other information given about the job – for example pay or holidays – would be expected to be totally honest.

The employees must also provide honest information regarding such details as their qualifications and experience. No information should be left out by the employee if it would influence the final decision – a criminal record, for example.

Objectivity

Both parties are expected to be totally without prejudice about each other. For example, the employer could not reject applicants simply because of their religious, political or social background. The employer has a responsibility to find the best person for the position, regardless of any other consideration.

Fairness

Total fairness is required by all parties. The employer, for example, must allocate equal time and consideration to each candidate in an interview and must ask the same questions to everyone. The same conditions must be applied to each person.

The employee must also be totally fair by disclosing full and accurate information.

Confidentiality

Both employee and employer must treat all information learned about each other as strictly confidential. The employee must not talk to others about details of the firm and the employer must not give personal details of the applicants to third parties.

Activity

In the following word search, find the words shown in the list. The words can be read in straight lines, horizontally, vertically or diagonally, either backwards or forwards. There is no overlap of words in the grid.

selection	applicant
form	letter
curriculum	vitae
interview	test
job	psychometric
shortlist	honesty
objectivity	fairness
confidentiality	

S	M	H	T	I	N	T	E	R	N	A	R	E	T	T	E	L	G
E	U	O	P	J	W	E	N	G	A	D	A	O	R	B	A	K	H
L	P	N	I	E	R	O	B	J	E	C	T	I	V	I	T	Y	A
E	W	E	L	I	U	A	A	S	B	R	O	C	H	S	K	G	S
C	L	S	R	S	H	O	R	T	L	I	S	T	L	P	D	S	D
T	A	T	X	S	L	E	K	C	C	G	T	I	C	M	P	O	Q
I	L	Y	C	J	O	B	E	I	N	T	E	R	V	I	E	W	T
O	U	P	E	N	C	T	T	P	Q	I	P	Y	C	M	U	A	Y
N	X	Y	E	Y	P	S	Y	C	H	O	M	E	T	R	I	C	I
X	O	D	D	E	R	Y	N	N	H	O	S	M	T	D	E	I	O
C	U	R	R	I	C	U	L	U	M	B	C	U	T	I	K	L	S
E	B	R	V	Y	T	I	O	I	U	Q	B	V	I	T	A	E	I
C	O	N	F	I	D	E	N	T	I	A	L	I	T	Y	R	P	L
E	I	I	X	A	I	P	R	T	U	E	M	A	U	T	U	Y	P
T	E	S	T	U	G	N	A	L	B	S	S	E	N	R	I	A	F
P	X	C	V	B	E	U	F	H	H	K	J	L	I	O	O	B	X
A	P	P	L	I	C	A	N	T	I	R	E	G	R	M	R	O	F

Checklist

At this stage you should be able to:

- understand the six main methods of selection and why they may be used
- understand and discuss the responsibilities of both employers and employees in the selection process – honesty, objectivity, fairness and confidentiality.

Theme 5.3

Training

Training is defined as 'the acquisition of knowledge and skills which can be applied to a particular job'.

Employers realise that their most valuable resource is their employees. Therefore they are anxious to have a highly trained and well-motivated workforce and are willing to invest considerable sums of money into training programmes.

Reasons for staff training

There are three major reasons for staff training.

1. Induction

Can you remember your first days in your present school? It is likely that you spent the first days being shown around and becoming familiar with the new surroundings. You were told how things were done in the new school and were introduced to the people you needed to know. That process was your 'induction'.

Induction is the name given to the training of new employees. It is designed to make new employees feel comfortable in the new workplace and to help them to fit in to their new surroundings. Induction enables new employees to understand the ethos and work of the organisation and to play their part more efficiently.

The content of the induction programme would vary from firm to firm. It usually includes a guided tour of the buildings, an introduction to work colleagues and line manager, a talk or video on the firm's aims and an explanation of the firm's health and safety procedures.

Activity

Answer the following questions:

1 Name two benefits which induction has for a new employee in a business.

2 Give details of one benefit which induction has for the company.

Change in procedures

Training is not only for new staff. Employees who have been working in that business for years also need to undergo training courses. This may be necessary because new technology has been introduced into the business and employees need to become familiar with its use and to have their skills updated.

Sometimes the firm's product changes and employees have to learn new information and be trained in the new methods required to make that change.

To become more competitive

Businesses also invest in training for employees in order to improve their competitiveness. Their aim is to maximise sales and profits. To do this they constantly are looking for ways to make their product or service better, and in a shorter time, than the product or service offered by other firms.

This requires training programmes designed to improve the efficiency of the employees.

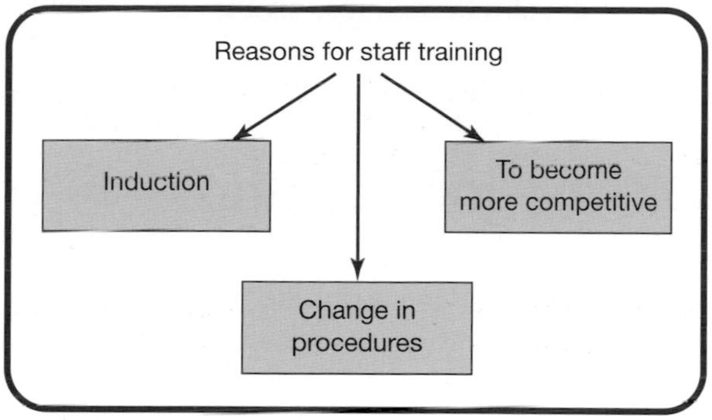

Benefits and importance of training

Businesses undertake constant training which they consider important and beneficial from the point of view of both the business and the employees for the following reasons:

- New employees will be properly inducted into the business
- Employees will be equipped to cope with constant changes in technology
- Employees will have updated skills
- Employees will have the required information for the introduction of new methods
- A highly trained workforce is more efficient and effective
- Having more effective employees improves the quality of the firm's products which will lead to increased sales and profits for the firm
- Training of employees helps the business to keep ahead of its competitors
- Training provides motivation for employees
- Training decreases the possibility of accidents in the workplace
- Training decreases the supervision required for employees
- Training reduces the risk of redundancy for employees
- Multi skilled workers are flexible and can undertake different jobs in the firm
- Highly trained employees have better opportunities for promotion in the firm
- A firm which has a highly trained staff and uses up-to-date methods earns a good reputation both as an employee and as a competitor in the marketplace.

Drawbacks of training

- Training programmes are expensive for the business
- Employees have to be given time off work to undertake training
- There is a risk that well-trained employees will leave to take work with the competitors
- Highly trained employees may demand higher pay levels.

Employees who do not retrain and keep up-to-date with modern trends risk becoming redundant.

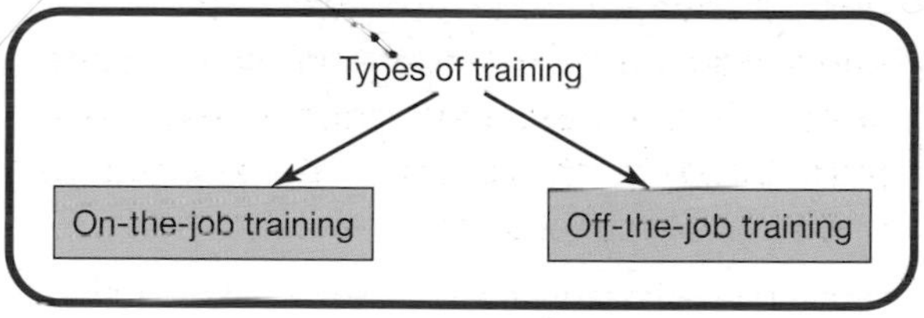

Types of training

On-the-job training

On-the-job training is the most common form of training for unskilled and semi-skilled workers. It is training given at the employee's normal place of work during his/her normal working hours.

On the-job training may be done in a variety of ways.

Internal courses

Sometimes employers run courses inside their own firm and use their own machinery and equipment. This means that the content of the course is designed specifically for that firm.

This method is very effective because the employee is shown how to do the work and can practise it under supervision.

Work shadowing

Sometimes the new employee 'shadows' an experienced employee. This means that they work alongside one another and the trainee learns from the experienced worker.

Role play

Sometimes role play is used. In this method a 'make believe' situation is created, and the employees have to work out how they would solve the problem.

On-the-job training has several advantages:

- the content of the course is designed specifically for the firm
- it is usually more economical because the work of the firm is not interrupted
- training is given to each individual
- everyone knows one another
- employees feel at home in their own surroundings.

Hairdressing: on-the-job training

Activity

In certain circumstances, on-the-job training can have one major disadvantage. What is that disadvantage?

Off-the-job training

Off-the-job training is training provided by a specialist and takes place outside the firm – perhaps at a training centre, college or university. The training is paid for by the firm and may be on a day release basis or for a longer period of attendance at a full-time course for a term or longer.

Off-the-job training may be done in a variety of ways:

Lectures

Sometimes employees attend lectures where they are given information which they can later apply in their work.

Demonstrations

Demonstrations are effective for showing how tasks should be done. The trainee watches the expert but then must be given an opportunity to practise the skill.

Role play

Role play is used in both on-the-job and off-the-job training and is undertaken to imitate a real-life situation.

Off-the-job training has the following advantages:

- since the training is done by specialists it usually is of a higher quality
- employees meet people from other organisations and can exchange ideas
- employees visit a new environment and perhaps are introduced to new equipment
- employees can attend evening classes which means they do not miss their work and this reduces the cost.

Activity

Name the most appropriate method of training for each of the following situations:

1. A business has replaced all its computers. All ten of the office workers need to learn how to use the new computers.
2. An engineering firm has installed one new machine. The firm has no experience of this type of machinery. Roisin will be working on the new machine but is unfamiliar with it.
3. A school is introducing a new subject to its curriculum and two teachers – Miss Todd and Mr Kenny – have been told they will be teaching the subject next year. They need help.
4. Brian is starting work as a hotel waiter next month. He has not done this type of work before.
5. Nadine is working as a hairdresser but would like to extend her hairdressing skills in order to get promotion in the salon.
6. Billy is tired of his work as a civil servant and has decided to open a garden centre. He needs to learn more about growing garden plants.
7. Molly has decided to join Billy in the garden centre to do the office work. She has been a housewife for many years but had done clerical work before her marriage.
8. A hi-tech business takes pride in using the latest technology. Recommend the methods of training it should use for its production staff.

Checklist

At this stage you should be able to:

- understand the reasons for staff training – induction, change in procedures, and to become more competitive
- describe the benefits/importance of training
- describe the drawbacks of training
- describe on-the-job training and off-the-job training
- justify the more appropriate method of training for particular circumstances.

Theme 5.4

Motivation

Motivation is the way in which a person can be encouraged to make an effort to do something.

Many studies have been carried out on what makes people want to work. Probably the most famous of these studies was by Abraham Maslow, an American psychologist who died in 1970.

Maslow's Hierarchy of Needs

Maslow concluded that people have five levels of need which he illustrated in a 'Hierarchy of Needs' pyramid. He placed the most basic needs at the bottom of the pyramid and the most advanced needs at the top of the pyramid. According to Maslow, when people satisfy one level of need they then move up to the next level.

In his theory, the most basic need is to survive – to have enough money to buy food, shelter and necessary clothes.

When they have satisfied the need for **survival**, they then need to feel safe and secure – perhaps from unemployment – so the second level of need is for **security**.

After that, people need to belong to a group and to have friends – these are their **social** needs.

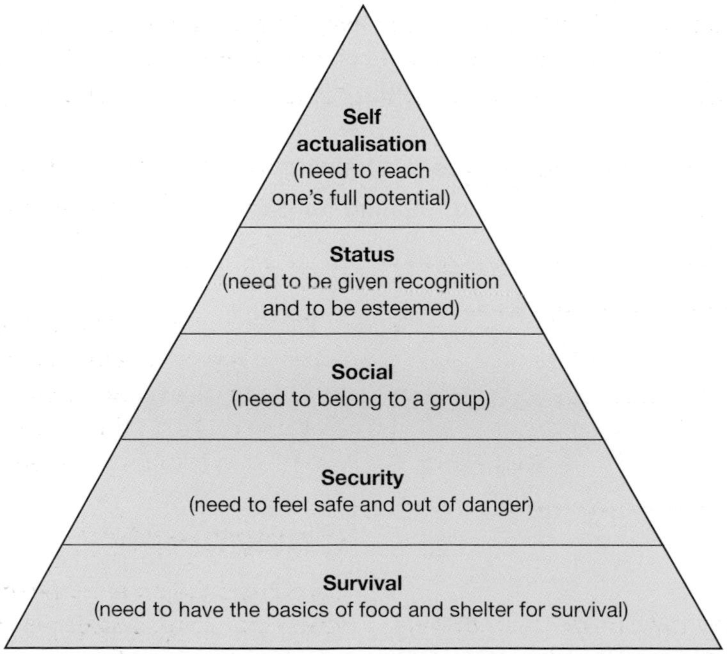

They then move on to needing **status.** At this stage they need to be respected in the community, to be esteemed, and to be given recognition for what they do.

When all these needs have been satisfied, people finally have **self-actualisation (or self-fulfilment)** needs. This is ambition to achieve as much as they possibly can – perhaps to be promoted to a high level position with more responsibility.

Importance of motivation

Obviously it is very important for a business to have well-motivated employees. If employees are highly motivated:

- There is likely to be a lower labour turnover. If employees are happy in their work, they are less likely to leave
- They would probably produce higher quality goods because they are more interested in their work
- There would probably be fewer accidents in the workplace since employees are working better as a team and are concentrating on their work
- They are less likely to take time off work. Reduced absenteeism improves production and overall profitability.

Activity

Employers are anxious to have a highly motivated staff.

1 Name two benefits for the employer if employees are well motivated.

2 How would work be more satisfying for employees if their motivation is high?

A generous pay system is a good incentive for workers, but money alone is not enough! Maslow's theory has shown that employees need to feel valued in the workplace, they need to feel they belong, and they need to be rewarded for good work.

For these reasons, employers introduce a variety of methods of motivation which offer rewards to employees in addition to their basic pay. These methods of motivation may or may not be for money – in other words, they may be either financial or non-financial.

Financial methods of motivation

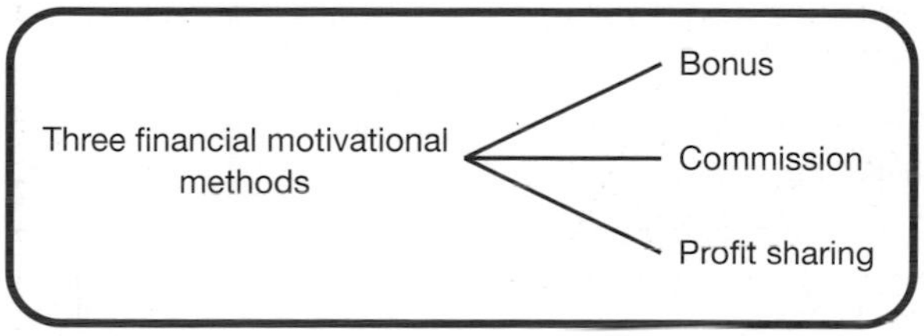

Bonus

A bonus is an extra payment made to employees who work well and help the business, for example, to complete its orders on time or to meet its sales targets. It is paid as a lump sum usually either at Christmas or at the beginning of the summer holidays.

Bonus payments encourage employees to work harder. The advantage for the employees is that they can increase their income while the employer has the advantage of greater production resulting in higher sales and profits.

Commission

Commission is an extra financial reward which is most suitable for a sales person. It is calculated as a percentage of the sales which that person makes. For example, if the commission is 10% and the sales person's sales amounted to £8,000, then the total commission which that person would earn would be £800 on top of his salary.

Commission payments encourage sales staff to increase their sales. In this way the sales staff increase their income while the business sells more goods and makes more profit.

Profit sharing

Under a profit-sharing scheme, employees receive a share of the profit made by the firm in addition to their basic salary.

Profit sharing acts as a good motivator for employees because it encourages them to increase the business's output and profits of which they can then own a share. It also has the advantage that the employees feel a greater sense of belonging to the firm and take a greater interest in its success.

Profit sharing is most usually found in the service sector because, in that type of work, it is not possible to estimate any single employee's contribution to the profits made in the firm. A slight unfairness of the system is that all employees benefit from the profits made in the business – even those who have worked less well and are less deserving.

Activity

Thomas, Jane and Katie all work for the same company. Study the following details and then name the method of financial motivation each one receives.

1. **Thomas has a management position and each year he receives some of the profits made by the company.**
2. **Jane is a sales person for the company and receives a percentage of the sales she makes.**
3. **Every Christmas Katie receives a welcome addition to her wages because the employees have worked hard all year.**

Non-financial methods of motivation

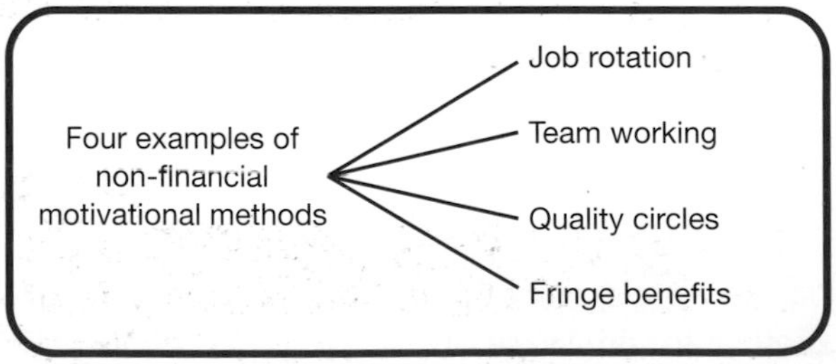

Job rotation

Job rotation is a system in which employees move around different jobs in the business in order to avoid the possibility of them getting bored by doing the same work all the time.

The system has the added advantage of giving opportunities for workers to learn more jobs. Job rotation is suitable for unskilled work and is frequently used for factory workers on production lines.

Team working

In a team working system, employees are grouped together in teams making sure that the team has the full range of abilities and skills required to make the product or carry out whatever task they have been set. The team may be given responsibility for how they carry out the work and organise it.

This system has the advantage of making the employees feel more responsible for their own team's decisions. In addition, employees feel committed and will be anxious to make their

own team successful so will work hard to make that happen.

Team working increases job satisfaction for employees and improves morale in the workplace.

Quality circles

Quality circles originated in Japan where they are widely and successfully used. They have now become very common in this country, possibly because of the spread of Japanese business in the British Isles.

The introduction of quality circles is really another approach to team working. Employees are organised into work teams and meet regularly to examine the quality of what they are doing and to try to find ways of doing the job better and improving the quality of the product even further.

Fringe benefits

Fringe benefits – sometimes referred to as perks – come with many occupations and are usually related to the seniority of the employee.

For example, directors and senior managers may be entitled to benefits such as company cars, free use of houses, education fees paid for their children, expense accounts, private health care for themselves and their families, pension schemes and trips abroad.

Factory floor workers may be entitled to benefits such as transport to work, free uniforms, discounts on the firm's products, recreational facilities, savings schemes, company shares and luncheon vouchers.

Activity

State which method of motivation you think is most appropriate in each of the following cases, giving reasons for your decisions.

1. **Catherine is a sales representative for a fashion company and needs encouragement to increase the company's sales.**
2. **David has been working as a swimming instructor in a leisure centre for several years. He feels that he is being isolated from the other instructors in the centre.**

3 Joyce is a factory supervisor and is good at her job. However, she often feels de-motivated because she works hard and she thinks her bosses get all the rewards.

4 Patrick is the financial director of the Northern Ireland branch of a multi-national organisation. He agrees that he is very well paid but needs some further encouragement.

5 Elizabeth loves her work as a shop assistant but feels she should have some fringe benefits. Which benefits would you recommend?

6 Jack is bored because for years he has been doing the same work on a production line in a toy factory.

Factors affecting job satisfaction

Job satisfaction is defined as the degree of happiness a person gets from his or her work.

If an employee is to reach his/her full potential and do his/her best work, it is extremely important that he/she enjoys his/her work and gets a high degree of job satisfaction from it.

There are several factors which increase a person's job satisfaction:

- **Wages/Salaries.** Money is obviously a very big factor in any job. People work in order to earn enough money to buy the goods they need and to be able to have some luxury in their lives. However, money alone is not enough!
- **Responsibility**. Employees need to be given responsibility in the firm. They want to achieve some status so they also need to have opportunities to apply for and be given promotion
- **Fulfilment**. People get job satisfaction from doing a good piece of work, so a sense of achievement is important
- **Enjoyment**. Enjoying the work is also an important factor in job satisfaction and it is vital to find work which you are happy doing
- **Good working conditions**. The conditions in the workplace can also affect job satisfaction. Such conditions could include a pleasant environment with warm, well-lit buildings for example. The other people in the workplace can also have a major effect. Liking the people working with you makes the job much more enjoyable and increases job satisfaction to a significant degree
- **Praise.** Everyone responds to praise and wants to feel valued as an employee. Job satisfaction improves if the employer has a good relationship with his staff and recognises their effort and contribution to the firm.

Activity

Make a list of the factors which give you job satisfaction in your GCSE work.

What steps could you take in order to improve your job satisfaction?

Checklist

At this stage you should be able to:

- explain the importance of motivation among employees
- identify and describe the main methods of financial motivation
- identify and describe the main methods of non-financial motivation
- identify the most appropriate methods of motivation in particular situations
- analyse the factors affecting job satisfaction.

Theme 5.5

Appraisal

Appraisal is the process of assessing an employee's performance in his/her job.

Reasons for appraisal and its importance

Employers are always anxious to know how to use their employees most effectively and to be aware of their strengths and weaknesses. Performance appraisal is used to discover this information.

Appraisal provides feedback to an employee on his/her performance. The system shows how performance could be improved and considers how the employee's career could be developed.

After identifying the employees' strengths and weaknesses through the process of appraisal, the employer may decide to reward employees who are performing well, or possibly to offer training to other employees where appraisal has shown weaknesses.

Appraisal is also frequently used to decide on the level of an employee's salary. In this case, the employee's effectiveness in the business is linked to his/her pay – a system known as 'performance related pay' – which is not appropriate for all types of work.

In summary, the reasons for appraisal are shown in the figure below.

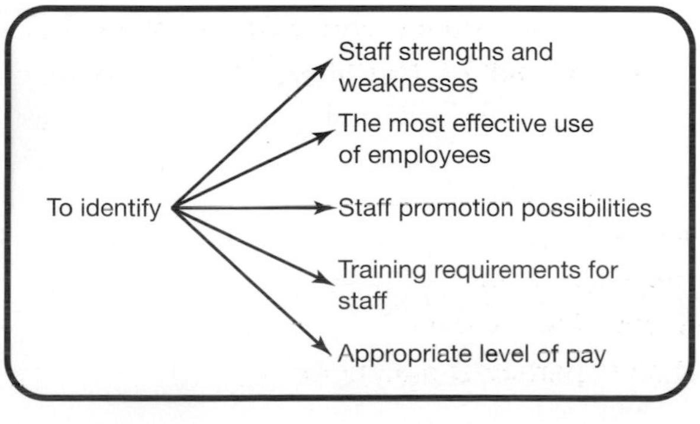

Activity

Name two occupations where performance-related pay would be unfair and give reasons why it would not suit those occupations.

Benefits of appraisal for employees and employers

Appraisal is beneficial for employees because it:

- gives them opportunities for promotion and sets pay levels
- makes sure that they receive training if necessary
- allows them to achieve their full potential
- lets them communicate with the employer on a one-to-one basis
- gives them an opportunity to discuss problems
- provides clear objectives and acts as a motivator.

Appraisal is beneficial for employers because it:

- helps in the planning and development of the firm's human resource provision
- shows up staff strengths and allows the business to use the best employees efficiently
- identifies staff weaknesses and helps the firm to plan an effective training programme
- increases staff competence and overall productivity
- improves the profitability of the business as a result.

Activity

Andrew is an employee in the accounts section of a large company. He has just been told that his appraisal interview will be held next week. He is nervous, and has come to you for help.

Write down the benefits which Andrew could get from appraisal.

Methods of appraisal and their evaluation

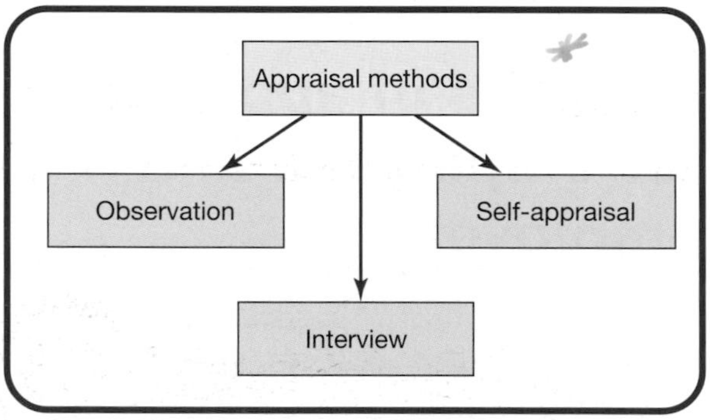

There are many methods of staff appraisal and the choice of method depends on the individual business and the type of work it does. The most commonly used ones are discussed here.

Observation

Observation is where the employee is watched doing his/her work, usually by the person who is that employee's immediate superior. For example a shop floor worker would be observed by a supervisor and the supervisor may be observed by a manager.

Observation is a useful method of appraisal because:

- it allows employees to be observed in their usual surroundings
- it gives a true picture of employees' work.

However, some employees may find it off-putting to be observed doing their work. Observation is usually accompanied by an interview.

Interview

An appraisal interview is a one-to-one discussion between the employee who is being appraised (the appraisee) and the supervisor or manager who is carrying out the appraisal (the appraiser).

The interview is a very useful method of appraisal because:

- it gives both parties a private opportunity to discuss the employee's work and progress
- it allows the employee to put forward his/her own ideas
- it diagnoses problems in work and tries to find solutions.

At the end of the interview, the appraiser completes a form which shows such qualities as:

- employee's level of initiative
- employee's ability to cope with pressure
- employee's leadership skills.

Self-appraisal

Nowadays employees are encouraged to undertake self-appraisal, which is simply looking critically at one's own work and seeking ways to improve its quality or finding easier, more efficient ways of performing it.

Self-appraisal has the advantage of making the employee more responsible for his own work. However, one disadvantage is that the worker may not be aware of his/her own faults or know how to improve.

Activity

This is an opportunity for you to carry out self-appraisal of your own performance in school for the school year so far. Take the exercise seriously because it could help you to improve your standard. Include all areas of your school life – examination subjects, sport, extra-curricular activity, etc.

1 Write down what you feel you have done well.

2 List the areas where you have not done so well.

3 Examine why you did not perform so well in those areas.

4 Finally, think of ways in which you could improve your weak points. It may be useful to get the help of your teacher to do this.

Activity

Match the appropriate sections in the following table. The first one has been worked for you.

Appraisal is	training requirements for staff
Performance related pay	is watched doing his/her work
Appraisal is used to identify	is known as the appraisee
Employees benefit from appraisal as it	profitability should improve
Employers use appraisal to help them	assessing an employee's performance
As a result of appraisal the firm's	an interview
Observation is where the employee	is known as the appraiser
Observation is usually accompanied by	is not suitable for all types of work
The employee who is being appraised	to increase staff competence
The person carrying out the appraisal	allows them to achieve their full potential
An appraisal interview is a one-to-one	at one's own work
Self-appraisal is looking critically	discussion between appraiser and appraisee

Checklist

At this stage you should be able to:

- explain the importance of appraisal and the reasons for it
- explain the benefits of appraisal for employees
- explain the benefits of appraisal for employers
- identify and describe the main methods of appraisal.

6

BUSINESS GROWTH

Theme 6.1

Business growth

Any form of expansion of the firm is an example of business growth.

Business success or failure

Present-day businesses cannot stand still. If they are not being successful, they will be unable to re-pay their loans to banks, to pay their employees or to pay their suppliers for stock. In this case, the bank and other creditors will force the business to close down in order to recover the money due to them.

The most obvious **signs of success** are:

- increased sales
- increased profit levels
- increased share of the market
- healthy cash flow
- business expansion
- opening more branches
- recruiting more employees
- up-to-date premises
- valuable assets
- improved product range.

The most obvious **signs of failure** are:

- decreased sales and lack of customers
- frequent discount offers
- cash flow problems
- decreasing profit levels
- dilapidated premises
- closing some branches
- staff redundancies.

A successful business will show signs of growth. Perhaps it will extend its premises and the range of its products. A business which does not keep up-to-date with the needs of consumers will not be as successful as it might be.

You will remember from your work on business aims that growth is one of a business's main aims. Theme 6.1 looks at growth in greater depth.

First of all, what is meant by 'business growth'?

Why businesses may grow

Listen to some of the reasons why business owners say they wish to achieve growth:

Growth would make my business more powerful and influential.

Business growth is likely to achieve increased profits.

If my business were bigger, it would make economies of scale possible.

A larger business would secure a larger share of the market and help my sales.

If my business grows, it may put some of my competitors out of business.

The positives (benefits) and negatives of growth are summarised here:

Benefits of growth	Negatives of growth
Increased profit	Poor communication because the business becomes too large
Increased publicity	Lack of motivation because the employees may not know the owners
Economies of scale (see following section)	Branches of the organisation may be difficult to coordinate

Economies of scale

Economies of scale are gained when an increase in production causes a decrease in production costs.

Economies of scale can be illustrated by an example from the newspaper industry. It would be very expensive to produce a single copy of a newspaper because all the major costs in newspaper production – costs of research, writing, designing and laying out the newspaper – would have to be met even for one copy.

However, when several thousand copies of the newspaper are printed the costs do not multiply in proportion to the number of copies. The costs of researching, writing, designing and laying out the newspaper are the same regardless of the number printed, and the only additional costs are extra paper, ink and electricity.

There are three main types of economies of scale (although there are several others as well).

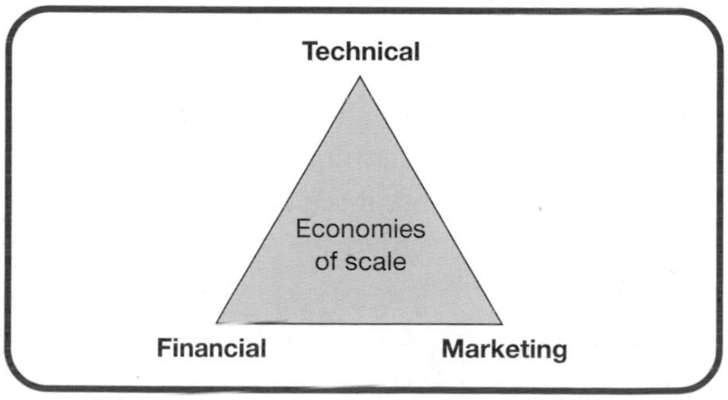

Marketing economies of scale

Marketing economies of scale are gained in situations where the business can save in expenses associated with marketing such as advertising and distribution.

For example, it costs the same sum to deliver ten boxes of goods in one lorry load as it does to deliver a single box of goods. For this reason, firms try to combine goods in one consignment and pick up other goods to use the vehicle economically on the return journey.

A large business is charged the same rate for advertising as a small business. However, in a large business advertising expenditure is less per unit of production than it is in a small business which is producing on a smaller scale. For this reason, a large firm can afford to undertake more advertising than a small firm can. The larger firm is also likely to increase its sales, as a result of the advertising, by more than the small firm.

Large firms such as Marks & Spencer can take advantage of economies of scale

Technical economies of scale

Technical economies of scale are gained in situations where the business can cut its production costs by introducing upgraded technology or by altering its production methods. Increased mechanisation will speed up production and allow the firm to use the mass production method. In this way, costs of labour and power are lowered and overhead expenses such as rates are more effectively used.

Large businesses usually can afford more advanced technology than small businesses, so technical economies of scale are often of more benefit to larger firms.

Financial economies of scale

Financial economies of scale are gained in situations where the business can borrow money or otherwise gain finance by cheaper methods.

Large businesses, in general, provide better security and fewer risks for banks therefore banks are willing to allow them to borrow larger sums for longer periods of time and at better rates.

Activity

Which type of economy of scale which is described in each of the following?

1 Fleet Delivery Ltd uses vans instead of lorries when small loads are being delivered.

2 The Premier Furniture Company has installed computerised machinery in its production plant.

3 A large group of supermarkets, Finest Foods, has been offered a lower rate of interest on a bank loan than Gillian Little who runs a small grocery shop.

4 Paul Kennedy, the manager of Finest Foods, uses the same advertisements to promote all shops in the chain.

5 The Fresh Bakery merged with The Daily Bread Company and increased its product range by using the flow production method.

6 The City Book Store is able to purchase books on credit from its main supplier because of the large size of its orders.

Main ways in which businesses may grow

Businesses may grow either internally (organically) or externally.

Internal (organic) growth

Internal growth (also referred to as organic growth) takes place inside the business, and without any reference to other businesses. Internal growth is slow to achieve and is a gradual process. The purpose of internal growth – like all growth – is to become better and stronger than other firms in the same type of business.

To achieve internal growth, a firm will:

- plough back its profits
- develop new markets for its products
- develop new products.

Activity

There are probably examples of internal growth in your town or area. To complete this activity you should do some local research to discover the information required.

1 Name any shops in your area which have increased their floor space or opened new branches recently.

2 Find out if any of your local hotels have plans to open, or have opened recently, new facilities such as a leisure centre or conference complex.

3 Find examples where any of the local factories are recruiting extra employees, introducing the latest technology, developing new products or expanding their markets abroad.

All of these are examples of internal growth in your local area.

External growth

External growth is a much faster type of growth and involves the bringing together of a number of organisations to form a single business. External growth may be achieved through amalgamations, mergers, integrations, takeovers or franchising.

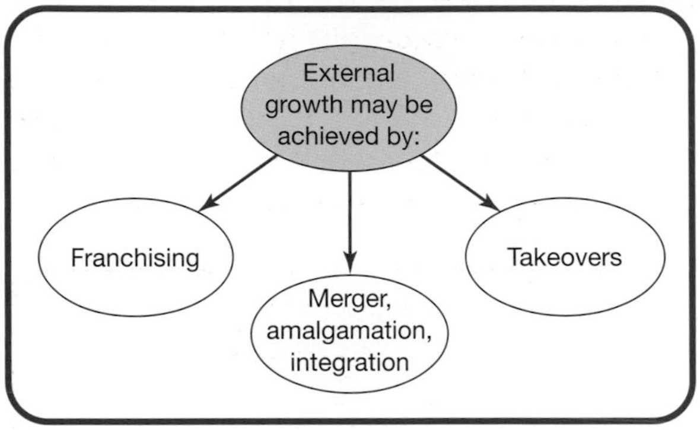

Franchising

Franchising is a popular method by which companies expand their operations and open shops in various parts of the country. McDonald's is the world's largest chain of fast food restaurants and is probably the best example of franchising. In 2009, there are 31,000 McDonald's restaurants, operating in 119 countries, all over the world. They claim to serve 47 million customers per day. This number grew, through franchising, from the first United Kingdom restaurant opened in 1974.

For further details on franchising, you should refer back to Theme 1.3 of this book.

Takeover

A takeover takes place when one business buys over the control of another business. To achieve a takeover, a firm would have to buy a large number of shares so that it could control the voting in the other firm. The firm wishing to gain control would offer very high prices to the existing shareholders for their shares in order to secure them.

Takeovers frequently are hostile and not welcomed by the firm which is being taken over. In other cases, takeovers are agreed and the firm being taken over would advise its shareholders to accept the high offers for their shares. In an agreed takeover, the firm being taken over welcomes the opportunity to be part of a larger organisation and gain from its resources.

Merger/amalgamation

A merger or amalgamation is a voluntary and agreed joining of two firms in order to form one larger business. It could be seen as a marriage between two businesses.

In the case of a merger, all the capital as well as all resources and assets such as premises, machinery and personnel are joined together in one organisation.

This arrangement has several benefits:

- Savings are made because one merged organisation is able to operate with less equipment and other resources than two
- There would be no duplication in running costs
- Fewer administrative staff and directors are required to run a single firm
- The business would be operating on a larger scale so would benefit from discounts for bulk purchases of supplies
- The market share would be increased and sales would be improved
- The firms would be working together rather than as rivals to one another.

Mergers have some drawbacks:

- There is a possibility of staff redundancies
- Consumers have less choice
- Competition is reduced.

Integration

To integrate means to 'combine parts into a whole'. In business, integration is achieved through mergers and takeovers. There are three main types of integration:

1 Horizontal integration.

2 Vertical integration.

3 Lateral integration.

Horizontal integration

Horizontal integration takes place between firms on the same level within the same type of business. For example, if two confectionery shops, 'Sweet Temptations' and 'Sweet Things' decided to merge it would be horizontal integration because they both had previously been selling sweets and chocolate to consumers.

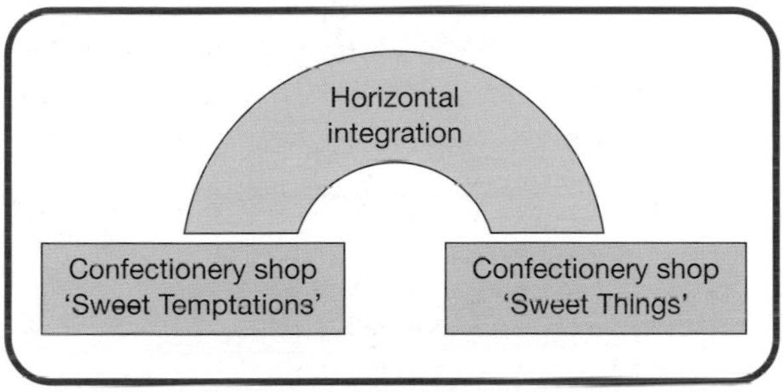

Vertical integration

Vertical integration takes place between firms on different levels within the same type of business. For example, if a chocolate factory decided to merge with a confectionery shop it would be vertical integration. This is because, although both firms were involved in the confectionery business, they were working at different stages of the chain of production – one was manufacturing the chocolate while the other was selling it.

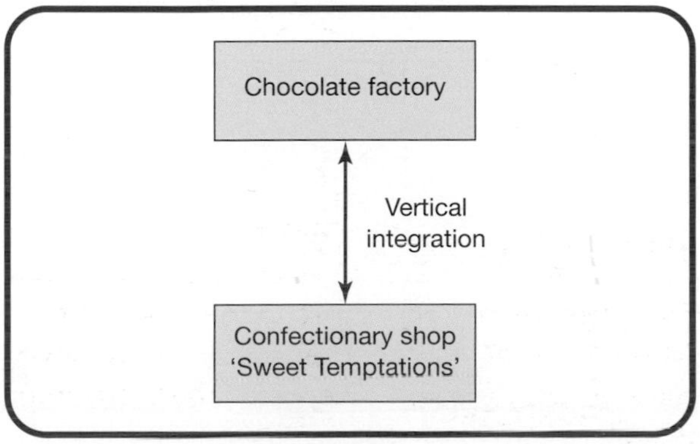

There are two types of vertical integration:

- **Backward vertical integration**. This is where a firm expands by taking over another firm which works with the same product but at an earlier stage in its chain of production. In the previous example, if the chocolate factory took over a cocoa plantation, it would be backward vertical integration because the factory actually makes the chocolate bars while the cocoa plantation grows the cocoa plants from which the chocolate is produced.

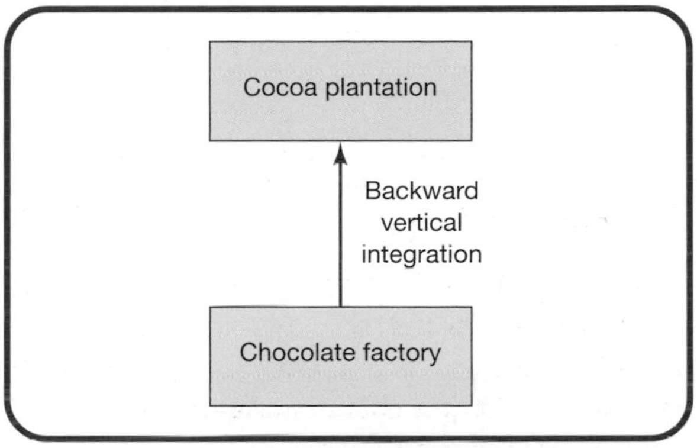

- **Forward vertical integration**. This is where a firm expands by taking over another firm which works with the same product but at a later stage in its chain of production. To use the same example again, if the chocolate factory were to take over the confectionery shop, it would be forward vertical integration because it makes the chocolate bars while the shop works with the chocolate at the later stage of selling it to the consumer.

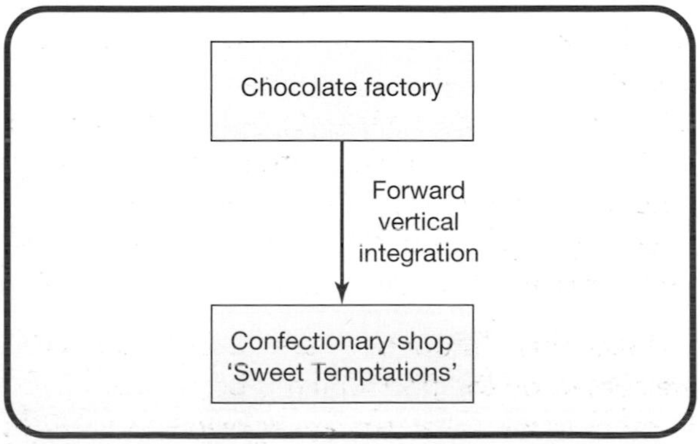

Lateral integration

Lateral integration takes place when a firm expands by merging with another firm which is in a related but different area. They were not in direct competition before integration took place. Their products may be similar but not identical and the types of skills required to make or handle the products are very alike. For example, if the chocolate factory were to merge with an ice-cream factory, the type of integration would be lateral.

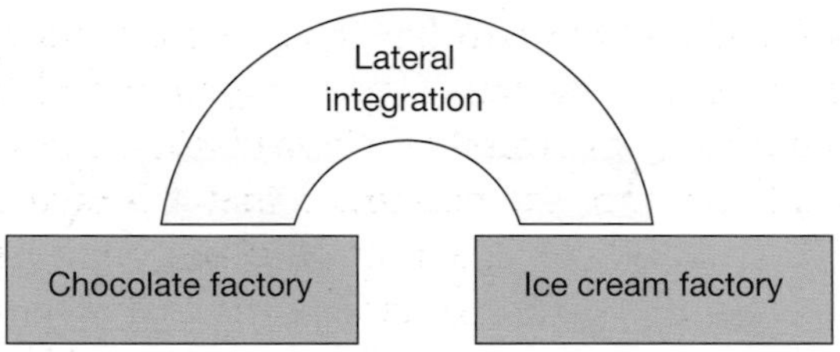

Conglomerate

This is the most usual type of merger and brings together firms whose products are totally unrelated and dissimilar. The firms may or may not be working at the same level of production.

This type of merger is also known as diversification, and it takes place mainly because the firm is expecting a decline in one of its markets and it is branching out into other lines as a safeguard. An example of a conglomerate would be the merger between the chocolate factory, a jewellery shop and a restaurant.

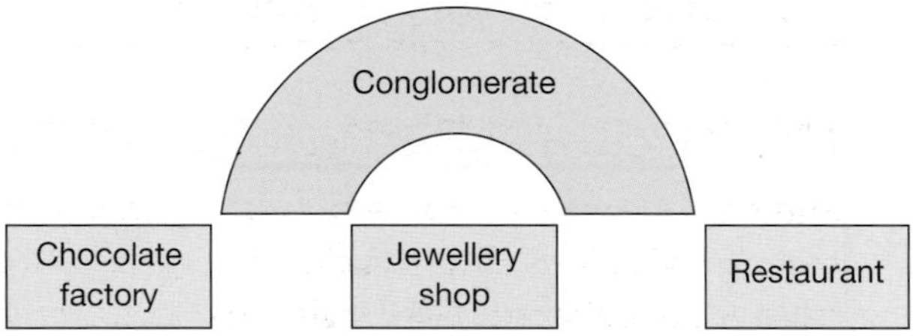

Activity

All of the businesses named here are based in one county. A number of them are considering some type of integration. Study each possibility and write down, in the spaces provided, which type of integration each would be.

Businesses	Type of integration
A filling station links with another filling station	
A bakery joins with a bread shop	
A filling station joins with a chip shop and the bakery	
A supermarket opens another branch in a different area of town	
A large public house and restaurant takes control of a smaller public house and restaurant	
Two hairdressers agree to join their businesses and work together	
A retailer of furniture links with a furniture factory	
The furniture retailer joins his business with a retailer of bathroom fittings	

Activity

Superfood is a chain of supermarkets with outlets in Belfast, Bangor, Ballyclare, Enniskillen, Portadown and Coleraine. It hopes to merge its business activities with Allworth Suppliers Ltd – a food manufacturer which supplies and distributes goods to food retailers including Superfood.

1 What type of merger is described here?

2 Why do you think that Superfood want to merge with Allworth Suppliers Ltd?

Implications for a business of the different methods of growth

Internal (organic) growth

Internal growth is very slow and gradual. The main implication of this is that the owners may have little personal gain from the business for many years as they plough back its profits. They will also have to look continuously for new markets and new products in order to gain some competitive advantage over its competitors.

External growth

The main implication of external growth is the loss of control of the business and the introduction of shared management and decision making.

Franchising

A franchised business has to accept that policy is dictated by the franchising company and that there is no opportunity for individuality. The main implication for the business is that it is seen as a branch of a large chain rather than a business in its own right. The owner is seen as a manager rather than as an owner. On the positive side, the implications are that the franchised business enjoys the reputation and ready made market which come with being part of a large enterprise.

Takeover

Where a takeover has been hostile, the main implications for the new business are strained relationships at managerial level and enforced control by an outside company. On the other hand, the new firm is likely to enjoy greater prosperity as a result of being part of a larger organisation.

Merger

The implications for a newly merged firm are the increase in business which comes from a larger operation resulting in economies of scale and greater profits. As with all joined organisations, methods have to be worked out whereby two workforces and two sets of managers can work as one. A merger has the added implication of shared resources without costly duplication. Another implication is the possibility of staff redundancies.

Horizontal integration

As well as all the implications of a merger, the most important implication in a horizontal integration is the elimination of a competitor in the marketplace.

Backward vertical integration

The principal implication in a backward vertical integration is that the company is assured a supply of raw materials over which it has total control. For example, the chocolate factory discussed earlier is assured supplies of cocoa for its production from its own cocoa plantation. It also has total control over the price of the cocoa.

Forward vertical integration

One of the main implications of forward vertical integration is that the company has an outlet for its products. For example, the chocolate factory, by taking over the confectionery shop, now has its own retail outlet where it can control sales of its own product.

Lateral integration

In lateral integration some economies of scale can take place through joint production. There are also opportunities for joint marketing campaigns for the benefit of both products.

Conglomerate

The main implication for a business involved in a conglomerate is the safeguard given through having a variety of commercial interests. If one aspect of the business should prove to be unprofitable, the other products can compensate.

Factors which may limit the growth of firms

While the majority of firms wish to grow and expand for the reasons stated at the beginning of this theme, others may not have the same ambition.

The very nature of specialised businesses such as dress designers or cabinet makers depends on those businesses being small-scale. Their work is done through expensive orders for hand-made articles for which mass production would not be appropriate. To grow into large organisations would take away from their high quality and individuality.

Other firms may, however, wish to expand but may be limited in their efforts to do so. This limitation could be caused by a variety of factors which also influence the firm's growth or decline:

- **Lack of finance**. Expansion and growth require capital. Capital would be needed to obtain the necessary premises, machinery and other resources for the enlarged operation. If the firm cannot raise the required capital it would be impossible for it to expand properly.
- **Competition**. A business may also be curtailed by very strong rivals who are much bigger and can sell products to consumers at lower prices. This is the case with small shopkeepers who are unable to expand because of the strength of large chain stores which take away their trade.
- **Consumer taste**. Some consumers prefer to shop in small boutiques where they are likely to be able to buy more exclusive goods than in large chain stores. However, it is difficult for such shops to compete with the chain stores because of the prices they have to charge.
- **Lack of entrepreneurial skills**. A spirit of entrepreneurship is also needed in a business

which would make it possible to see the opportunities and take the risks involved in expansion.

- **Lack of expertise**. A business could also be hampered by a lack of expertise. If expansion opportunities arise, the business needs to have a well-trained staff who are capable of undertaking the more advanced work.
- **Lack of information and poor communication**. In order for a business to expand, it is necessary for it to have a good communications network. This would give the firm the necessary information about the market and its up-to-date requirements.

Social and moral implications of growth

The modern tendency in retailing, especially in grocery and light hardware items, is for very large supermarkets to be situated in shopping centres in larger towns or on their outskirts. These large stores are very attractive to shoppers because they offer a wide variety of goods under one roof and at low prices. In addition they offer the convenience of being able to use trolleys and the car parks provided. All of these factors lead to the further success and growth of the large supermarkets.

The growth of the large firms has taken place at the expense of the traditional small retailers in town centres and villages throughout the country. Those situated in towns have been hardest hit because they are close to the large supermarkets and also have parking problems. Small retailers situated further away in villages have survived because of their convenience to local communities although they too are struggling.

The social implications of this drift to towns could become serious for the rural community in Northern Ireland. It is taking jobs and business away from villages. It is also damaging rural community life and increasing traffic on the roads as people are forced to travel to towns to shop.

Castle Court Centre, Belfast

Perhaps the groups who are most adversely affected are the elderly and non-drivers who are losing the convenience of local shopping.

There is also a moral debate centring on the growth of large shops at the expense of small retailers. It is true that the big get bigger while the small struggle, and everyone has a personal view on the situation. On the one hand, it could be argued that the large shops are providing a necessary service because they are supported and people obviously wish to shop there because of their lower prices and convenience. On the other hand, it could be argued that there will always be a role for small shops because of their personal service and local situation.

The Competition Commission

The Competition Commission was established to investigate mergers and to make sure that mergers between businesses are fair to consumers.

The Competition Commission (CC) was set up in 1999. It is an independent body which has been established for the purpose of investigating mergers and monopolies. It conducts in-depth inquiries into mergers and the regulation of major industries.

Such inquiries are necessary in order to protect consumers. This is because a merger between businesses could make one very large business and could eliminate competition. Without competition, it would be possible for a business to charge customers very high prices. The aim of the Competition Commission is to make markets work well for consumers by increasing the level of competition.

The Commission has two functions:

- It carries out inquiries into monopolies and mergers
- It hears appeals against decisions made on monopolies and mergers and on the abuse of market power.

The Competition Commission publishes the results of its investigations and its decisions on mergers and monopolies are made on the basis of the public interest.

Checklist

At this stage you should be able to:

- identify signs of business success or failure
- discuss why a business may grow
- describe the main ways a business may grow
- evaluate the implications of the different ways a business may grow
- discuss the factors which limit growth
- describe and explain 'economies of scale'
- analyse the social and moral implications of growth
- understand the role of the Competition Commission.

International trade

International trade is the selling and buying of goods to and from foreign countries.

It is impossible for any country to be totally self sufficient and to be able to meet all its own needs. This is the reason why international trade is actively encouraged by the government.

Benefits and drawbacks of international trade

Benefits of international trade

- **Increased market and profits.** Through international trade, a business can sell its goods in increased quantities. This situation leads to increased profits for the firm.
- **More employment.** Increased sales lead to higher levels of production in the business. This situation gives employment to a greater number of people.
- **Economies of scale**. Increased production creates opportunities for economies of scale. This ultimately results in higher profits for the business.
- **Greater variety.** International trade increases the variety of goods available for consumers. This generally creates a better standard of living in the country. For example, the climate in Northern Ireland is unsuitable for the cultivation of citrus fruits, tea or coffee and, without international trade, these goods would not be available in Northern Ireland. Martin Luther King had this in mind when he once said: 'Before you've finished your breakfast this morning, you'll have relied on half the world.'
- **Political reasons.** The government encourages international trade because it establishes and develops good relations with other countries.

Drawbacks (or difficulties) of international trade

- **Competition.** When a business enters the international market, it will meet stiff competition because there are so many more producers trying to sell their goods. To succeed, a business's marketing and product have to be better than those of its competitors.

- **Production.** Increased markets and increased production may require capital investment and recruitment of additional staff. Accommodation and financial arrangements would have to be made available to undertake this. The firm has to be aware of its capacity for production. If this capacity is exceeded, it will have to make sure that the increased investment would be economical and viable.
- **Distribution.** Distribution on an international scale is much more difficult than for a business which is marketing and selling to the domestic market only. Secure packaging and efficient transport systems all have to be in place. Unless the business is using the internet, it may need to employ agents in the foreign country or else set up a base there.

- **Documentation.** Businesses trading internationally have to be familiar with the documentation required for sending goods abroad. Within the European Union documentation has been simplified, but the problem remains in trade with other countries outside the European Union such as America or the Far East.
- **Language.** Businesses which trade internationally must have at least some members of staff who are capable of speaking, writing and translating the language of the country in which the marketing is taking place.
- **Currency.** Businesses need to be familiar with the currency of the foreign country and be able to sell their products in that currency. Within Europe, this problem has been eased somewhat since many European countries have adopted the euro as its single currency.

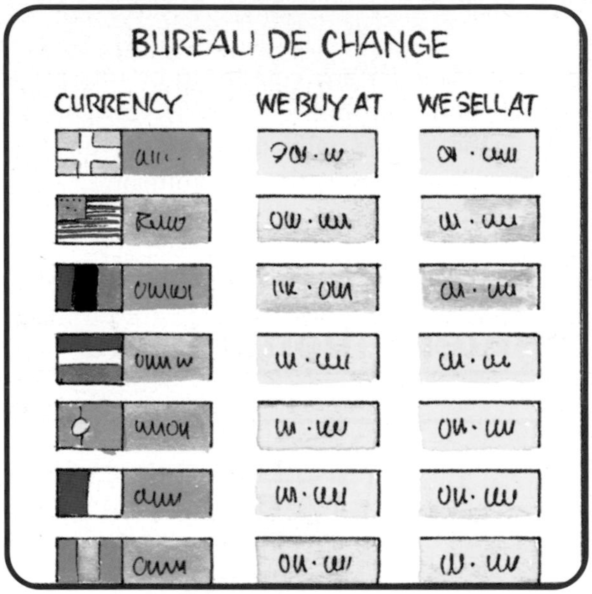

- **Promotional activity.** Increased promotional activity may be required abroad and the promotional material must also be modified to suit the foreign country.
- **Cultural differences.** Exporters have to be conscious of the values and traditions of the country to which they are selling. It is vital that those values and traditions are respected.

Activity

Technoland is a firm which produces computer games. It has decided to market some of its games abroad.

1 Give two reasons why it should market its products abroad.

2 Advise the firm of two drawbacks it may experience in international trade.

How the marketing mix would be affected by international trade

	EFFECT
PRODUCT	• May have to change to suit the legal requirements of the foreign country • Must suit the technical set-up in the foreign country. For example, electrical sockets are different in the UK from other European countries
PRICE	• Needs to reflect what the market in the foreign country would be willing to pay • Has to be set at a level to cover taxes • Has to consider exchange rate variations • Has to be quoted in the appropriate currency
PROMOTION	• Must be in appropriate language • Must consider any possible cultural differences • Must be a style suitable for the product and the market
PLACE	• Product must be available in places where the target market would be able to buy it • Suitable transportation must be arranged • Suitable packaging has to be available

Implications of the global market for the local economy

The global market simply refers to trading on a worldwide scale (around the globe).

Every business, no matter how small, can now think of the whole world as being its marketplace if its product is the type of product which is demanded in other countries. The present situation has been thought of as a second industrial revolution.

Many of Northern Ireland's businesses are small. Previously those smallest businesses had a narrow market base and would not have considered exporting to be a viable option. The global market now presents that opportunity. It also presents massive competition from businesses around the world.

The business which can overcome the competition will survive and its market will continue to expand. This will result in increased employment and further opportunities. The business which cannot overcome the competition will fail and result in redundancies for its employees.

However, it may be beyond the scope of small businesses to respond positively to the competition. For this reason, mergers of businesses into larger units may be the answer to the need for increased capital in order to take advantage of economies of scale.

Globalisation has been made possible partly by:

- the lifting of import controls between countries
- the advances of technology in general but especially due to the continuing development of the internet. It is estimated, that the internet

population has doubled each year since 1988, and now the internet is available in nearly every home throughout the developed world. Other components of technology are also developing continually.

Northern Ireland is a small country and, as part of an island on the extreme western side of Europe, it is geographically remote. These facts present difficulties for businesses in Northern Ireland which do not have to be considered by businesses in other, more central locations. Technology succeeds in reducing the effects of that remoteness and offers connection with potential customers all over the world.

The global market provides many challenges for local businesses, but it also presents definite opportunities. The questions now are 'How can those opportunities be grasped?' and 'How can the difficulties be overcome?'

The main implications of the global market for the local economy are as follows:

- **The need for the cultivation of a wide vision**. The Report by the Economic Development Strategy Review Group 'Strategy 2010' recommends that students should have language skills in a variety of languages and should have opportunities to participate in international exchanges. The Report also stresses the value of town twinning arrangements which develop opportunities for exports and joint ventures as well as other inward investment projects and links. These are seen by the Review Group as being ways of widening the vision of Northern Ireland's population.
- **Businesses need training and practical experience**. Training and practical experience of export marketing is required in order to be able to avail of marketing opportunities abroad.
- **Local businesses need to be able to use the available technology competently**. Local businesses need to be using modern technology fully, and at an equal level to any of the other regions of Europe. The practical implications of this fact are capital investment in technology accompanied by training in the use of technology.
- **Stiffer competition for businesses in Northern Ireland**. This could result in the closure of some manufacturing companies and the redundancy of employees. On the other hand, stiffer competition could have beneficial results for businesses in Northern Ireland. It could be fought with the use of advanced technology and skills, and could result in increased trading and employment. The outcome of competition is largely determined by how globalisation is regarded and the degree to which it is welcomed.
- **The opportunity for Northern Ireland to trade equally with all other countries**. Using modern technology, communication is equally easy throughout the world. Trading opportunities are equally available everywhere.

If those trading opportunities are taken up, they will result in Northern Ireland having more investment and employment which will lead to improved living standards and a growth in national wealth.

The greatest opportunity for businesses is that of expanding their markets throughout the world. To be able to grasp that opportunity, businesses have to be prepared in advance.

In order to make use of the opportunities of international trade, the business has to:

- research the market abroad to discover if its product has to be modified
- decide on suitable forms of transport for the goods
- cater for the type of packaging required
- understand the documentation required for sending goods abroad
- ensure that its employees are properly trained to undertake extra commitments
- train some staff to speak the foreign language required
- research the political and legal system of the foreign country concerned
- make sure that its machinery and equipment are capable of coping with increased demands
- examine the culture of the foreign country concerned
- put in place a suitable pricing policy
- make provision for the return of goods

Careful packing is needed for this product

International trade has also opened up opportunities for every other business as well, and this results in a situation of increased competition. Where there is competition, producers have to compete to persuade consumers to buy their products. The reality is that only the best survive.

In order to combat the competition and keep ahead, the business has to:

- innovate by changing its product in a way which makes it unique and more desirable than other products in the same market
- make sure that the quality of the product is of the highest possible standard
- reduce its prices below the level of the competitors
- offer special inducements with the sale
- supply the goods in the shortest possible time
- offer a personal service.

Cultural dimension of international marketing

Any business which is trading internationally needs to have an appreciation of the traditions, culture and legislation of the countries with which it is dealing. It is important that those aspects of the foreign way of life are respected.

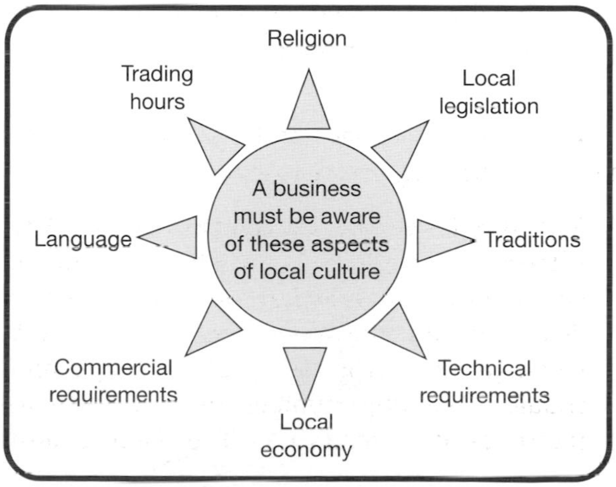

Language

A knowledge of the foreign language is a basic requirement. This is needed for complete understanding of the transaction taking place, and also for the correct translation of instructions on the packaging of the product.

Traditions

It is important that local traditions, beliefs and customs are not offended. For example, some Indians do not regard black clothes as being fashionable, as is the case in this country. Instead, they connect black with evil spirits and therefore would not wish to wear black. This fact has to be understood if successful trade is to be completed.

Religion

The religious culture of a country needs also to be understood and respected. A practice in McDonald's illustrates how one company does this. In McDonald's restaurants in Israel, Big Macs are served without cheese in order to separate meat and dairy products. This separation is required in kosher restaurants in order to fulfil the requirements of Jewish law.

Hours of trading

Climatic conditions are very different abroad and this results in variations of trading hours. For example, it is too hot to work in the afternoon in Italy and shops are closed from 1.00 pm to 5.00 pm. Contact has to be avoided with Italian businesses during those times.

Commercial and technical requirements

Technical specifications, particularly in electrical goods, differ throughout the world. Products may have to be modified for use abroad.

Local legislation

Laws vary from country to country. It is important to understand these thoroughly so that they are not broken.

Local economy

It would be impossible to set a price for a product and sell it at the same price in every country. What the local market would bear and what the local people could pay must be considered.

McDonald's are found throughout the world offering the same products for sale. However, the price at which those products are sold varies according to what local people could spend, and also according to the price charged by their competitors in that particular country.

Activity

Match the parts of the sentences in the following table appropriately.

Knowledge of a foreign language is needed	must be respected in international trade
Prices vary throughout the world	differences in trading hours
Local traditions, beliefs and customs	particularly in electrical goods
Climatic conditions cause	to suit the religion of the other country
Products may have to be modified	to suit the local economies
Technical specifications differ throughout the world	to understand the transaction taking place

The role of the European Union (EU)

The United Kingdom and Ireland are members of the European Union which is an economic and political union of a total of twenty-seven member states (at the time of writing).

The full list of members

Austria	Belgium
Bulgaria	Cyprus
Czech Republic	Denmark
Estonia	Finland
France	Germany
Greece	Hungary
Ireland	Italy
Latvia	Lithuania
Luxembourg	Malta
Netherlands	Poland
Portugal	Romania
Slovakia	Slovenia
Spain	Sweden
United Kingdom	

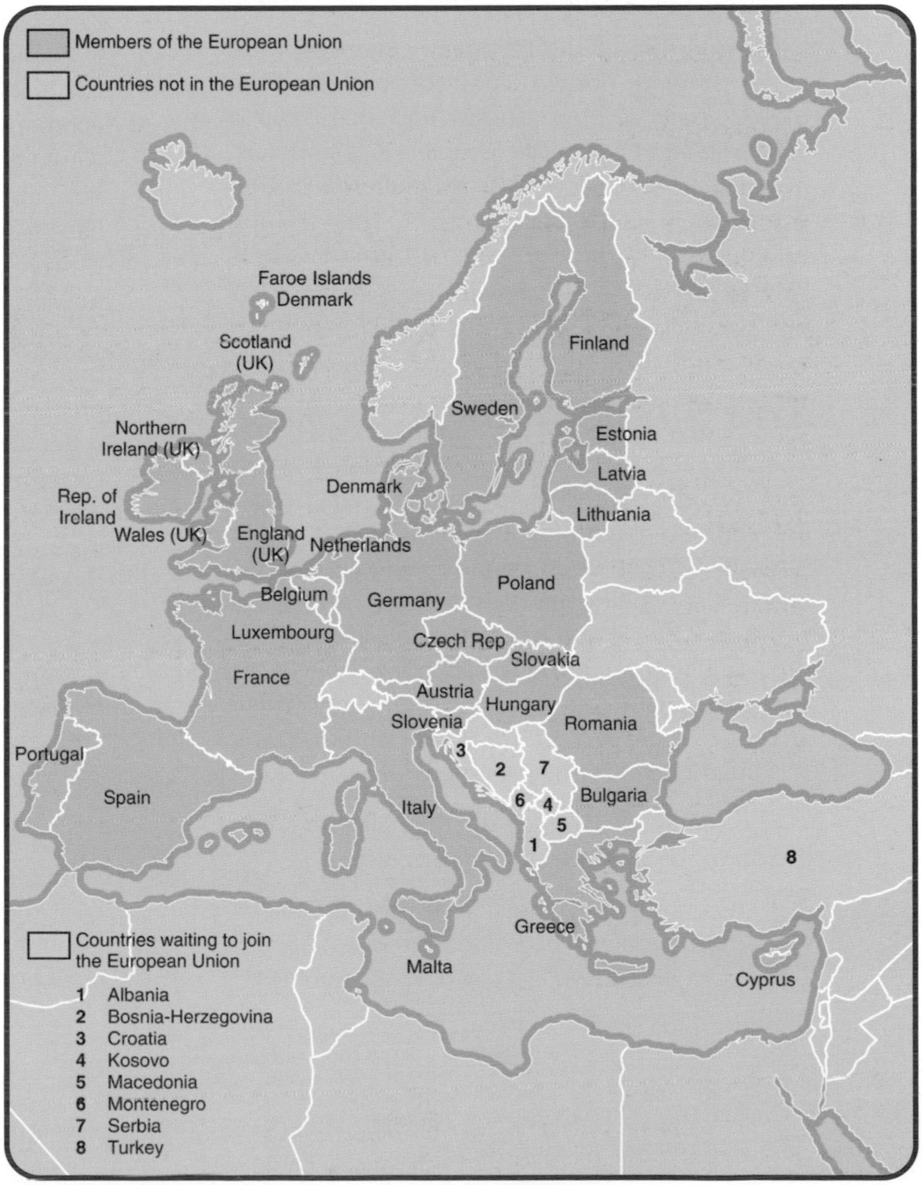

Altogether there are approximately 500 million citizens in the European Union and the area generates an estimated 30% of the world's trade. A variety of languages are spoken by the member states and a variety of currencies used, although many have adopted the euro. The European Union's aim is to promote social and economic progress among its members.

All member states are represented in the European Union Parliament from where directives (Community laws) are issued. Directives outline the objectives which the EU wishes to achieve and are binding on all member states, but it is up to the government in each country to choose how to implement those directives in that particular country.

Membership of the European Union provides better trading opportunities for businesses in those twenty-seven countries and opens up a wide market of potential customers and suppliers. It is easier to trade in this market than other overseas markets as many of the trading practices, regulations and standards apply throughout the European Union. This is largely due to the introduction of the Single Market.

The Single Market

The Single Market freed up the trade of goods and services and the movement of people between EU countries. The aim is that doing business with other EU countries should become more like doing business within your own country. The Single Market also intended to provide better opportunities for the people of the European Union by providing full employment and lead to improved standards of living and sustained economic development.

The Single Market set up the following four freedoms, details of which are given here.

1. Freedom of movement of people and labour
   - Citizens of any part of the European Union can live and work in any other part of the EU
   - Professional qualifications should be recognised in any area of the EU
   - Social Security benefits would be transferable between EU countries
2. Freedom of movement of goods
   - Companies can sell their products anywhere in the European Union and consumers can buy where they want
   - There are no quotas or tariffs
   - Standards of goods have been made the same to ensure that they are acceptable throughout the EU
   - The major benefit of this freedom is that a business has the possibility of expanding its trade over the entire area and increasing its productivity
   - Efficient businesses could benefit from economies of scale and lower costs. This would result in increased profit
   - Administrative procedures and taxation have been simplified
   - Custom duty is not charged on good moving between EU countries
   - The major drawback of this freedom is that competition would become much greater and inefficient companies would suffer a loss of market share.
   - Consumers benefit from a wider range of products in the market
   - Increased competition should also make goods cheaper for consumers
3. Freedom of movement of capital
   - Currencies and capital can flow freely between any areas of the European Union
   - EU citizens can use financial services in any European Union country
   - Foreign exchange controls were eliminated
4. Freedom of movement of services
   - Professional services such as banking, insurance or advertising can be offered in any European Union country.

Checklist

At this stage you should understand:

- the benefits of marketing abroad
- the drawbacks of marketing abroad
- how the various elements of the marketing mix of a business would be affected by international trade
- the implications of the global market for the local economy
- the role of the European Union (EU).

Theme 6.3

E-commerce

E-commerce (electronic commerce) is the on-line transaction of goods and services, and the transfer of funds through digital communications.

E-commerce involves carrying out business over the internet and operates by linking computer systems between buyer and seller. Most people are familiar with electronic transactions between a business and a consumer (B2C). Amazon.com is a popular example. E-commerce may also take place between businesses (B2B).

Using modern technology, trading opportunities are available throughout the world. However, e-commerce has opened up those same opportunities for every other business as well, and this results in a situation of increased competition. Where there is competition, businesses have to compete to persuade consumers to buy their goods or services. The reality is that only the best survive.

This section gives details of the advantages and disadvantages of e-commerce for both businesses and consumers. You will notice that sometimes these will be similar for both groups.

Advantages of e-commerce for a business

- Business can be conducted at any time – even when the store is closed
- The business can source and use products and services from a range of international firms
- E-commerce provides opportunities for increased sales on a world-wide basis
- It expands the market from regional to global
- It leads to increased productivity
- It increases turnover and profits
- It allows the business to become better known
- Payment for the goods is made immediately
- Payment is more secure than by cheque
- Transactions can be processed very quickly
- E-commerce allows the business to access a greater range of customers
- Therefore e-commerce is excellent for specialist markets where customers would be few
- Overhead costs are reduced – e.g. sales can be made from warehouses instead of high street premises where rates are high
- Marketing costs are reduced
- Fewer sales personnel are required for e-commerce, saving wages
- Processing errors are less likely to occur
- It is easy to deal with repeat orders as all details are stored on computer
- Direct communication with customers can be made by e-mail
- It saves having to print catalogues and update price lists regularly. Instead web pages are easily edited.

Advantages of e-commerce for customers

- It is possible to log-on to the internet at any time of the day or night
- It is possible to access the websites of firms throughout the world
- Gives a greater choice of goods so customer can 'shop around'
- It is possible to research and compare prices between businesses
- Customers are not charged according to the distance they are from the business

- Websites give maximum information about products
- This leads to better customer satisfaction
- It is very convenient to shop from home
- Time is saved by not having to visit shops
- Transactions are almost immediate unlike via a catalogue which takes a longer time
- Goods are generally cheaper as business expenses are reduced
- Repeat orders are easy as information can be stored on computer
- Direct communication with the business can be made electronically
- Electronic price lists are up-to-date.

Disadvantages of e-commerce for a business

- Competition is increased
- An attractive website and efficient electronic system are essential
- Efficient packing and reliable transport systems must be in place
- E-commerce is not suitable for perishable goods
- Customers dislike buying very expensive goods, such as jewellery, without seeing them
- The business must be aware of differing cultures of customers
- The business must understand different legal requirements in other countries
- The business needs to be able to cope with many languages
- Payment providers, e.g. PayPal, usually charge commission for their services.

Disadvantages of e-commerce for customers

- Lack of trust of payment system is the greatest disadvantage
- Security issues and fear of personal information being wrongly used by hackers
- Customers must have credit cards for payment
- Customers must be linked to the internet
- Customers must understand the technology
- If goods are required immediately, it is necessary to buy from a shop
- There are some poor websites which may offer poor value
- There is no guarantee of product quality
- E-commerce is not suitable for perishable goods
- The customer is unable to handle the goods before purchase
- Returning goods can be a nuisance
- Some customers resist change and dislike faceless, non-physical transactions
- A few websites require special software not common in standard systems
- Some customers may find the use of foreign currencies confusing.

Activity

Beetroot Blue is a delivery service of sandwiches and finger foods to homes and meetings. It operates in Scotland. To see an example of this service being offered through the internet, visit www.beetrootblue.com

Activity

Copy the following table and match the parts of the sentences appropriately.

E-commerce increases competition	to have a credit card for payment
Security issues in e-commerce	sales staff are not required
In e-commerce a customer's needs	perishable goods
Wages are saved in e-commerce because	to have an attractive website
In e-commerce it is necessary	greatly concern customers
E-commerce is not suitable for	which is a disadvantage for a business

Checklist

At this stage you should be able to:

- understand what e-commerce is
- analyse the advantages of e-commerce for a business
- analyse the advantages of e-commerce for customers
- analyse the disadvantages of e-commerce for a business
- analyse the disadvantages of e-commerce for customers
- understand how e-commerce supports international trade.

7 BUSINESS PLAN

7.1 Business plan

Theme 7.1

Business plan

A business plan is a detailed description of what a business hopes to do over a period of usually one to five years.

The business plan shows the business's:

- costs during that period
- expected level of sales and income
- timescale for starting to make a profit
- expectation of when it would be able to repay loans.

If you were travelling by car from your home to Cork, you would consult a map before you started out and that would act as a guide for your route. On the actual journey you would refer frequently to the map or to the signs along the road to make sure that you were going in the right direction.

A business plan is just like a map because it acts as a guide for the business and can be referred to frequently to make sure the business is meeting its targets.

The name 'plan' indicates that a business plan is for the future, but it has to cover quite a short period of time because it is not possible in business to predict what will happen in the longer term with any degree of certainty.

The importance of planning in business cannot be over-emphasised. According to a study carried out by the Federation of Small Businesses, 400,000 small businesses were set up one year, 55,000 of which failed. The major factor for failure was given as inadequate planning. Another study found that companies which had planned properly had 50% more income and profit growth than firms which did not have clear plans.

Going into business without a business plan is like trying to drive a car without a steering wheel – there is no way of directing it!

A business plan would be worked either by a new business or by a business wishing to expand – perhaps by bringing out new products or by selling in new markets.

Reasons for developing a business plan

- **To show to the bank.** A new business, or one which is hoping to expand, is likely to need to borrow money from the bank or other source. The bank manager would be unwilling to lend money unless he/she was reasonably sure that the business would be able to repay both the loan and the interest on the loan. The purpose of a business plan is to work out accurately the amount of money which is required, and then to convince the bank manager that the business idea is viable and that the loan is a safe investment from the bank's point of view.
- **To show to shareholders.** The business would probably have shareholders who have invested finance in the business. They will use the business plan to gauge the strength of the business, and to decide whether or not they wish to remain as shareholders.

- **To show to other possible investors.** The business may hope to encourage other investors to put money into the business. These potential investors would also study the business plan to see if they would receive a worthwhile return on their investment.
- **To ensure proper planning of the business.** The actual process of compiling the business plan is a valuable one because it forces the business owners and managers to think about every tiny detail of the business. This makes sure that nothing is left out and that there are no forgotten costs to be discovered later. This fact also adds to the confidence of the bank manager and other investors who can see that the business idea has been carefully thought out.
- **To monitor actual performance against the plan.** The business plan is also very useful to the managers in the firm who can monitor the actual progress of the business against the plan. The firm's managers will be constantly comparing its performance with how it expected to perform, and they will also compare their performance against that of their competitors.
- **To keep a check on spending.** The accounts produced as part of the business plan will be used to check the monthly figures and any differences can be investigated before they become too great.
- **To ensure that aims are being met.** The business owners and managers would also use the business plan to monitor whether and how the stated aims are being met in the running of the business.

Style of the business plan

Most businesses go to great trouble to make their business plans very professional. Some are bound, but all are presented in covers with the business name and logo. This is to present an image to potential financiers and to make them interested in the business.

Business plans are usually written in the third person, and should be word-processed.

The best way to learn about a business plan is to work one. However, that would be a very long activity so this one has been broken down into sections. By the end of this theme, you should have a complete business plan if you proceed through the theme, step by step.

You are not ready to do this activity unless you have previously studied the different forms of private sector business ownership, business aims, market research, the marketing mix, forecasting, final accounts and the balance sheet.

Activity

This is your chance to put your big ideas into practice! You can now plan to open that business you have always dreamed of and which you just know would be a success.

For those of you who can't think what type of business you might like to run, the following ideas may be helpful. Choose one which would suit your talents and interests, and one which would be likely to be successful in the area where you live.

It is useful if you know some people in that type of business because they could act as your consultants and give you the benefit of their experience.

Some ideas to get you going:

Garden centre and landscape gardening	Music shop
Leisure centre	Day crèche
Artist	Printer
Restaurant or café	Hairdresser
Any type of shop	Fun fair

1 When you have chosen, you should start by thinking of a name for your business and designing a logo for it.

2 You should also carry out some market research at this stage to help you to estimate the demand for your product, your niche market, and the price at which the product will sell.

Components of a business plan

Business plans differ in design and layout but the following information is common to all of them. The sub-headings, and their order, may vary according to the type of business being planned. For example, many business plans have ten to twelve headings, so the following are suggested only as a framework.

- Introduction to proposed business
- The business and its objectives
- Resources plan
- Marketing and marketing mix
- Production plan
- Financial plan
- Appendices.

Introduction to proposed business

- This is where the business makes its first impression and therefore it is very important to get the introduction right. The impact of this page should make people reading the business plan want to invest in the business. The introduction should be short and attention grabbing
- Include the business name and address in the introduction
- The introduction should give a description of the business idea. Describe very clearly what goods or services are to be produced
- Briefly state why that product is marketable and its benefits – for example, it may be especially easy to use.

Classic Computers is the name of a proposed business in Armagh. The business is being planned by Danny Brennan and he is preparing his business plan which he hopes to submit to his bank manager.

Danny has previously carried out market research and he has discovered that there is little competition in the area. He has also found out that there is a demand for high quality computers and for all types of computer software. His research has informed him that his niche market is mainly from the local business community which would like to be able to buy computer supplies locally and quickly. There are large numbers of students in Armagh who would also be an important part of his market.

This is the 'Introduction' which Danny prepared.

CLASSIC COMPUTERS

Business Plan
for a new retailing outlet selling high-quality computer hardware and associated software products

by Danny Brennan

The computer products for sale will be sophisticated models offering the best technology at keen prices

Activity

You are now ready to design and write your introduction. Using the guidelines provided here, prepare the 'Introduction to your Proposed Business' and file it.

The business and its objectives

- This section gives details of the business and explains its work
- The strengths of the business should be shown clearly and its past achievements should be included
- A brief summary of the value of the business and how it has been funded are needed
- This section must show the legal status of the business – is it run and owned by a sole trader, partnership or company?
- Has the business been given any service awards in the past? If so, they should be detailed here
- The goals or objectives of the business should also be described. These are likely to include levels of profit, sales expectations, future product development, etc.
- A mission statement would be appropriate in this section
- The personal details of the owner should be included in this section.

Danny Brennan's proposed business in Armagh is a completely new one so it has not got any past achievements or awards to show.

This is the 'Business and its Objectives' section which Danny has prepared.

Classic Computers – the Business and its Objectives		
Ownership	Danny Brennan and Anne Brennan	
Rented Business Premises	32 High Street ARMAGH	
Private Address	Deanne House 88 Church Spires ARMAGH	
Legal Status	Partnership with two equal partners	
Purpose of the business	Classic Computers is being established for the retail sale of: high quality computers other hardware components high quality software products such as floppy disks and ink cartridges high quality stationery for computer use	
Strengths of the business	Danny Brennan has an established good reputation in this trade and a firm knowledge of this type of business	
Value of the business	Danny and Anne Brennan have joint savings of £20,000 for investment in Classic Computers. Additional funding of £20,000 is being applied for from their bank.	
Business objectives	Projected turnover: £75,000 per annum	Projected gross profit: £40,000 per annum
Mission statement	We aim to match the highest quality products with the highest quality service	

Activity

You are now ready to write the next section of your business plan. Using these guidelines, prepare the 'Business and its Objectives' section and file it with your introduction.

Resources plan

- This section describes the people involved in the business together with details of their special contributions to the business
- It also includes a description of the premises – its size, location and special features
- Details of the equipment available would be appropriate here
- Description of raw materials required – if the business is a manufacturing one
- Required levels of working capital should be estimated.

Danny Brennan's proposed business is a retailing business so it will not have raw materials.

Here is the Resources Plan which Danny has prepared.

Classic Computers – the Resources Plan	
Management	Danny Brennan. In year 1 he will take only £1,000 per month from the business for living expenses
Managerial experience	Danny Brennan has been the manager for ten years with the firm of 'Technology Supplies' in Craigavon. He has established contacts with suppliers in this trade
Clerical assistant	Anne Brennan, working on a part-time, voluntary basis, will assist in the preparation of accounts while retaining her part-time job in the offices of a local accountancy firm
Employees	No other people will be employed at the beginning. Later, it is planned to employ one assistant
Premises	Situated at 32 High Street, Armagh. Premises rented for £300 per month comprising one shop area (40m x 30m), one store (50m x 25m) with street access
Equipment	Shelving and display stands for small items Six desks for computer display with six chairs New delivery van (on credit until July)
Working capital	£15,000 in Year 1 rising to £20,000 in Year 3

Activity

It is your turn now to write the next section of your business plan.

Using the guidelines provided, prepare the resources plan and file it with the remainder of your work.

Marketing and marketing mix

- This section gives details of the likely types of customers for the new product
- Details of the competition should also be shown
- Estimations of the overall demand for the product, projected as far as possible into the future, are included here
- Information received from previous market research about the demand for the new product should be given
- Include a description of where you propose to market the product and how you will distribute it – the *place* part of the marketing mix
- Give details of any expected future developments to the product – the *product* part of the marketing mix
- Details of the price at which the product is to be sold need to be given – the *price* part of the marketing mix
- This section should include details of how the product is to be promoted and advertised – the *promotion* part of the marketing mix.

Have a look at the following marketing plan which Danny has prepared.

Classic Computers – the Marketing Plan and Marketing Mix	
Customers	The main customers are the many business organisations in Armagh and the surrounding area which have indicated that they would value a local supplier. A large number of schools and their students as well as university students living in the area would be part of the market.
Competition	There is one other computer retailer in Armagh. The market is too large for one supplier.
Demand	In the first year, the demand is estimated at 50 computers. Demand for supplies of software is estimated at £15,000 per year and £5,000 for stationery. With increased lines these figures could be doubled within five years.
Suppliers	Main supplier will be 'Ever Ready Technology' who will supply on one month's credit. A second supplier will deliver extra goods in December for cash.
Market place	Sales will be conducted at the premises in Armagh.
Distribution	All computers sold will be delivered and installed. A personal back-up service would be guaranteed.
Future development	Product lines would be extended in later years to include a range of popular computer games and educational packages.
Price	The average prices are: Computer – £1,100 including printer Ink cartridges – £25 Floppy disks – £6 High quality 100g computer paper – £10 per ream
Promotion	Weekly advertising during the first six months in each of the local papers. An opening launch of the business to include viewing and demonstrations of computers. Free mouse mat with every computer sold.

Activity

You can now go ahead with writing your marketing plan. Use the guidelines provided here to help you, and then file your marketing plan with the remainder of your work.

Production plan

- (This section is required only in a manufacturing business)
- A full description of the production process is included in this section
- Details of how the premises will be used in the production process are given
- Details are needed of the layout of the equipment and the design of the work area
- Evidence should be provided that features such as health and safety requirements and ergonomics have been catered for.

Classic Computers is a retailing business and none of the details normally shown in a production plan, apply to it. Danny Brennan, therefore, did not write a production plan.

Activity

If a production plan applies to the business you are setting up, you should prepare it now. When you have it completed, check it against the details of a production plan provided above, and then file your production plan with the remainder of your work.

Financial plan

- A breakeven analysis is required here – in order to show the point at which profit can be expected. This will also show sales estimates
- A cash flow statement is included to explain the likely timing of the firm's income and payments
- A statement of the capital invested by the owners to show the funding of the business
- Details of other loans already given to the business must be shown together with details of the terms of those loans
- Details of mortgages on the premises
- Most recent trading accounts, profit and loss accounts and balance sheet would be included to show the financial history of the business.

Danny Brennan's business is a new one so he has to present forecasted final accounts and balance sheet rather than actual ones. The premises for Classic Computers are rented so Danny does not have a mortgage. He does not have any loans other than the one he is hoping to get from the bank.

The following accounts have been prepared by Danny as his financial plan.

Statement of Capital Invested on 1 January 20....

	£
Danny Brennan	10,000
Anne Brennan	10,000
	£20,000

Cash Flow Forecast for Danny Brennan for Year 1

	Jan	Feb	Mar	Apr	May	June	July	Aug	Sept	Oct	Nov	Dec	Total
Receipts													
Capital	20,000												20,000
Loan	20,000												20,000
Sales	2,648	2,900	3,885	4,298	5,888	6,915	7,850	5,300	6,250	7,541	11,990	9,535	7,5000
Total Receipts	**42,648**	**2,900**	**3,885**	**4,298**	**5,888**	**6,915**	**7,850**	**5,300**	**6,250**	**7,541**	**11,990**	**9,535**	**115,000**
Payments													
Rent	300	300	300	300	300	300	300	300	300	300	300	300	3,600
Purchases		3,125	4,150	5,000	2,500	3,700	1,000	1,000	1,500	8,500	775	23,125	54,375
Rates	100	100	100	100	100	100	100	100	100	100	100	100	1,200
Electricity			200			200			200			200	800
Shelves	750												750
Desks	720												720
Chairs	300												300
Décor	1,500												1,500
Wages	1,000	1,000	1,000	1,000	1,000	1,000	1,000	1,000	1,000	1,000	1,000	1,000	12,000
Advert	200	200	200	200	200	200							1,200
Van							40,000						40,000
Telephone			120			120			120			120	480
Insurance	500										1,000		1,500
Office Stationery	50												50
Loan Interest	80	80	80	80	80	80	80	80	80	80	80	80	960
Total Payments	**5,500**	**4,805**	**6,150**	**6,680**	**4,180**	**5,700**	**42,480**	**2,480**	**3,300**	**9,980**	**3,255**	**24,925**	**119,435**
Opening													
Balance	0	37,148	35,243	32,978	30,596	32,304	33,519	–1,111	1,709	4,659	2,220	10,955	220,220
Add Receipts	42,648	2,900	3,885	4,298	5,888	6,915	7,850	5,300	6,250	7,541	11,990	9,535	115,000
	42,648	40,048	39,128	37,276	36,484	39,219	41,369	4,189	7,959	12,200	14,210	20,490	335,220
Less Payments	5,500	4,805	6,150	6,680	4,180	5,700	42,480	2,480	3,300	9,980	3,255	24,925	119,435
Closing Balance	37,148	35,243	32,978	30,596	32,304	33,519	–1,111	1,709	4,659	2,220	10,955	–4,435	215,785

Forecasted Trading Account of Classic Computers for the year ended 31 December ....

	£	£
Sales		75,000
Less Cost of Sales:		
Purchases	54,375	
Less Closing Stock	20,000	
Cost of Sales		34,375
GROSS PROFIT		£40,625

Forecasted Profit and Loss Account of Classic Computers for the year ended 31 December ....

		£	£
Gross Profit			40,625
Less	Electricity	800	
	Stationery	50	
	Rates	1,200	
	Rent	3,600	
Interest on Loan		960	
Wages		12,000	
Insurance		1,500	
Decoration		1,500	
Advertising		1,200	
Telephone		480	23,290
NET PROFIT			£17,335

Forecasted Balance Sheet of Classic Computers as at 31 December ....

	£	£	£
FIXED ASSETS			
Fixtures and Fittings		750	
Furniture		1,020	
Motor Van		40,000	41,770
CURRENT ASSETS			
Debtors	3,125		
Stock at close	20,000	23,125	
CURRENT LIABILITIES			
Bank Overdraft	4,435		
Creditors	3,125	7,560	
Working Capital			15,565
			£57,335
LONG-TERM LIABILITIES			
Capital		20,000	
Add Net Profit		17,335	37,335
Bank Loan			20,000
			£57,335

Activity

You should now prepare the accounts needed for your financial plan. Go ahead and prepare:

1 A statement of capital

2 A cash flow statement

3 Details of loans and mortgages

4 Most recent (or forecast) trading accounts

5 Most recent (or forecast) profit and loss accounts

6 Most recent (or forecast) balance sheet.

When you have the accounts finished, file them with the rest of your business plan. Be warned that the financial plan is the slowest part of the business plan!

Appendices

An appendix is usually added and acts as a place to show any additional background material. This material might include:

- Any technical information on the product which has not been included previously
- Any additional material from market research
- CVs for the staff
- Photographs and drawings
- Copies of legal documents such as partnership agreements or loan agreements.

Danny Brennan decided to include the following in his business plan:

1 His own CV

2 A copy of his partnership agreement with his wife and business partner, Anne

3 A photograph of the premises he was planning to rent.

Activity

If there are any documents which you can attach as an appendix, you should do so now to complete your business plan.

Well done!

Evaluation of a business plan

Activity

The GCSE specifications require you to be able to evaluate a business plan. It is extremely unlikely that you would have access to a real business plan, but that doesn't really matter.

Instead you should now swap the business plan you have just prepared with another student in your class. Evaluate each other's work constructively – that means that you look for its positive points but also should point out any omissions or details which are unclear.

As you study the business plan you are evaluating, ask yourself:

- Would I lend money to the proposed business?
- Does this business sound profitable?
- Would I want to buy from or sell to the proposed business?
- Do I need any additional information about it?

Checklist

At this stage you should understand:

- the reasons for developing a business plan
- the components of a business plan
- how to construct a business plan
- how to evaluate a business plan.

ASSESSMENT OBJECTIVES AND COMMAND WORDS USED IN THE GCSE (CCEA) BUSINESS STUDIES EXAMINATION

The GCSE examination must examine three assessment objectives and the following table sets out the weightings for each one in the GCSE qualification.

Assessment Objective	Controlled Assessment Weighting	Paper 1 Weighting	Paper 2 Weighting	Overall Weighting
AO1	6%	16%	11%	33%
AO2	10%	12%	14%	36%
AO3	9%	7%	15%	31%
TOTAL	25%	35%	40%	100%

A variety of key terms – known as command words – is used to do this. This list is presented to show the exact requirements of each term used.

AO1

The first assessment objective finds out if candidates can recall, select and communicate knowledge and understanding of concepts, issues and terminology.

Define	Explain the meaning of a term precisely. An example should also be given
Explain or What is/are	Give the details of a topic to show understanding. An example makes the explanation clearer
Name or Give or State or List	Present examples or a list
Identify	Name or list the required information
Outline	Write a short description or a brief summary
Show your calculation	Show the steps leading to the final answer

AO2

The second assessment objective finds out if candidates can apply their knowledge and understanding in a variety of contexts.

Apply	Put into effect in a recognised way
Comment on	Write an explanation or make remarks on the situation
Calculate	Work out the answer to a mathematical question. The formula should be written down, then the appropriate figures should be substituted and finally the answer should be given

Demonstrate or Show or Why	Explain understanding of the business concept being discussed
Describe	Write about the main features of the topic in order to show knowledge of it
Distinguish between	Show the difference between two terms
Examine	Investigate a situation and look closely at the facts and interpret them
Explain	As for AO1
Suggest	Give views on reasons why something has occurred or perhaps on ways to solve a problem
Use the data etc.	Select the required data and apply it to the question asked
Which	Choose the best option

AO3

The third assessment objective finds out if candidates can analyse and evaluate evidence, make reasoned judgements and present appropriate conclusions.

Advise	Give ways in which a problem might be solved or show the best way to do something
Analyse or Examine	Break down information and identify its characteristics. A thorough explanation is necessary but a conclusion is not
Compare/contrast	Consider the similarities and differences between two options. To do this involves looking at the points for and against each option
Discuss	Investigate or examine the topic giving reasons for and against it. A conclusion is necessary
Illustrate	Clarify the topic by means of either an example or visual material
Interpret	Examine and translate the data
Organise	Select relevant information and put it in
Select	Choose from a variety of alternatives and pick the most relevant
Assess	Make an informed judgement about how effective something is. The candidate must show both the strengths and limitations and must make a definite judgement
Consider	Weigh up the arguments for and against two courses of action
Criticise	This type of question also makes the candidate weigh up the strengths and weaknesses of a situation
Decide	Make a judgement between the alternatives being discussed
Evaluate	Make an appraisal of a situation to judge its value. Weigh up both strengths and weaknesses of something and reach a conclusion
In your view/ opinion	Make a personal judgement by considering the positive and negative points
Judge	Make a personal judgement based on evidence and backed up with reasons
Justify or Recommend	Make a decision and show that it is the best decision in the circumstances

Predict	Forecast what will happen as a result and make a judgement about the consequences	Suggest	State ways in which something should be done or improved, giving reasons

Glossary

A

Accounts The records of the financial transactions of a business

Acid Test Ratio Shows a firm's ability to pay its current debts without having to sell some of its stock

Additional Capital Extra capital brought into a business, perhaps for expansion

Amalgamation A voluntary and agreed joining of two or more businesses in order to form one large business. Can also be known as a merger

Appraisal The process of assessing an employee's performance in his/her job

Appraisee The person who is being appraised

Appraiser The person who is carrying out the appraisal

Arbitration The second stage of a process in which the Labour Relations Agency provides a solution to the parties in a dispute

Articles of Association A legal document used in the setting up of a limited company

Asset An item owned by a business such as premises or vehicles

B

Balance Sheet A list of assets and liabilities and shows the accurate value of a business on any given date

Batch Production A method of production in which several of the same product are made at one time

Bonus An extra payment made to employees who work well and help the business to achieve its objectives

Breakeven Point The point at which a business's total costs equal the total of its sales income. It is the minimum point at which the firm can survive

BSI The British Standards Institution is a body which tests products to ensure that they are reliable, safe and of good quality

Business Growth Any form of expansion of a business

Business Plan A detailed description of what a business hopes to do over a future period of usually one to five years

C

Capital The factor of production which is contributed by the owners and is wealth which is invested in order to create further wealth

Cash Flow The flow of money into and out of a business

Cash Flow Forecast A prediction of the level of spending and level of income which a business will have during the following period of time

Channel of Distribution The means by which goods are passed from the producer to the consumer

Commission An extra financial reward for sales staff. It is usually expressed as a percentage of sales

Communication The passing of information from a sender to a receiver

Competition Act Passed in 1998, this Act is the major anti-competition legislation and brings it into line with European Union law

Competition Commission An independent body set up in 1999 for the purpose of investigating mergers and monopolies

Competitive Marketing Any market in which there are many firms competing for customers

Competitive Pricing See Market-led Pricing

Conglomerate Is where a number of businesses merge but their products are totally unrelated

Consultation Is the process by which management discusses with employees and seeks their views

Consumer A person who is the final user of the product

Consumers' Association A body which gives advice and information to consumers and aims to improve the standard of goods and services

Consumer Protection Act Passed in 1987, this Act lays down rules which ensure that prices advertised are genuine, and also is designed to protect consumers from unsafe products

Contract of Employment It is an agreement between the employer and the employee and its main purpose is to define the rights and duties of both parties

Cost-based Pricing A pricing policy which is based on the firm's total fixed and variable costs plus a percentage profit

Cost of Sales A firm's opening stock plus purchases less closing stock

Current Assets Items owned which can be quickly exchanged for cash, for example stock

Current Liabilities Amounts owing which must be paid immediately, for example to creditors

Current Working Capital Ratio Shows the relationship between a firm's current assets and its current liabilities

Curriculum Vitae A list of a person's qualifications, work and achievements which is used as a method of selection

D

Decline The sixth and final stage of the product life cycle when sales have fallen and the product is unprofitable

Deed of Partnership A legal document which may be drawn up for business partners to replace the Partnership Act

De-industrialisation A situation where there is a decline of manufacturing industries in an area

Demand The quantity of goods which will be bought at a given price

Desk Research See Secondary Research

Destruction Pricing A pricing policy which is designed to destroy competitors' sales and drive them out of the market

Director A person who is appointed to a company's board and has responsibility for the running of the company

Disability Discrimination Act Passed in 1995, this Act makes it unlawful to treat disabled people less favourably than other people in employment

Discount A sales promotion method in which a percentage is taken off the price of the product

Dismissal Is where an employer discontinues an employee's work because of incompetence or dishonesty

Division of Labour A type of specialisation in which the manufacture of a product is divided into a number of small stages

E

E-Commerce Stands for electronic commerce which is buying and selling via the internet

Economies of Scale Economies which are gained when an increase in production causes a decrease in production costs

Entrepreneur A person who has a business idea and is willing to take a risk in order to make it work

Equal Pay Act Passed in 1970 and amended in 1984, this Act states that men and women performing the same, or similar work, must be paid the same and must be given the same conditions of service

External Business Growth Growth which takes place outside the business. This may be by takeovers or amalgamation for example

External Recruitment A system in which advertising for new employees invites applications from people who do not work in the firm

F

Factors of Production Four resources of land, labour, capital and enterprise which must be present before production can take place

Fair Employment Order Passed in 1998, this Order ensures that people of all religious beliefs and political opinions have equal opportunities in employment

Field Research See Primary Research

Financial Economies Economies which are gained in situations where a business can obtain finance by cheaper methods

Fixed Assets Items owned by a business which are more permanent, for example machinery

Fixed Costs Costs which are not affected by the quantity of goods produced or sold, or by the scale of services rendered

Flow Production A method of production in which one product is made continuously and in large numbers. Also known as mass production

Food Safety Order Passed in 1991, this Act ensures that all food offered to the public is safe to eat and is properly described

Franchise A system in which a business idea is hired out to other businesses

Franchisee A person who buys a franchise

Franchiser A person or company who sells a franchise

Fringe Benefit Is a non-financial method of motivation and includes such perks as company cars, pension schemes, private health care and free housing

Full-time Employment A system in which an employee is engaged to work the total number of specified hours per week

G

Generic Advertising A method of advertising which advertises a whole industry or a particular type of goods regardless of where the goods are sold

Global Market Trading on a worldwide scale

Gross Profit The difference between a firm's income from sales and the cost of sales. It is found in the trading account

Gross Profit Percentage The amount of gross profit which a business has made on sales. It measures a firm's trading efficiency

Growth The third stage of the product life cycle when sales are growing rapidly

H

Health and Safety Order Passed in 1978, this Order sets out the responsibilities of both employers and employees to ensure that the work environment is safe

Hire Purchase A medium-term method of finance used for the purchase of assets. A deposit is paid at the beginning and the remainder paid in instalments while the business uses the asset

Horizontal Integration Is the joining together of two businesses which are at the same level of production and work with the same type of product

I

Induction Is the training given to new employees and is designed to make them fit into their new workplace easily

Informative Advertising A type of advertising which is intended to give information

Internal Business Growth Growth which takes place inside a business such as ploughing back profits. Also known as organic growth

Internal Recruitment A system in which advertising for new employees is done inside the firm

International Marketing Marketing which takes place between different countries

Interview A method of appraisal in which a one-to-one discussion takes place between the appraiser and the appraisee

Invest NI Northern Ireland's economic development agency which was created in 2002

Investors in People An award given to a business organisation which has invested in the training of the people working there

J

Job Analysis A process in recruitment where the employer identifies the duties and needs of a given post

Job Description A document used in the recruitment process to define the duties and responsibilities of the post being offered

Job Production A method of production in which one single item is made at a time – often to a customer's individual specification

Job Rotation A system in which employees move between different jobs in order to avoid boredom

Job Satisfaction Is the degree of fulfilment and happiness which an employee gets from his/her work

Job Sharing A system in which two employees undertake one job and share its duties between them

Just-in-time Production A method of stock control in which products are manufactured just in time for them to be sold

L

Large Enterprise A business which has more than 250 employees

Launch The second stage of the product life cycle when the product is introduced to the market

Leasing A medium-term method of finance used for acquiring assets. Similar to renting, the business makes regular payments for the use of the asset

Liabilities Amounts owed by a business, for example to creditors

Liquidity The ability of a business to pay its debts

Long Term Liabilities Amounts owed by a business which may be owed over a longer period of time, for example a mortgage

Loss Leader A sales promotion method in which the price of one or two products is reduced to a very low level in order to attract customers to the shop

Loyalty Cards A sales promotion method in which each purchase in the store earns points which can be exchanged later for cash or air miles

M

Manager A person on the second layer of authority in a business who has responsibility for its day-to-day running

Manufacturer See Producer

Margin of Safety The amount which a business is able to sell in excess of its breakeven point

Market-led Pricing A pricing policy in which a firm accepts the price which competitors are charging and prices its product at the same level. Also known as 'competitive pricing'

Market Research The collection of information from consumers to find out if they like, or will buy, certain products

Market Segmentation The selection of groups of people with similar tastes who would be most interested in a particular product. Segmentation may be by age, gender, background, class or geography

Marketing The process which identifies, anticipates and satisfies customers' requirements profitably

Marketing Economies Economies which are gained in situations where a business can save in expenses associated with marketing

Marketing Mix All the key activities which are used in marketing a firm's goods – price, promotion, place and product

Mass Production See Flow Production

Maturity The fourth stage of the product life cycle when sales levels are maintained and the product has become established on the market

Memorandum of Association A legal document used in the setting up of a limited company

Merger See Amalgamation

Micro Business A business which has fewer than ten employees

Mission Statement A statement of a firm's main aims and objectives

Monopoly A situation in which one firm controls more than 25% of the market

Mortgage A long-term method of finance often used for the purchase of premises.

Motivation The way in which a person can be encouraged to make an effort to do something

Municipal Undertaking An activity organised by a local authority

N

Needs Analysis The first stage in the recruitment procedure where the employer decides exactly what the firm needs from new employees

Net Loss Arises when a firm's expenses exceed its gross profit

Net Profit The true profit of a business which is found in the profit and loss account by subtracting all expenses from the gross profit

Net Profit Percentage The amount of net profit which a business has made on sales. It measures a firm's trading efficiency and also its ability to keep expenses low

O

Observation A method of appraisal in which the employee is watched doing his/her work

OFT Stands for the Office of Fair Trading, which is an independent body set up to promote and protect the interests of consumers

Off-the-job Training Training which is provided by a specialist outside the employee's normal place of work

On-the-job Training Training which is given at the employee's normal place of work

Operative Is a shop floor worker and is responsible for making the firm's product

Organic Growth See Internal Business Growth

Overdraft A short-term means of finance in which the business is allowed to write cheques beyond the amount of the balance in the account

Owner A person who has invested money in a business

P

Partnership A business which has between two and twenty owners and is most often found in professional businesses and those giving a service

Partnership Act Passed in 1890, this Act governs the formation and running of business partnerships

Part-time Employment This is where an employee works less than a full week – three mornings per week, for example

Penetration Pricing A pricing policy in which a low price is set at the beginning. The price is increased when the product's place in the market has been secured

Permanent Employment Is where an employee is contracted to work for a business until he/she leaves because of retirement, resignation, redundancy or dismissal

Person Specification A document drawn up as part of the recruitment procedure to identify the qualities, skills and experience which an ideal applicant for the post should have

Persuasive Advertising A method of advertising which is intended to create a need and to encourage members of the public to purchase the advertised product

Ploughed Back Profit See Retained Profit

Price War A pricing policy which cuts the price of some products to a very low level in order to attract customers

Primary Production The first stage of production which is extracting raw materials and using the earth's resources to grow crops

Primary Research A method of market research which collects original information and is carried out by making direct contact with consumers and members of the public. Also known as 'field research'

Private Sector Businesses Businesses which are owned by private people

Private Limited Company A company which cannot sell its shares on the Stock Exchange. Its shares are owned by a small group of people

Producer A person who manufactures goods or services

Product The goods or services which a business is offering for sale

Product Life Cycle The lifespan of a product showing the path from the beginning of the product to its withdrawal from the market

Profit and Loss Account One of the final accounts. Its purpose is to find net profit

Profit Sharing A financial method of motivation whereby employees receive a share of the profit made by the business

Promotion (in Employment) Is where an employee has been given a job at a higher level in the same firm

Promotion (in Marketing) All methods by which businesses inform customers about their products and encourage them to buy those products

Public Corporation A government-controlled market body

Public Limited Company The largest type of private sector organisation. Its shares are traded on the Stock Exchange

Public Private Partnership A business activity organised and funded jointly by a public body and a private company

Public Relations Any activity where the public's awareness of a business is raised and the business is seen to be generous and public spirited

Public Sector Businesses Businesses which are owned by the country and run by the government

Q

Quality Assurance The need to achieve constant, high standards in all that customers require

Quality Circles A similar system to team working. Employees are organised into groups and meet regularly to examine the quality of what they are doing and try to find ways of improving it

Questionnaire A means of primary research and is a list of written questions which members of the public are to be asked in order to find information

Quota Sampling A method of sampling in which interviews are held with a set number of people who fall into pre-determined categories, e.g. male or teenager

R

Race Relations Order Passed in 1997, this Order states that people of all races, colours, nationalities and ethnic origin must be treated equally in employment, recruitment and training

Random Sampling A method of sampling in which people are randomly selected and questioned

Recruitment Is the employment of new workers

Research and Development The first stage of the product life cycle which takes place before the product is put on the market

Resignation Is where an employee leaves a firm voluntarily because he/she has decided to give up work or is leaving to go to a different job

Retailer The shopkeeper who is the final seller of goods to the consumer

Retained Profit Profit which the owner re-invests in the business. Also known as 'ploughed back' profit

Retirement Is where an employee leaves a firm because he/she has reached the end of his/her working life

Return on Capital Employed Shows the net profit which the owner of a business has received on the capital invested

Returns Inward Goods which are subtracted from sales because they have been sent back to the business by another business

Returns Outward Goods which are subtracted from purchases because they have been sent back by the business to another business

S

Salary Payment given to an employee in return for work done. Usually paid monthly

Sale and Supply of Goods and Services Act Passed in 1994, this Act ensures that goods and services supplied and Services Act by a business are of satisfactory quality

Sales Promotion See Marketing Promotion

Sampling A method of primary research which questions a sample of people as being representative of the whole population. Sampling may be random, quota or target

Saturation The fifth stage of the product life cycle when sales are at their highest and new customers cannot be found

Secondary Production The second stage of production which works on raw materials to manufacture finished goods

Secondary Research A method of market research which uses published statistics, data and other information all of which have been collected previously. Also known as 'desk research'

Self Appraisal The process of assessing one's own work to find ways of improving its quality

Self Employment An employment system in which a person sets up his/her own business and works for himself/herself

Sex Discrimination Order Passed in 1976 and amended in 1988, this Order states that men and women should have equal treatment and opportunity in employment and recruitment

Shareholder A person who has invested money in a limited company by buying shares. This makes the shareholder a part owner in the company

Short Contract Is a system of temporary employment in which the employee is engaged to work for a short period – over Christmas, for example

Skimming A pricing policy which sets a relatively high price initially in order to skim the market. The price is reduced later when other firms enter the market

Sleeping Partner A partner who contributes capital to a partnership business but does not work in it or take part in its organisation

Small Enterprise One which has fewer than fifty employees

SME Stands for small to medium-size enterprise and usually has between fifty and two hundred and fifty employees

Social Enterprise A business which has the interests of the community at heart

Sole Trader A person who owns and runs his/her own business

Sponsorship A method of promotion in which a company meets the costs involved in running an event or providing a service.

Stakeholder A person who has an interest in the activity

Start-up Capital The capital needed to get a business started

Stock Exchange The place where shares in companies are bought and sold

Stock Turnover Rate The number of times in a year that a business is able to sell the value of its average stock. It measures a firm's trading efficiency

Supervisor A supervisor is on the lowest level of management in a business and has direct contact with the workforce

Specialisation Is when an employee concentrates on one particular operation and does it all the time. Specialisation may be by product, process, function or country

T

Takeover Is when one business buys the control of another business

Target Sampling A method of sampling in which people from only a particular market segment are interviewed

Team Working A system in which employees are grouped together in teams, making sure that each team has the full range of skills and abilities required to carry out the task required

Technical Economies Economies which are gained in situations where a business can cut its production costs by introducing upgraded technology or by altering its production methods

Temporary Employment A system in which an employee is engaged to work for a specified period of time – one year, for example

Tertiary production The stage of production which provides services to members of the public and to other industries

Total Costs The sum of a firm's fixed and variable costs

Trade Descriptions Acts Passed in 1968 and 1972, these Acts prohibit the giving of false descriptions of goods and service for sale

Trade Union An organisation which represents the interests of workers

Trading Account One of the final accounts. Its purpose is to find gross profit

Training Is the acquisition of knowledge and skills which can be applied to a particular job

V

Variable Costs Costs which change according to the level of work being done in the business

Vertical Integration Is the joining of two businesses which are at different levels of production but are in the same industry. Vertical integration may be either backwards, forwards or lateral

W

Wage Payment given to an employee in return for work done. Usually paid weekly

Weights and Measures Order Passed in 1981, this Order protects consumers from being sold goods which are underweight

Wholesaler The wholesaler purchases goods in bulk from the manufacturer, stores them, and sells them to retailers in smaller quantities

Working Capital Capital required to pay the day-to-day running expenses of the business

Index

Bold figures refer to glossary.